A FAR CORNER

A FAR CORNER

Life and Art
with the
Open Circle Tribe

SCOTT EZELL

University of Nebraska Press
Lincoln & London

Chapter 17 previously appeared, in different form, in
Kyoto Journal, no. 57 (July 2004).

Portions of chapter 19 previously appeared as "Biung
Home Again," *Kyoto Journal*, no. 58 (November
2004).

To my father

CONTENTS

A Far Corner

Far is a relative term, based on a conception of a center. In 2002, after living and playing music in Taipei for some years, I received an advance from a local record label and moved to Dulan, a village on a remote stretch of Taiwan's Pacific coast. There, fifty miles south of the Tropic of Cancer, I joined a community of aboriginal artists, the Open Circle Tribe, and built a recording studio in an old farmhouse above the sea.

The Open Circle Tribe was acephalous and amorphous. It was anarchic in the original sense of the term, having no internal ruler or authority, no one to say what was right or wrong, no administration or hierarchy. It had no phone tree, no newsletter or list of members, or even a concrete definition of itself. It was a loose confederation of woodcarvers, painters, and musicians, splitting apart and reconverging to work on collective projects that came up periodically. These artists cultivated a living connection to their indigenous heritage, and to their ancestral landscape, while navigating the social and economic terms of the Republic of China. They were not primitive or "pure" in maintaining past tradition—they used chainsaws and drove four-wheel-drive trucks, and they never dreamed of boycotting the products of the government-run Taiwan Alcohol and Tobacco Monopoly. But within the terms of their creativity, their distance from centers of authority, and this landscape of mountains and the sea, my friends in Dulan did not sacrifice their identities at the altar of progress, that laughing god with a stomach of oblivion.

I related instinctively to the Open Circle Tribe. I felt at home with the gift exchange nature of their social commerce, their spontaneous gestures of friendship and welcome, and their love of art as an infusion of creativity into a fluid present, rather than as some wingbone of the human social apparatus that had to be kept behind glass in a museum. Time here was an elastic continuum, distinct from the gridded fragmentation of the metropolis. We had no fealty to the hegemon. We existed within the hierarchy of the nation-state, but within this structure we lived out a desire for freedom of identity and occupation. For the Open Circle Tribe, autonomy was connected to indigenousness, an identification with place and culture, in the wake of decades or centuries of assimilation, relocation, and repression. In the previous fifty years of the Republic of China's occupation of Taiwan, aboriginals had been mostly confined to roles such as construction workers, coal miners, truck drivers, and often, in the case of women, prostitutes. I arrived in Dulan with only the desire for cheap rent, open space, and the sea, but over the period of my residence I experienced my friends' issues of identity, marginalization, and belonging, which reflected back upon my own sense of individual and cultural identity.

• • •

Dulan is a village of the Amis (Ah-MEECE) tribe, who originally settled much of Taiwan's Pacific coast. I was in my midthirties when I moved there and had first come to Taiwan to study Chinese ten years before. Because Mandarin was the lingua franca of the various ethnicities in the area, I communicated fluently with nearly everyone, with the exception of the aboriginal elders. Taiwan was colonized by Japan from 1895 to 1945, so in addition to their indigenous languages, the elders had learned Japanese when growing up. They were only exposed to Mandarin as adults, and for them it always remained a foreign language.

In and around Dulan, vestiges of indigenous culture remained, such as a belief in the sacredness of the land, an affinity for gift exchange rather than strict monetary accounting, and an oral transmission of stories, songs, and history. The Amis, Puyuma, Bunun, Paiwan, Rukai, and other indigenous peoples here did not feel they were far from anything. Rather, they were at the center of their traditional cultures and landscapes; they were home.

At the same time, these ethnic minority peoples were fully aware of their marginal social and political status. When I arrived, the population of Dulan was approximately half Amis and half ethnic Chinese. The flank of Dulanshan, Dulan Mountain, which rose behind the village, had been wild and unbroken a few decades before but was now quilted with fruit orchards and hog farms owned by Hakka farmers who had migrated from the north. A luxury resort was slated to be built by a distant conglomerate upon Dulan Point, a rocky promontory sacred to the Amis. When I went on a two-week "cultural re-establishment" trek organized by the Bunun tribe, high in Taiwan's central mountains, we ventured into land where the Bunun were not allowed to live and hunt, though they had resided there until they were relocated to the lowlands by the Japanese in the 1930s. (Chapter 13, "Hunting with the Bunun," is an account of this trek.)

Taiwan's aboriginal languages belong to the Austronesian language family. Most scholars believe Taiwan was the origin of Austronesian languages, which today comprise about 1,200 of the roughly 8,000 living languages in the world. (See, for example, "Taiwan's Gift to the World" by Jared Diamond, in the journal *Nature*.) It's generally accepted that Taiwan was the source of the great Austronesian sea migrations from which Malay and Polynesian languages are descended, and which reached as far as New Zealand, Madagascar, Hawaii, and Easter Island. Arriving in this "far corner" of the world, I stepped into a further vector, the starting point of the largest dispersion of a language group before the European conquest of the Americas.

• • •

In the introduction to his book about seventeenth-century Taiwan, *How Taiwan Became Chinese*, Tonio Andrade writes: "I decided to study Taiwan because it is a place where European and non-European colonialism met."

I had no such perspective on Taiwan when I arrived for the first time in 1992. I loved ancient Chinese poems of nature, wine, contemplation, and letting go of social or material ambition, and I came to Taiwan to study Chinese on a friend's recommendation, almost by chance. Tang Dynasty poets like Wang Wei and Li Bai, from the eighth or ninth century, or Tao Yuanming, from much earlier, wrote about stepping away from positions of power and returning to the essence of things (though this was usually only after they had been banished from the capital). These old exiles, writing from the margins, created bodies of work that now stand at the center of Chinese culture.

I arrived in Taiwan with visions of Taoist recluses drinking wine in bamboo groves and Zen monks cutting cats in half to prove that the world is an illusion, and I did not know the then-longest-running martial law regime in the world had existed in Taiwan until 1987. After its first, partial colonization by the Dutch from 1624 to 1661, Taiwan became a loosely administered province of China's Qing Dynasty. It was ceded to Japan in 1895; then at the end of World War II it was handed over to Chiang Kai-shek, whose Nationalist government, the KMT or Guomingdang, was fighting Mao and the Chinese Communists. When the Nationalists lost the civil war in 1949, they retreated to Taiwan and established their government-in-exile of the Republic of China, the ROC. This was a dictatorship ruled by Chiang and, after his death in 1975, by his son. Though the ROC proclaimed itself "Free China," and received huge amounts of financial and military support from the United States, the KMT was a brutal regime that killed twenty thousand Taiwanese in the course of its White Terror period, starting in 1947, in response to civilian protests to its rule. An ethnic, cultural, and political rift remains today between the different Chinese peoples of Taiwan—between the "Taiwanese" Minnan and Hakka from southern China, whose immigrations began during the Dutch period, and the "Mainlanders," who originated from all over China and mostly came with Chiang Kai-shek in 1949.

In the mid-1990s, my fellow grad school dropout Doug and I used to go busking in Jilong, the major port of northern Taiwan. We sang and played guitars in the pedestrian underpasses of that swampy harbor city, and sailors urged us to gulp vodka as they dropped foreign currency in our guitar cases. There was no sign of Jilong's history as a Spanish fort surrounded by aboriginal villages, or of the battle the Spanish lost to the Dutch there in 1642, forcing them back to their base in Manila. Years later when I read in Andrade's book, "The loss of Jilong to the Dutch signaled a change in the balance of power in the Far East," I was astounded to imagine Jilong as a pivot point of global power.

In the early 2000s a disproportionate number of the most interesting and successful musicians and singers in Taiwan were Amis and Puyuma from Taidong. This included everyone from A-mei, a pop diva whose albums sell in the tens of millions, to Chen Jian-nian and Panai, folk singer-songwriters who recorded with an independent label in Taipei. These musicians contributed to a shift of national identity, from a Chinese province at war with the mainland toward a pluralistic culture and de facto sovereign nation. From their cultural and geographic margins, aboriginal singers and artists helped transform the social center, just as ancient poets, writing from the edge of the empire, now occupy the heart of Chinese civilization.

• • •

I first went to Dulan a year before I moved there. Xiao Lu, a Puyuma bass player, invited me to drive the seven hours south from Taipei to Taidong to join a gig he was playing with his cousin Chen Jian-nian. We wound our way up and out of the Taipei basin and back down the mountains to the northeast coast, then drove the two-lane coast highway south along the Pacific Ocean. The sea was gray and undulant beyond the fields that spread along the apron of the coast, with clouds moving over low and brooding. We drove past aquaculture farms, duck pens, and patchwork fields of corn and rice with power lines striding through. We also passed glass booths enclosing beautiful young women wearing almost nothing.

"Holy hell, did you see that?" I said.

"That's nothing. Wait till you see what's up ahead," Xiao Lu said, driving onward unperturbed, cool as Danish butter.

They were selling betel nuts (*binlang* in Mandarin), a mild palm nut stimulant that turns saliva blood-red when chewed. In addition to *binlang*, these roadside stalls sold anything else you might need for a long-distance drive, including cigarettes, canned tea, and Wisbih, a bubblegum-tasting liqueur infused with caffeine. The betel nut merchants each tried to purvey a sexier girl wearing less clothing to reel in drivers as they sped down the highway.

"We need cigarettes," Xiao Lu said.

"How can we decide where to stop?"

"It's not easy," he agreed. "I've got to concentrate on the road. When you see one you like, shout out."

We were flying down the road and had just whipped past a blue farm truck stacked with cages of chickens when we passed a girl in a booth more seductive than any we'd seen so far.

"Stop!" I shouted. "She's the best one!"

Xiao Lu had seen her too. He hesitated and almost jammed his foot on the brake, but grimaced and stomped the gas instead.

"They get better and better up ahead," he said. "You can't believe how polite some of these girls are."

"How could they be any more polite than that? Did you see the tassels on her bikini?"

"Trust me, that's just the beginning," Xiao Lu said, though

he gripped the wheel hard, tendons straining in his wrists, perhaps still considering cranking us around and doubling back. As if to reassure himself, he said, "Some of them are so polite it's almost illegal."

However, we were out of cigarettes, so had no choice but to pull over a few minutes later. Xiao Lu swerved to the side of the road, where a girl tottered out of her booth in a miniskirt and high heels. She paused and took a half step back when she saw me, but Xiao Lu threw out a few strands of testosterone-laced banter and ordered two pouches of betel nuts, two packs of 555 cigarettes, and two Mr. Brown coffees (a saccharine brew with a caricature of a leering Panamanian on the can). He implied he might have to fight me if I even thought about making a move for my wallet. The girl wiggled back to her booth, brought us the goods, and bent far forward to hand it all in to me. Xiao Lu passed her some bills and flashed a smile, and he gunned us back onto the road.

"Man, you're right," I said, slamming down my Mr. Brown like it was liquid salvation. "She was extremely polite."

"Damn it, that was nothing. You should see when they're *really* polite. Don't worry, we'll try another place up ahead. Shit, did you see her face when she caught a glimpse of you? She didn't expect to see a giraffe in the passenger seat."

"No," I said, "they never do."

I'm six and a half feet tall, with gold-colored hair, and in Asia I stood chest, shoulders, and head above almost everybody. When I first arrived in Taiwan, I felt like a circus bear unicycling through a crowd. In no time I could lip-read "*hen gao!*" from twenty paces, "So tall!" But soon, as if a switch were clicked off, I simply stopped registering this physical gulf between myself and others. Only when someone called my attention to it did I recall that I was a giant in this land.

• • •

South of Hualian, the coastal mountains rose up beside the sea. The central range retreated inland, and a rift valley opened in between. We stayed on the coast road. Xiao Lu clenched cigarettes between his teeth and spat betel nut juice out the window as he wrestled the car through the mountain curves, his arms bulging where they emerged from his embroidered vest. I reclined into his gregariousness as he told me stories of signing on to a deep-sea trawler at sixteen, ranging out as far as South Africa to strange ports he never knew by name. Below us an ocean of three blues stretched to the horizon—a milky cornflower blue gave way to periwinkle, and then to deep cobalt, all separated distinctly as if by drawn lines. We crossed the Tropic of Cancer as sunlight poured ripe and liquid from the sky and sparkled across the sea.

In Taidong the streets were caramelized with heat, glassy and dusty. We joined Chen Jian-nian on his cousin Tero's porch, playing guitars and talking about nothing. Jian-nian had won a Golden Melody Award in 2000, the Taiwanese equivalent of a Grammy, and was a genuine star, especially here in the Puyuma homeland. Tero presided over the scene with bohemian panache, pouring tea and homemade rice wine, explaining the origins and virtues of each. Men and women drove up in work clothes and rubber boots, parked their motorbikes by the chain-link fence, sat down for a cup of tea or wine or both, and joined in singing harmony on a song or two without bothering to take off their helmets, then stood up and stepped back out into the molten heat.

Jie-ren sat in the background with a Japan Railways (JR) baseball cap pulled low over his eyes, tapping along with the guitars on a hand drum. He was a music friend of mine from Taipei, the producer of Jian-nian's albums, as well as those of various other aboriginal and indie artists, and had caught a flight down for the gig.

"What are you working on these days?" I asked him.

"Nothing. I've had enough of Taipei, I'm ready to make a change."

"Yeah, to what?"

"Chicken farming."

"Layers?"

"No, fighting cocks. Tero offered to let me keep some cages here in the back yard."

Hao-en, a Puyuma guitar player, had flown down from Taipei with Jie-ren.

"Hey, what are you doing here?" he said, and slapped me on the shoulder.

"I just drove down with Xiao Lu to have a look around," I said. "What about you?"

"Here for the gig with Jian-nian, you know. And to practice dancing, my group has a performance next week. What, you don't believe me?"

Hao-en was rotund, and had a slightly crippled foot, and seemed to think I doubted his ability to dance. He immediately folded his arms and dropped down into a squat, from where he executed vigorous dance moves, kicking out his legs as he chanted to accompany himself. Then he smiled and lifted a glass of *mijiu* to welcome me.

"That's how we do it here," he said. "That was a war dance. But don't worry, it wasn't aimed at you."

We rumbled out into town in a phalanx of beat-up cars, cruising through the sun-strafed afternoon like ice sharks, cool and melting everywhere we went. Steam boiled up from roadside stalls, the streets were turgid with motorbikes and their blue two-stroke exhaust. We went to a music shop to buy a harmonica, did a soundcheck at the gig venue, then stopped at someone's cousin's restaurant, where we ate glutinous rice and roasted wild pig.

As I looked out the window of Xiao Lu's car, Taidong appeared to me as just a far-flung provincial town, a bit bland, a bit miasmic, a bit gray and straight despite the hip wavelength of my friends. The city was a listing grid, half-heartedly industrialized, seeming to have fallen off the map of its own consciousness.

However, I'd forgotten that *Taidong* is both a city and a county designation. Commerce, development, and population were concentrated in the city, which differed little in character from other Taiwanese urban centers, apparently slapped together with a bit of rebar and some low-grade cement. For decades the KMT defined itself by the imperative to defeat the Communists and retake to the mainland, and had therefore invested little in local infrastructure. But the broader designation of Taidong included the coast north and south of the city, and the vast high mountains inland, which were still raw and plangent with natural beauty and open space.

· · ·

Our last day in Taidong, Xiao Lu and I were preparing to drive back up the coast when he got a phone call from Panai. She was a folksinger we knew from Taipei, but she came from this area, and was half Amis and half Puyuma.

"How'd you like to see the real Taidong?" Xiao Lu asked when he hung up.

"Sure," I said, "but where have we been the past few days?"

"Ah, that's just the city, man. I'm talking about the ocean, the mountains! That's the real Taidong. We're going out to lunch with Panai, then I'll show you what I'm talking about. We'll head back to Taipei after that."

We picked up Panai and drove twenty minutes north to the Feiyu Café, just south of Dulan. The café fronted the coast highway, and the back opened onto the sea. We sat in the back yard, where Feiyu, an artist from the Tao tribe on Orchid Island, had arranged driftwood logs like sentinels, standing them on end with their twists and contortions lifted against the sky. Feiyu was stocky and strong, with a round, solemn face and a long ponytail, and showed us pictures of himself in Utah wearing a cowboy hat.

"What are you doing down here?" I asked Panai while we waited for our food.

She shrugged and half-frowned, as if it were a gratuitous question. "My mother tongue is here," she said.

Panai never said much, as if she believed most words weren't worth speaking, and those that were didn't need to be said. Xiao Lu and I were already weary at the thought of the seven-hour drive before us. But when we finished eating, Xiao Lu was his usual cheerful self, and said, "Okay, now I'm going to take you to a place you won't believe."

I said nothing and climbed in the car. We drove straight across the two-lane highway and onto a dirt road into the foothills. We wound up and up, along tongues of land, twisting higher and higher above the sea. The mountains spread green all around us as the coast receded below, till we arrived at the top of a broad bluff. We got out of the car and looked down onto the shore a thousand feet below. The ocean was a blue and purple swirl of currents, like a billion saltwater eyelids receding to the horizon. The coastal range rose behind us, lovely shapes and lines moving north in jungle-green ridges. To the south the Beinan River emerged from the throat of the rift valley and flowed out to the sea.

"That's Dulanshan. It's sacred to the Amis here," Xiao Lu said, pointing to the peak behind us.

My weariness melted away. I felt lifted and liberated, at a midpoint of geologic perfection between the mountains and the sea. I felt at peace and at home, though I'd never been here before, had never even known this place existed.

"I'm going to move here," I said, with a certainty unmitigated by logic.

"Sure you are," Xiao Lu said. Panai just smiled and looked out to the sea.

Xiao Lu didn't believe me, and who could blame him? This lip of earth at the edge of infinitude would make you prone to irrational talk, and made rational talk sound crazy. Taidong was Xiao Lu's and Panai's home, and even they didn't live here—what chance, then, that I would be able to unzip from the convenient speed and opportunity of the metropolis and inhabit a slower wavelength, to choose the gentle ridges of the coastal mountains over a skyline of apartment buildings and office complexes and antennae towers? What chance did any of us have to step away from the industrial glossolalia of the modern nation-state that nobody understands but to which we all jump in time like we're skipping rope with live electric wire?

We headed down the mountain and took Panai home, then drove back to Taipei. But this landscape began to grow inside me like a seed of tranquility, spreading roots through my blood and bones, opening like a blue-green flower in my mind. A year later I relinquished my life in Taipei, moved to Dulan, and met the Open Circle Tribe on this stretch of coast I had only glimpsed once, from high atop a hill, between Dulan-shan and the sea.

· · ·

The Open Circle Tribe salvaged driftwood that washed from the mountains to the sea, then back up onto land, and carved it into sculpture, partaking of this cycle of return. I learned from them and used driftwood to build the counters, shelves, and tables in my studio, as I wrote guitar music to express the color and texture of the ocean.

This narrative is an evocation of a place and community where I became at home across the ocean from my native land. Among other things, *A Far Corner* may be a long-gestated contribution to the oeuvre of the Open Circle Tribe. However, my friends might disagree that Dulan is peripheral or marginal, as the title suggests. They might say instead that there is no such thing as a far corner of the world, that every place is a center, every piece of earth is sacred, everywhere is home.

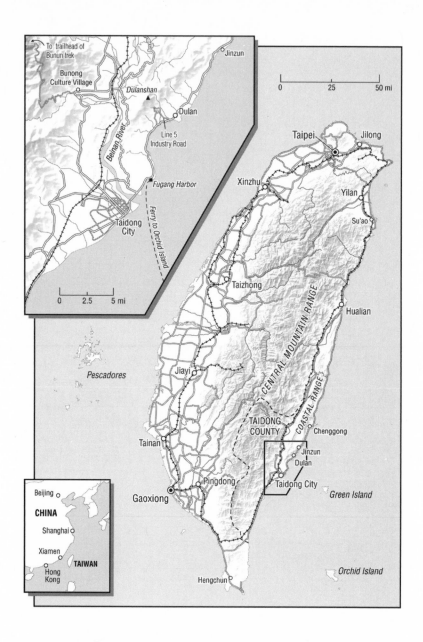

Map of Taiwan, circa 2002. Cartography by Erin Greb.

ONE

E-ki on the Beach

The day I arrived at Jinzun, seven miles north of Dulan, I walked up the beach from the woodcarvers' camp to where E-ki (EH-kee) was chainsawing a driftwood log. Waves rolled in silver-blue beneath a blue-gray sky, and fountains of wood pulp and sparks erupted from the saw, along with dark blue smoke from the two-stroke engine. E-ki's belly was a round ballast, keeping him weighted into the cut as tendons strained and pulled taut the skin of his throat. Sweat or the spray of waves condensed into a crust of salt at the corners of his eyes. The smell of seaweed and engine exhaust mixed with the tannin scent of cedar, as the saw ripped a thick kerf into the wood, re-exhuming sun and soil from within this tree that had washed ashore here at the edge of the Pacific Ocean. E-ki leaned into the saw and levered it back and forth, pushing and thrusting, sometimes almost caressing the groove, as burnt oil from the chain blackened the lips of the cut. He wore oversized sunglasses for safety glasses, and as he worked they slipped down to the tip of his nose, so he had to tilt his head back to keep them from falling, regarding his work with distance, like an old man reading. It was February, a cool steel-colored day. E-ki wore a sweater and denim pants though we were south of the Tropic of Cancer. The seasonal northeast wind blew in cold and blunt, and out toward the horizon a curtain of rain slanted down into the sea.

E-ki sawed through the log; it opened into two faces of golden grain within its skin bleached silver by salt and sun.

E-ki shut off the engine and hailed me like an old friend, though we'd never met. He set the saw down amid a splash of sawdust the color of sunset or whiskey, lit a cigarette, and offered one to me.

"Ho there," E-ki said, looking over the top of his shades, "where do you come from?"

"America," I said. "But now I'm moving here from Taipei."

"Hmm, America, tough country. Look at this chain saw, made in America. American tools don't mess around. You have a chain saw?"

"Not yet."

"Let me know when you need one. Most important thing with chain saws, aside from not cutting your pecker off, is to keep 'em sharp. This driftwood is full of sand, dulls the teeth. The young guys around here, they don't sharpen their saws, they use muscle to cut. Don't matter. I was the same when I was thirty-five. But now I want the saw to do the work."

E-ki reached up and gave me a high five, apropos of nothing; then he took out a rat-tail file and began sharpening the saw teeth along the chain with a twisting movement, testing each point with the pad of his thumb. Sand sloped down along the edge of a half-moon bay, and further north a narrow spit extended to a rocky promontory that stood amid the surf. The wind blew streams off the crests of waves as they curled in. E-ki topped up the fuel with a mixture of petrol and motor oil and tightened the chain.

"How long have you been doing this?" I asked.

"Well, I learned from my father. But he told me to make money. So I went north and had a job in a hotel for a while, a coupla years. But then I came back home, came back to work with wood. Not much money in woodcarving, but what the hell. Come on out to my workshop any time you need a hand with anything. Where you live anyway?"

"Nowhere yet. I just arrived here from the north, I'm looking for a house around Dulan."

"Ho ho!" E-ki stood up and released a burst of laughter like a flock of birds. He stripped off his sweater and tossed it aside, beneath it he wore a frayed tank top. His arms and shoulders were thick and hard as if they themselves were carved from wood, though his hair was iron gray. He stroked his belly like a pet, man's best friend, and his eyes were quick and lively, filled with liquid light.

"Ho ho, look around, my friend! Look no further! We can build you a hut right here, why not? Or if you like, over there beneath those trees. You can live here, eat with us, don't have to pay rent. Whaddaya say?"

E-ki spoke so openly and amiably that his words seemed saturated with laughter, a blossoming of aliveness. But a few days before, I had loaded all my books, guitars, and recording gear into a rented truck and driven south from Taipei with a vague and possibly impossible plan to build a recording studio in the mountains above the sea. I still felt fragile with the precariousness of departing the structures and connections accrued through years in the metropolis, shedding them like an exoskeleton, and couldn't respond to E-ki's geniality in kind.

"I need a house," I said. "I've got recording equipment, guitars, books. I need solid walls to work within, a desk where I can sit and write, a room for my machines."

"Hmm, big plans. Sounds like you know what you need," E-ki said, light still spilling from his eyes. He stubbed his cigarette out on the face of the log he'd just sawed open, ran a finger along the chain saw blade, and ripped the cord. The engine disgorged a mass of smoke and roared to life.

· · ·

When I first arrived at Jinzun I knew nothing about the Open Circle Tribe, their chain saws and driftwood sculptures, or Taiwanese aboriginal communities with their circles of songs and wine. Jie-ren had mentioned the gathering of artists to me in his usual laconic way, saying, "Some friends are doing a project up north of Dulan. You can check it out if you feel like it," with no further clue as to what was happening.

I came down the stairs from the coast highway to the wood-carvers' camp, where everyone was at ease, in a state of symbiosis with the place and community. Feiyu was there, but he was gruff and distant, barely tilting up his chin in acknowledgment we'd met the year before. Maybe he was already contemplating his "work-piece," a protest against the storage of nuclear waste on Orchid Island. I stood wondering where I was and what I should do, and was starting to think about returning up the stairs, when Shen-hui offered me a cup of coffee. An artist from the Rukai tribe of the southern central mountains, Shen-hui was warm and personable, dark and diminutive, and asked me the usual questions about where I was from and what I was doing. After a few minutes she began to introduce me all around, and I stepped from my sense of displacement into these ritual questions of welcome, which Shen-hui offered as a bridge between myself and the collectivity. I began to feel at home in my body in this place and looked out at the sweeping curve of the shore, and to the cliffs that rose behind us in a jungled tangle. Shen-hui reclined in a hammock next to her driftwood coffee bar, which was hung with mossy seaweed as if ensconced in an old man's beard. Feiyu sat with a cowboy hat pulled low over his eyes, solemn as if predicting the day Armageddon would arrive but listening to Zhiming's banter and every once in a while erupting into a bellow of belly laughter, as if opening some time-breach to a ludic, joyous past. Monkeys rustled and chattered as they scattered by in the bluffs above, and Dafeng and Yiming shouted back and forth to each other as they worked fitting pipes together for the fresh water supply.

At dusk the group started preparing a communal dinner, and Dou-dou asked me to go collect wood for the cooking fire. The beach was covered with driftwood of all shapes and sizes, I walked through the soft sand picking up sticks. The sky shone like heated tin above the sea, as the sun descended beyond the mountains. The beach had a short steep break. The waves were raw and muscular, hauled in by the moon across the long yawn of the Pacific. They curved up like blue-green ribs to crash quickly down into froth and wash hissing across the sand, then subsided back to where the next wave had already risen from the lap of the sea. I returned with an armload of wood and chucked a few pieces on the fire. Zhiming jumped up and grabbed a thick piece of red-orange wood out of the fire before it could catch.

"Whoa there," he said, "this is *hong jumu*. Don't let Shen-hui see you burning this. She's nuts about this stuff. She uses it in all her pieces. There's not much of it around anymore, so we'd better not waste a single scrap." Zhiming smiled and leaned back, looking up at the sky. "Don't worry," he said, "all the rest is fine." We each threw a couple of sticks onto the blaze.

. . .

The project at Jinzun involved a core of about a dozen artists living and working together as a community in a landscape as primary as possible—a step away from *civilization*, with its complexes, abstractions, and market demands, and a step toward *culture*, sustaining, generative, whole.

In the coming months each artist developed a *zuopin*, a "work-piece," of his or her own. Some were hewn with chain saws and carving knives, while others were manipulations of original forms. However, the living space and collective lifestyle were creative expressions antecedent to these pieces. Art was a corollary product of the experience of this place, not an overriding ambition. Creative energy was invested in such tasks as running a water line from a spring atop the cliffs to a barrel with a spigot, building benches and tables from driftwood logs, or gathering grasses and vines to decorate the communal space for impromptu rituals and parties. Huts and dwellings were built with lavish imagination, and a fairytale village grew amid the grove of trees at the base of a cliff. Feiyu had erected a tepee; Shen-hui's coffee bar was built in the mouth of a cave, and she festooned a lattice of branches with seaweed and shells; Zhiming built a toadstool-shaped hut that looked like something from *Alice in Wonderland*. Yiming and Ai-qin cleared the top of a low rise and built a broad deck to set up Ai-qin's paints and brushes, and for canvasses she used lengths of driftwood chainsawed into boards.

Each artist had a personal fire pit with a smoke-blackened pot hanging over it to make tea or a midday noodle snack. Within the group dynamic, individual autonomy was respected—there was an implicit understanding of the benefit and need of solitude. Nobody minded, or even seemed to recall, that I was from another continent. I was always greeted like a friend and invited to share whatever was for dinner, and before long I was as local as the locals, a strand in the fabric of the group. Later, when these friends stopped by my house, they'd feign anger if I offered them something to eat or drink, saying, "Don't treat us like guests, we're friends! We'll help ourselves to what we want and leave when we feel like it." I was similarly welcomed as a non-guest, with the same lack of pretense or formality. In other words, I was offered a home.

A direct translation of the community's name, *yishi buluo* (意識部落), is "Consciousness Tribe," but in English I called it the "Open Circle Tribe." We ate, drank, talked, sang, and danced in a circle. Like a circle, the group was self-defined and self-enclosed, yet open to whoever showed up—always whole, never closed.

This community began in the late 1990s, when a group of Amis artists were invited to Hualian to work on an installation sculpture project. At that point they had not worked together and were not personally acquainted. The artists lived in the exhibition space and were simply let loose to create as they pleased, to work when they felt like it, and not to work when they felt like doing something else. They were provided with everything they needed, and they occupied the space with complete freedom of lifestyle, working both communally and individually, and coming together to sit around a fire at night. The group formed a synergistic whole that provided support without imposing limitations on individual expression.

After the Hualian project, the artists began gathering at Siki's workshop at the Dulan sugar factory, sometimes working together even though they all had workshops of their own. They were then invited as a group to do an installation project at a park in Taipei. They took the gig but from the start were frustrated by its limitations. They weren't allowed to light fires within the park, and in general their work and lifestyle were constrained by city ordinances, subject to the authority of the organizing body of the project, the Taipei city government.

The gathering at Jinzun was a response to the sense of what had been missing at the Taipei project. This was an intentional return to the self-determining and autonomous mode of communal living they had experienced in Hualian. The Amis core of the group had expanded to include artists from other tribes and ethnicities. There were no limitations, no restrictions, no parameters, no agendas other than to come together and live and create in an organic way. No official body oversaw the project. The only administrative act of the group was to write a formal letter to the East Coast Management Department declaring their intention to occupy the beach, to live and work there. In this way these indigenous artists assumed agency over their traditional lands, not asking for permission from the state authority, but still making a gesture of dialogue. The letter was never answered, nor were they issued formal permission for the project, but neither were they evicted from the beach.

Some months before the Jinzun project, at a gathering at the southern end of the central mountain range, Dou-dou overheard the woodcarver Vadsuku and an Amis writer named A-biao talking about the ethos of the group. One of them said the community had a "tribe consciousness," *buluo yishi.* But in Dou-dou's mind this phrase got turned around, and became *yishi buluo*, "consciousness tribe." When the group started talking about a name for themselves, she recalled this phrase, and they chose it by consensus. Even the naming of the community was a nonhierarchic process that evolved holistically, percolating through the experience and language of several members of the group, and was ratified by collective agreement.

The "tribe" was predominantly aboriginal in ethnicity, but bloodlines weren't a criterion for inclusion. There were individuals from several indigenous tribes, including Amis, Puyuma, Paiwan, and Rukai, and also Hakka Chinese, ethnic Taiwanese, and me. It was a gift community, where all who stopped by were invited to eat and drink, were welcome to stay as long as they desired, and were free to give back to the community whatever they chose.

After several months, driftwood sculptures rose along the beach, forming an interface between human culture and the natural landscape. The Open Circle Tribe spent half a year living and working at Jinzun even though everyone knew the first typhoon of the summer would wash everything away.

• • •

The day I met E-ki and the other artists at Jinzun, I pitched a tent in a grove of trees up the beach from the main camp. That night six or eight of us sat around a fire, drinking *mijiu*, rice wine, from a plastic bottle. Among the Open Circle Tribe, as for all the aboriginal communities of this region, *mijiu* was a communal libation, part of a ritual of giving and receiving. Now Zhiming moved around the circle, person to person, pouring shots into a cup made from a hollow joint of bamboo. Stopping before Dou-dou, he swung the cup back in his right hand, his long hair swaying around his body, then swooped forward, bringing the cup in low to the ground and lifting it with a stomp of his right foot. "Why thank you," Dou-dou said when the cup appeared before her. She drank the *mijiu*, handed back the cup, and Zhiming moved on to the next person in the circle. Sometimes one would accept the drink but then offer it back, saying, "This one's for you!" Some people dripped out three drops of wine with an index finger as an offering before each drink, to touch the spirit to the earth. Some did that for the first drink of the night and then let it ride, others just drank what came before them with no questions, apology, or remorse.

"Hurry up," E-ki said. "Get that bottle around the circle. You know, my doctor said my health's no good, I got to drink and smoke while I can!"

"What doctor says that?" Dou-dou said as she smoothed the tassels on her leather jacket. "He must be jealous of all your girlfriends."

"Ah, you know my heart!" said A-dao in English as a shot materialized out of the dark before him, flames reflected off the skin of the bamboo cup. Like E-ki, A-dao was in his early fifties, but wiry and gnarled as E-ki was broad and strong. He had long gray hippie hair perpetually tied back with a wrinkled cloth. "You know my heart" was his most beloved dictum, which he repeated with undiminished zest in lieu of "please" or "thank you," an existential thumbs-up to the universe, especially when it appeared in his hand as a cup of wine.

"Look here, we got a new friend from America among us," E-ki said. "Is it really the *beautiful country*? Get some drink in him so he'll sing us a song. Say there, know any cowboy songs? We got a guitar here for ya."

E-ki was making a pun on *Meiguo*, the Mandarin transliteration of "America," which means literally "beautiful country."

"All American songs are cowboy songs," I said, and took a shot of proffered *mijiu*.

"Even 'The Star-Spangled Banner'?"

"Especially that one, and I'd sing it right now to prove it, but I'd rather play a song of my own instead."

"You know my heart!" cried A-dao. "Even better!"

"Somebody pour him another drink, loosen up his throat—"

"Yes," I said, "can't hurt, mmm-ahh . . ."

E-ki became suddenly serious and leaned forward to observe me as I tuned up the five strings on the guitar, cleared my throat, and crooned out a song.

"Ho," E-ki said after a minute, "hmm, hum. You all hear that? This is a serious man we caught here. Who hooked him, who dragged him up out of the sea?"

"What do the words mean?" Shen-hui asked from where she sat on a driftwood log.

"Well," I said, "it's called 'Between You and Me.' It means, between me and you there's no difference—we have different skins, different faces, different language, but we're really the same. We breathe the same air, our hearts beat with the same blood, we all have the same loves and needs."

"Ah, that's our theme song!" said Dou-dou.

"You know my heeeaaarrrtttt," said A-dao, and fell over backward, legs spraddled skyward.

"It's not true, there's a big difference—you've all had more to drink than me," said Ai-qin, who stepped into the circle, joining us from her hut.

"You snooze, you lose," Dou-dou said.

"I wasn't sleeping!"

"Whatever you were doing, you were doing that, not this, there not here!"

"Somebody play the guitar . . ."

"E-ki, sing a song!"

"What, you want me to follow this A-marry-can? Who would dare to?"

"E-ki," Dou-dou said, "he brought that song from the other side of the ocean! You're Amis! We have to give one back. Here, take the guitar, sing one of our songs."

E-ki caressed the guitar, resting it on his belly. He played a few notes, mellow light gleaming off the varnished wood. He looked down at his hands on the strings and frowned, then looked into the fire and began to sing a haunting, melancholy song. It was sinuous and slow, deeply moving without being depressing or mournful.

"Understand that one?" E-ki asked, turning to me. "Of course you didn't, that's 'cause it's in my mother tongue, Amis. It's a song about these mountains, this ocean. It's about coming home. It's the only song you need, and if you can sing it right you're already there."

In the quiet and dark, the song seemed to open and breathe between us as we sat listening to the murmur of the fire and the hush of waves.

I did not realize it at the time, but sitting around a fire, passing *mijiu*, songs, and a guitar around a circle of friends would essentially comprise my social life for the coming two and a half years I lived in Dulan.

E-ki squinted down the neck of the guitar, played a few flamenco licks he'd picked up somewhere, then pushed it away in disgust. "See this?" he said, holding his left hand out to me. "I can't play. It's no good." The tip of his left middle finger was missing.

"How'd that happen?"

"Ah, don't matter, it happens to everyone who works with wood. Lemme tell ya, you want to play guitar, don't be a woodcarver." He reached into a satchel and pulled out a pint of whiskey. "Now, who's still thirsty? Didn't I tell you my doctor says I've got to drink while I can?"

He took a hit of liquor and passed it on, then lifted a burning branch from the fire to light a cigarette.

TWO

The Sugar Factory

From Jinzun beach, where I lived in a tent, an American-in-residence with the Open Circle Tribe, I climbed the hundred-plus stairs to where a small café sat next to the parking area atop the cliffs, then hitched south to meet Siki at the Dulan sugar factory. Taiwan's coastal mountains were pushed up by the Philippine tectonic plate as it drifted north—they are sea bottom stood on end. The coast was undulant here, a series of bluffs that rolled down to the sea before being lapped at and eroded by the waves. Light hung from the midday sky like glass thread, the ocean shining platinum-blue beneath.

Most of Taiwan's Pacific coast had been settled for centuries by the Amis, who are the largest aboriginal tribe in Taiwan. The Amis are a lowland people, who originally occupied the narrow strip of land between the coastal mountains and the sea, as well as the inland rift valley that runs from Taidong to Hualian. When I arrived in Taiwan in 1992 the Amis and all other indigenous peoples were termed *shandiren*, "mountain people," reflecting the traditional dynamic between primarily agricultural Chinese, who settled lowlands, and indigenous inhabitants, who were pushed to the mountains. The Alliance of Taiwan Aborigines, established in 1984, advocated the term *yuanzhumin*, "aborigine," but this term was outlawed by the KMT until the 1990s. Most Taiwanese still thought of indigenous peoples as "mountain people," regardless of their tribe.

As a plains people, the Amis had early contact with colonizing Chinese and Japanese forces. But due to their position on the further and less hospitable east coast, the Amis were not assimilated into Taiwanese culture, ethnicity, and society the way the *pingpu* plains aboriginals of the north and west were, to the point of the latter's disappearance as distinct peoples. Because of this early contact, the Amis were considered more "civilized" or "cooked" than mountain tribes such as the Bunun, who had more recently been integrated into the state social and economic system. Many Amis and members of other tribes had migrated to cities to work and now navigated their own polarities between traditional and contemporary identities, "between the city and the sea."

The sugar factory, *tangchang* in Mandarin, was an enormous U-shaped compound built around an asphalt lot, with the open side fronting the highway and the sea. Built during the Japanese occupation of Taiwan, it was a sprawling phantom of a gone time, a gone industry, a gone government, where water-stained walls sheltered moldering gunk, old work clothes, shift records from lost decades, rotted wood, rusted cans and cabinets, and the odd plastic sandal like something out of a time capsule, so impervious to senescence that you could slip it on and wear it away like you'd just bought it from a shop, unless a rat had gnawed the sole. Chutes and turrets towered up from the processing buildings, so otherworldly that they were never even an object of curiosity or wonder—they just seemed stenciled onto the sky at the edge of the village.

Sugar was integral to Taiwan's history. There had been no significant Chinese presence in Taiwan until settlers were encouraged to immigrate by the Dutch, who needed workers for sugar and rice plantations beginning in the seventeenth century. Sugar's role in Taiwan was similar to that on "sugar islands" in the Caribbean, where demographics were dictated by a massive colonial investment—though with the distinction that Chinese immigrants were enticed to Taiwan by economic opportunities, while islands such as Jamaica were populated with African slaves forcibly "imported" by European colonizers.

A couple of Siki's apprentices sat outside the workshop, Amis teenagers with spiky hair and silver earrings. They scraped halfheartedly at driftwood logs with fluted chisels, knocking wooden mallets *cack-cack* against the metal ends. The Dulan *tangchang* had continued sugar production after the Japanese left in 1945, but it had now sat idle for years. Siki's parents had worked in the factory, and he had bathed in the communal showers as a child. Its concrete hangars abandoned, Siki had recently negotiated with the sugar factory management to occupy two of the cavernous warehouse bays, turning them into workspaces.

The *tangchang* was home to Siki's workshop, and it also functioned as a general hangout and meeting point for the Open Circle Tribe. Chain saws, carving knives, wood scraps, and a helping hand were always available. Inside, the concrete floor was covered in wood shavings and sawdust. Carvings in various states of completion were propped against the walls along with uncut driftwood logs. The ash of a fire and a half-dozen bottles lay scattered by the bay door. The windowless interior was filled with the sweet scent of wood grain peeled open, and with the thick atmosphere of machine oil and smoke and sweat.

Across the asphalt lot, on the opposite arm of the U-shaped structure, the sugar factory's former administrative office had been converted into a café-cum-bar. Since it was managed by peripheral members of the local bohemian crowd, Xiao Ma and Xiao Zhu, mostly serving friends at friends' prices, the business always ran at a loss—it was practically an alcohol subsidy program for local artists.

· · ·

A chain saw revved within the recesses of the warehouse. It ran furious and violent, the pitch rising and falling as the saw grasped and tore the wood grain, the sound like a mechanical anger at the organic world. The engine cut out, and silence descended like a balm. Dafeng emerged from within and stood with his arms folded across his chest. One of the Amis woodcarvers of the Open Circle Tribe, he was among the most taciturn men I have ever met. He had worked in a furniture factory near Hualian before transitioning into creative art. In this respect he was like most aboriginal artists I knew, who had begun their work lives as laborers, like Xiao Lu with his stint at deep-sea fishing, or Zhiming, who had worked as a plumber and electrician. Dafeng wore a baseball cap turned backward, and when I said hello he nodded in a reserved but not unfriendly manner, not ignoring or rejecting words, simply sidestepping them, as if refusing to acknowledge their primacy.

Dou-dou drove up on her motorcycle. Dafeng said a few words to her in a language I couldn't understand—it was Amis, the indigenous language of this place. She answered briefly in Amis, before switching to Mandarin (her Amis was not as fluent as Dafeng's). All languages other than Mandarin had been repressed for forty years in Taiwan—from 1946 to 1986 only Mandarin could be legally written, published, or spoken in public. Until recently children had been punished for speaking their mother tongues in school. The indigenous languages still held on, in fragmented form, though they were fading. Some aboriginal children, raised in a Mandarin environment, could not communicate with their grandparents, who spoke only aboriginal languages and Japanese.

I was astonished to hear someone my age speaking an aboriginal language in conversation. It was one thing to hear E-ki pull an Amis song out of the bag to sing around the fire, but I had only conceived of aboriginal languages in terms of museums and mausoleums, as existing in the past and in paper lexicons. Well, how else could you imagine indigenous languages from the freeways and department stores of southern California, from the rivers of cars and mountains of manufactured goods? Hearing Dafeng speak Amis was tantamount to walk-

ing through a shopping mall and hearing Chumash spoken—
though since *Malibu* was originally a Chumash place-name,
we've all spoken an indigenous American language without
knowing it. Malibu Beach, the Chevy Malibu, the Malibu of
an extinguished culture.

· · ·

Dou-dou was a large-boned woman in her late thirties. She
had softly rounded features and long silken hair, but generally packaged these feminine qualities within camo pants, an
army jacket, and work boots, though accented with a purple or green scarf around her neck, a woven grass belt, or a
paisley bandana. Traditionally, the Amis were a matrilineal
culture, and this seemed to imbue Amis women with greater
confidence and independence than are found in social structures where women are expected to unilaterally defer to men.
Strength of character was projected from Dou-dou's physicality and her personal bearing. Her face was smooth and dim-
pled like a polished apple and could go from severity to jollity
in a blink. In fact, these were mutually engendering, and if
she made any kind of reprimand or criticism she could only
hold her seriousness for the few seconds necessary to give it
credence, before dissolving into quick risibility, her eyes crin-
kling with laughter.

Dafeng and Dou-dou strolled off toward the *tangchang*
café, she talking and gesturing animatedly, he nodding at the
ground. In front of the other warehouse bay, Zhiming and
Feiyu worked together to pry a segment of barbed wire out
of a cylindrical piece of driftwood. It looked to have been a
pile in a dock once, knocked loose in a typhoon, perhaps, and
washed ashore, where Feiyu had salvaged it to integrate into
his café installation space.

Both Feiyu and Zhiming had long black hair, both were
stocky and muscular and browned by sun. They looked like
brothers sweating and working arm to arm. Zhiming was a
ponytailed lothario, an Amis woodcarver and general handy-

man from a few hours up the coast near Hualian. Every few months the local grapevine would flare up with the news that this or that young woman had threatened to commit suicide because of the way Zhiming had forsaken her, or shamed her, or loved her. He was a guitar-playing crooner, with a compassionate smile eternally radiant, which I suppose convinced the objects of his affection that he was incapable of doing them any harm. He was irrepressibly friendly and cheerful, always happy to lend a hand to any work or project, as when some months later I was connecting my kitchen pipes for an outdoor sink and he drove up to help me, just for the pleasure of shared work and camaraderie. His own creative work had a whimsical quality, like the toadstool hut he built at Jinzun. At an open-air art exhibit at the *tangchang* he later created an installation sculpture like an elongated, open-ended whale skeleton, a cage of driftwood ribs that entunneled visitors as they walked through. He hung shells and shards of glass from the "spine" of this skeleton, which tinkled and jingled in the breeze all up and down its length.

Feiyu is Mandarin for "flying fish," which are central to the Tao people's culture and economy. For his self-styled moniker, Feiyu had chosen the Mandarin rather than the Tao word, as if to make sure the Chinese knew how he was identifying himself. Zhiming and Feiyu made a seemingly unlikely pair, not because Feiyu was Tao and Zhiming was Amis, but because Feiyu had converted to Mormonism and was somber and staid in a way that was foreign to everyone else in the community, except perhaps Vadsuku when he wasn't drunk. I heard rumors that before his religious conversion, Feiyu had been the greatest hellion of all—but now he had an ethnic Chinese wife and a baby son, and a code of conduct that didn't even let him drink.

Zhiming was so good-natured that he wouldn't hold Mormonism or anything else against anyone, and so lent Feiyu the benefit of his jocularity with no thought of whether it would be well received—because of this, naturally it always was. Around

Zhiming, Feiyu was light-hearted and loose in a way I never saw him otherwise, except once at his café when he emerged from the sea with a mesh bag full of fish he'd speared, wearing the beatific smile of a fisherman who doesn't even have to lie about his catch.

The barbed wire was not cooperating. Feiyu hollered and groaned as he wrapped it around a crowbar and leaned into it with all his weight and strength, but it was frozen within the wood. Zhiming sat down, lit a cigarette, and stroked his chin with exaggerated dispassion as he watched Feiyu strain and heave, until Feiyu finally dropped the bar, spent from lack of progress.

"Why don't you try that bar you've got that's a little harder?" Zhiming said, and they both collapsed in laughter. Zhiming tossed his cigarette aside, and they worked together to twist and pry the wire inch by inch from the swollen clasp of the wood.

"What are you going to do with that piece of wood, anyway?" I asked Feiyu when they paused for a moment.

"I don't know," he said, wiping the sweat from his face. "I just like the look of it. Maybe I'll use it in a piece of sculpture, maybe make a table or chair from it, maybe just leave it as it is and stand it up behind my café."

The distinction between utility and art was blurred here. Driftwood tables and chairs were sometimes hard to distinguish from sculptures, unless someone was sitting in or eating dinner off of them. Bottle glass, seaweed, rushes and vines, feathers, shells and stones all became part of a context in which the distinction between found objects, raw nature, and human design was often blurred.

When Marcel Duchamp put a toilet in a museum, it became art. Was it also art, then, if a lamp shade was made of woven reeds and sea grasses, or if beer bottles were cut in half and hung in a row above a doorway, or if a driftwood log was chainsawed lengthways and used as a table, the wood grain and saw-cut face comprising an interface of wilderness and machine, a texture as myriad and evocative as a Rothko painting? Intention transforms the way an object is perceived—Duchamp's toilet is just a bowl to shit in without his intention to label it as art.

There was no lesser degree of intention here, except that creative expression and beauty were considered to belong to life, rather than to a museum or gallery. The Open Circle artists recognized the function of their work as fine art—they all did exhibitions at galleries and museums. But their creative idiom was an organic process, not cut off from daily life, but rather informing and augmenting and absorbing life as it unfolded day by day.

Down at Jinzun, I once asked Ai-qin what she'd painted lately. "I haven't painted anything," she said. "My heart's been too heavy."

Mystified, I blurted out, "Well, paint a heavy-hearted painting!"

After all, van Gogh didn't stop painting just because he was feeling a little down or had been thrown into the local lunatic asylum. I still held to the van Gogh ideal of art as a transcendence of mundane life, rather than a part of it, which implies a basic division of experience or consciousness, the usual dichotomy of civilization.

My suggestion merely provoked a burst of laughter from Ai-qin. She didn't bother to answer or rebut it, but repeated it with increasing jollity to everyone around. This phrase was later attributed to me as a dictum, always accompanied by hilarity, as if it were a polished jewel of wisdom I had hoped to present to the community, rather than a spontaneous remark that I would have forgotten five seconds after uttering it. In his essay "On a Streetcar Named Success" Tennessee Williams says, "It is only in his work that an artist can find reality and satisfaction, for the actual world is less intense than the world of his invention." For the Open Circle artists this wouldn't have made any sense. Creativity was an expression of life, so how could you separate it from the "actual world," where life takes place? How could you paint a picture with meaning or wholeness if you didn't feel those within yourself at that moment? And, as Ai-qin might have said if she'd felt any need to reply to me, who wants to look at a heavy-hearted painting anyway?

. . .

Siki pulled up in his van. He scowled at his apprentices, said something derogatory about their work, and told them to make a pot of tea. But a minute later, when he sat down on one of the half-carved logs that served as a bench around the fire pit, his frown resolved into a grin, and he looked around at the rest of us as if to make sure we knew he didn't take this role too seriously. In his late thirties, Siki was the de facto junior chief of Dulan. He spoke Amis fluently, as well as Mandarin and Taiwanese, and acted as a liaison not only between the tribe and the outside world, but also between the elders and the younger generations of the village, since many of the latter did not speak Amis. He was expected to exert authority over the youngsters, and they in turn were assumed to be lazy and recalcitrant, to justify his reprimands—but Siki's personal nature had nothing to do with this authoritative veneer.

When we met at Jinzun, Siki had offered to drive me around the hills to look for a house. In doing so, he extended courtesy on behalf of the Dulan Amis and also had the chance to learn what kind of person was settling in the neighborhood. In addition to his social responsibilities, Siki possessed charisma derived from genuine caring about others and was liked by everyone.

Dou-dou and Dafeng returned just as the apprentices began pouring tea. "Ah, Siki," Dou-dou said, "we don't often see you drink tea!"

Dou-dou never missed an opportunity to sass anyone, and Siki was one of her favorite targets. However, it was the most good-natured ribbing in the world, for everyone's enjoyment, even Siki's, without malice or self-aggrandizement. Siki just laughed and took a sip of tea.

"He was drinking *mijiu* earlier. He's just come back from a nap," Zhiming called out, as Feiyu jerked the crowbar and fell over backward, the wire finally freed from his log.

With his wedge-shaped face and bristling crew cut, Siki would have had a threatening mien if there'd been a mean bone anywhere inside him. His body was ridged and rippled with muscle, lean and cut as a weightlifter's, though the only weight he lifted was logs and chain saws. He poured some tea into the severed end of a bottle and offered it to me. In this community, glasses were made by heating a strand of wire red-hot in a fire, twisting it taut around a beer bottle with pliers, then plunging it in water. The bottle fissured where the wire encircled it, and would break apart with a slight pressure. Then, by filing down the edges, you had a glass, which was not only free, and fit nicely in the hand, but also had a bit of style, as the edge was never straight, but formed a curved lip along the seam where things had broken open.

"Now tell me," Siki said, looking at me intently, eyes hooded beneath his heavy brow, "what it is you're looking for."

I was probably overearnest in those days and tried to talk myself into believing I'd done the right thing by moving here, though I didn't know if I'd be able to find a house to rent, or if my thirty-year-old recording machines would run once they were plugged in and linked together, or if the whole endeavor was an exercise in self-delusion. I told Siki about the sterility of city recording studios, how I disliked the way the world was shut out of music made in them, how artificial it was to freeze, like a lemming atop a cliff, with a guitar in your hands and a song in your throat, and then, when someone on the other side of a soundproof window pushed a button, to play, to leap into the abyss, to sing out something supposedly inside your heart, your heart that had already been cauterized by a dozen practice takes and sound checks, and how you were not even allowed to tap your foot in a session, because that might get picked up by the mics, but how could anyone play music without tapping his foot to the beat? And so here I was, with a truckload of guitars and analog tape machines, looking for a place to build a studio of my own, where I could open the windows and roll the tape, where the world would be part of my music, not cut off from it, and where I would stomp my foot as loud as I wanted when I sang a song.

"I see," Siki said, squinting at me through his cigarette smoke and the scrim of his own agendas. He bit off the cap of a betel nut, put it in his mouth to chew, and offered the pack to me. He glanced left and right, his prelude to a question, then asked, "Have you ever recorded aboriginal songs?"

"Siki!" Dou-dou said. "No one wants to listen to you sing!"

"Not me," he said, trying not to crack a smile and refusing to glance at her. "The elders of the village. We should record them, especially the old Chief."

"It's easy," I said. "I've got the mics, the machines, everything. It will just take a little time to get the studio set up once I have a place."

"The old Chief, ah . . . he has a good voice. We have to document it. The elders, the ones who grew up speaking our mother tongue . . . they won't be around forever."

Siki's phone rang. He stood up and walked away as he answered, standing at the center of the open lot surrounded by the geometric dilapidation of the sugar factory buildings, the strange outlines like wrecked metal that foregrounded the gentle ridges of Dulanshan behind. He kicked at the loose gravel scattered across the asphalt, scuffing at it with the soles of his boots. In his sleeveless shirt, his arms bulged and glistened in the sun, hanging out to the side of his torso like sides of beef. Siki was a powerful man, with a physical presence of solid muscle and bone, and yet the theme that recurred in his work was feathers—as if some part of him desired lightness or flight, to drift rather than be anchored. His contribution to the Jinzun project was a large, curved feather, about twelve feet long, carved from a single driftwood log. It reclined like it had fluttered from the sky and come to rest there on the sand. Maybe everyone has a latent desire to be the opposite of what he is, and maybe as the cotter pin that held various and sometimes conflicting elements of Dulan together as a whole, Siki dreamed of feather lightness, the unfettered freedom to fly high and far. Or, maybe he just liked feathers.

We got in his van and drove south from the *tangchang*, past the edge of the village, and turned up the mountain at "Water Running Up," a tourist attraction with an optical illusion that made a stream in a concrete bed appear to run uphill.

"See that?" Siki asked, pointing to the supposed miracle.

"See what?"

"Exactly."

We drove through taro fields and rice paddies, past foul-smelling pig farms where livestock squealed beneath metal roofs, past yards with hundreds of ducks and chickens enclosed within wire fences. We turned along a lane traversing the mountain slope, and hounds bayed at us where they were chained outside square concrete farmhouses. Down below, waves curled in along the curve of Dulan Bay and broke over beaches strewn with boulders. Trucks chugged along the coast highway, moving from the Beinan River bed outside Taidong City, where backhoes loaded them with sand, to cement factories to the north. The land we drove through lifted gradually from the sea into a patchwork of farms and orchards, with wild ravines cutting down where streams carved through the declivity. A few miles to the south I saw the high bluff where I'd stood with Xiao Lu and Panai a year before. The earth rose to about a thousand feet of elevation and then erupted into the naked cliffs and ridges of Dulanshan, the southernmost peak of the coast range, which then subsided into the alluvial plain where the rift valley opened outward to the sea. Further south, the high peaks of the central range crowded back in along the coast.

"It's not easy to find a place around here," Siki muttered, hunched over the steering wheel and peering through the windshield. "Just a lot of farmers—they don't move out until they die."

"Is it Amis land?"

"Used to be." He spit the mangled fiber of a betel nut out the window. "Now it's all Han tribe, Hakka from up in Xinzhu. They came down and bought everything up thirty or forty years ago. All these plum and peach orchards were planted by them. But there are still things buried here they don't understand."

We passed a farmer walking barefoot along the road, a wood-handled mattock over his shoulder, his pants rolled up to his knees and his feet caked with mud. Siki pulled over, offered him a cigarette, and chatted a few minutes in Taiwanese with the engine running; then we drove on.

"He doesn't know of anything for rent around here. You sure you don't want to live down in the village? I can show you a few places there. A lot more convenient than living up on the mountain, too. You don't even have a car. There you've got friends, neighbors, all the shops nearby. What do you think?"

I looked out the window, up the slope into the quilt of orchards and fields, and to the deeper green beyond. I was barely able to articulate what I wanted to myself, let alone to another person. I wanted solitude, remoteness, an isolation to retreat to when necessary, but I didn't know how to express or define these, or explain why they mattered. Anyway, this idealized vision was being quickly eroded by the situation at hand. I had simply arrived here with the intention to live in the mountains above the sea, but without having ascertained whether such a thing was possible. Every place we passed was full of barking dogs and chicken coops, each apparently holding about a thousand chickens in a ten by ten box.

. . .

Back down at the *tangchang*, Siki apologized for not being able to help me. I stepped out of his van, where he remained as he answered a phone call. Feiyu had returned to his café. A sleek, sexy woman got into a car parked at the edge of the sugar factory lot. I sat down on a log next to Zhiming.

"Who was that?" I asked Zhiming, as we watched the car pull out the gate and onto the road.

Zhiming looked at me with his famous smile, which made his brows knit together, the expression of concern and affection so irresistible to women.

"Siki's wife Ming-ling," he said. "You like her?"

Before I could answer, Dou-dou chimed in from behind us, saying, "No, no, no, don't be naughty!"

I just shrugged. The last thing I had in mind was to move in on anyone's wife. However, as time went on, I learned that Siki and Ming-ling were no longer married, but in fact had been divorced from each other twice—married, divorced, remarried, and divorced a second time. It was a bit of a paradox that everyone still called Ming-ling Siki's wife (no one ever referred to him as Ming-ling's husband), but this was not uncommon here. Legal definitions were one thing, and the way relationships were interpreted by the community was another.

"Are you coming to the Chief's tonight?" Dou-dou asked me.

"Chief? What Chief? Where?"

"Siki, invite him!" Dou-dou said, as Siki strolled over from his van.

He looked at her with his sideways grin, mischievous and playful yet inhabiting authority, as if acceding to her request was a favor he could grant or refuse.

"You know where the old Chief's house is?" he asked, turning to me.

"No." I didn't know anything. I'd just been here living on the beach for three days.

"Okay, you can come with me. There's a big dinner. Meet us here at six, and we'll go together. Now I've got to go and see some people . . ."

Siki shouted to his apprentices. They ran and jumped into his

van, and they drove out into the stillness of the village afternoon. When I turned around, Zhiming and Dou-dou had dozed
off in the shadows of the warehouse bay. I reclined on a half-
carved log, along the grain laid open by chain saws and chisels, and drank the dregs of tea from the pot I'd shared with Siki
as the sky yawned and turned, glassy and blue, streaked with
feathery clouds between green mountains and the silver sea.

THREE

Dinner with the Chief

At six o'clock the usual suspects and I sat around the fire at the *tangchang*, waiting for some critical mass of will or hunger to accrue before we headed to the Chief's. Siki poured out a shot of *mijiu* and handed it to Zhiming, who smiled in mock astonishment, as if this were the most unlikely thing in the world. He tossed it back, smacked his lips, and said, "The doctor told me, Drinking's no good for your health. I told him, Doc, not drinking's no good for my heart."

This was just a clichéd anecdote, tossed out like a hockey puck to slap around a bit—in fact, Zhiming was one of the least devoted drinkers of the group. Still, there was a residue of insight in this mini-fable. According to the story, what is prescribed for physical health by the doctor (that is, by linear objectivity, social authority) may not be good for one's spirit—and alcohol, with its aspect of communal celebration or release, may be necessary for one's spirit, even if it degrades the body.

Siki poured out two mouthfuls of *mijiu* and handed one to me. We raised our cups and paused. Siki stared at me with all the gravitas he could muster.

"Welcome," he said. We clicked our cups and drank. "We'll find a place for you soon, don't worry . . ." Then his sternness flaked away, as usual, and he grinned, ". . . unless you're getting used to your tent down on the beach . . ."

Dou-dou and Ai-qin sat together talking and laughing, slapping each other's knees. Dafeng sat silent and stoic, staring into the fire, and Zhiming sang snippets of melody beneath the splash and ebb of conversation. The apprentices stood off by themselves sharing a cigarette.

Yiming, a woodcarver from the Puyuma tribe, was bearishly strong and broad, but affable and warm as Bacchus, with a childlike enthusiasm for life-as-play, however it manifested, however it appeared. Yiming had studied gymnastics and was seldom content to sit still. Now he did cartwheels across the asphalt just beyond the fire's illumination, then stood in place and did a backflip, exhibiting astonishing agility though he was bulky as a tank.

"What's this dinner at the Chief's for, anyway?" I asked of no one in particular.

"For eating!" Yiming called out.

That was enough. We got up and drove the two minutes through the village back streets to the Chief's, Ai-qin and Yiming in his truck, Dou-dou on her motorcycle, and the rest of us in Siki's van. We always traveled this way, massing together like conspirators and then launching out into the world, as if to ambush any mundanity that lay ahead, slit its throat, let it bleed into colorful possibility. We parked and spilled out into firelight and the smell of meat cooking over an open flame.

"*Meiyou jiu meiyou pengyou!*" roared Kala-OK when he saw us. He was a stringy old man, an elder Amis, with enormous hands hanging down from arms that seemed barely thick enough to contain blood vessels. This was his famous Mandarin dictum, "If you got no wine, you got no friends." *Kala-OK*, the Mandarin transliteration he had chosen for his Amis name, means "karaoke." Like most of the Amis elders his Chinese was halting and disjointed, but he always announced his arrival or presence by calling out, "OK!" Maybe he'd selected his moniker for just this purpose. Kala-OK always looked like he'd been swept up by a tornado and set down by the vortex a moment before, his hair wispy and wild, long strands extending out into the air like tentacles, a look of harried mischief on his face as if he were keeping just a half-step ahead of someone taking everything far too seriously. Like most male Amis elders, he had devoted a lifetime to manual labor, and his hands were rough and calloused even though the physical vitality had begun to drain from his body. At Siki's direction, A-zai, one of his apprentices, ran over with a bottle of *mijiu* and poured Kala-OK a shot. He licked his lips and drank it down. A-zai tried to take the cup back, but Kala-OK shook his head and said, "No, one more, one more." The apprentice poured another shot into the cup, whereupon instead of drinking it Kala-OK handed it back, motioning A-zai to drink it, which he did with a shy but grateful smile.

The gathering was loose and relaxed. There was no structure, no governance, no time frame—just clusters of people, activity, food and drink that converged and swirled, everyone bouncing off each other like molecules in a hot air balloon. The Amis men stood around in their truck tire sandals and worn T-shirts; the elder Amis women sat in small groups, chatting among themselves. Three dozen plastic chairs were set up in a circle in a concrete yard abutted to a row of squat concrete housing blocks, one of which was the Chief's. A couple of youths orbited with bottles of *mijiu*, pouring as they went. Traditionally, *mijiu* was an offering for ancestors and spirits, a product of surplus cultivation, a community blessing for weddings and harvest celebrations. Now it came in plastic bottles, a product of agribusiness, government monopolies, and industrial distillation. A week after this dinner, I saw a group of village elders gathered around a flatbed truck stacked with cases of *mijiu*, political banners draped across the vehicle, party propaganda playing through a megaphone, while suit-and-tied men handed out bottles and sample ballots. A gutload of wine might be enough to buy a vote today, even if a man was hungry again tomorrow.

With the erosion of the more holistic aboriginal cultures

of the Amis and other tribes, alcohol as a sacramental link to ancestors, spirits, and tradition became a primary element of pan-aboriginal identity. (Hunting was another aspect of indigenous culture that was amplified into an identity.) Any time I refused a drink, Yiming would shake a finger at me and say, "No good, no good!" as if I were forsaking the fraternal bond between us, the spiritual truth immanent beneath the sober surface of things. But etiquette sometimes trumped the chemical fact of alcohol. A year after this night, Siki and a few other Amis men invited me to their table in the *tangchang* café and asked me to share their *mijiu*. When I told them I wasn't drinking, without a word of question or argument Siki went to the bar and got a bottle of water and a glass for me, so that I could complete their toasts of friendship without alcohol.

Zhiming and Yiming gravitated to where the meat was being roasted and soon appropriated the barbeque tongs. Dafeng carried an armload of wood over from Yiming's truck and threw a few sticks on the fire. At the other end of the gathering I said hello to a group of Taiwanese and Hakka men in polyester shirts and pomaded hair. One of them was introduced to me as the "mayor" of Dulan, though something made me suspect this was a localized epithet, rather than an official position. He doffed his Dulan Agricultural Co-op cap to reveal a buzz cut with angles and planes like an illustration from a geometry book. Rhombus? Decahedron? Inverse trapezoid? There were planes and angles everywhere. We were handed cups to toast each other, and he gave me his business card, which featured a photo of him in a maroon blazer and broad striped tie.

Someone said I was an American musician, and everyone began to shake my hand like I was a star. "Sing us a song!" said the mayor, holding out his cup to be refilled and toasting me again.

"I can't, I don't have a guitar," I said. It was not really true. Anyone can sing a song any time, but I was self-conscious. All the friends I'd made here sang gorgeously, as if their throats opened to a chasm of centuries, their melodies shaped by this sea and these mountains, their voices cultivated by a hundred generations of sitting around a fire. Here in the Chief's courtyard, at an audience with the mayor, I didn't feel my homemade folksongs, held together with guitar strings and the wispy hope of poetry, could stand up to what was expected.

"Next time," I said.

"We'll have another party, at a karaoke bar. You can sing one then, whooeee!" the mayor said, lining us up for a third shot of wine. His face was already red and glowing, like a cross between polished plastic and raw meat. Kala-OK appeared in our midst and sang a verse of an old Taiwanese folksong to the mayor, the tendons in his neck stretched like twine as he crooned in a hammed-up vibrato. He handed me a bottle and motioned me to take a turn pouring the *mijiu*. I started moving around the circle with a bottle in one hand and a cup in the other, sloshing out a shot and cocking it behind me as I took a half-step back, then pivoting forward and bending at the knees and waist, grazing the concrete pavement as I stepped forward and swung the *mijiu* to the waiting grasp of the recipient. There was a rhythm and flow to this ritual pour—it was a dance step, a graceful swoop harmonic with the "happy bantering poem of the living" (Pierre Clastres's phrase) that was manifest here, culminating in the foot stomp that said, *Friend, here you go, enjoy!*

Zhiming and Dafeng carried a long table over and set it outside the circle near the fire. Dou-dou and Ai-qin helped stir-fry a big pot of wild bitter gourd over a roaring gas ring. *Ye kugua*, wild bitter gourd, nubbly, bright orange, two or three inches in length, grew all across the hills here and was a staple down at Jinzun, where no one had any money, and where everyone preferred to forage rather than shop anyway.

I poured out the last shot of *mijiu* and stomped it forward to Dafeng. He dipped out three drops, drank it in a gulp, and handed the cup back to me with a nod. I raised the bottle and let the remaining vagabond drops drip into my mouth as I walked over to get a new bottle from the box, but Siki intercepted me and told a young woman to take over pouring. "There's the Chief," Siki said. "I'll introduce you in a minute."

The Chief emerged into the half-lit margin of the gathering and set a bundle of betel nut fronds and a few stalks of bamboo against a low brick wall. He was in his seventies, but he stood strong and broad as an old thick tree, and he moved with deliberate ease. The Chief drew a machete from an open-faced wooden sheath banded with copper wire, which hung at his hip from his belt. He lopped the leaves and twigs off a length of bamboo, then cut it into segments just beneath the nodes, the solid, woody membranes within the hollow cylinder. Sectioning the pieces again a few inches up from the node created a cup an inch or two in diameter and a few inches tall—a *mijiu* shot glass. He trimmed the top edge to a beveled lip, paring away the splintery bamboo skin so that it wouldn't scratch one's lips, and making the cup more pleasing as a work of handicraft. The bamboo was mottled like the skin of a tree frog, dappled-green and mud-brown, shining and smooth in the firelight.

Betel nut is a tall, skinny species of palm that bears a fibrous, acorn-like nut, which is a mild stimulant, producing red spit and heart palpitations when chewed with lime paste (calcium oxide). As new growth emerges from the top of its crown, the lowest frond on a betel nut tree browns and dies, and droops down suspended by a few fibers, until it drops to the ground. Ridged nubs left behind where fronds were attached give the trunks of betel nut, palm, or coconut trees their ribbed texture. With their longitudinal strength, betel nut trunks are often used as roof rafters. And the betel nut heart—the interior of the crown—is edible, a layered delicacy, like a cross between artichoke heart and bamboo shoots.

The Chief took a betel nut frond in his left hand, held the fan-like end extended and sliced it off. The frayed ends of the ridged lamina were brown and crinkly, kinking off in all directions, so in silhouette it looked as if he had decapitated a Rastafarian with a single easy stroke of his machete. A broad, leathery stem remained, with a lateral curve from where it had once emerged from the crown of the tree in a tightly rolled cylinder before unscrolling outward.

The Chief sliced the rubbery, striated material into a slightly concave rectangle. He folded the edges up an inch or two on each side, and put a sliver of wood through the corners to hold them, making a viand tray of about six by eight inches. The Chief worked through the bundle of betel nut fronds this way, and as he finished Siki and I walked over to where he was working.

"*Toumu*, Chief, this is Scott, an American singer. He's just moved down here from Taipei. He's looking for a place to stay." Siki said this in Mandarin, and repeated himself in Amis.

The Chief reached out to take my hand in both of his, not so much shaking my hand as embracing it with his. This gesture was so warm and personal that it seemed incongruous with the conventionality of Siki's introduction. The Chief didn't articulate any word of welcome, but repeated "hello" in Mandarin, "*Ni hao ni hao ni hao*," with a rhythmic intonation that made it sound more like an incantation than a greeting in the standardized tones of Mandarin.

The Chief had never left Dulan to work on ships or in factories, as most aboriginal men of his generation had. He was born in Dulan, and had stayed, and was considered one of the most "pure" members of the tribe. He was a solid, palpable presence, both physically and culturally. He exuded dignity, a centeredness in place, and wore a humble, toothy smile. Unassuming, self-contained, self-possessed, he came from a time when songs and singing were integral to the estimation of a man.

As in many primary societies, the role or function of "chief" as a wielder of power never existed in Amis society until it was imposed by colonizing forces, who projected their own concept of political authority onto the peoples they contacted.

In primary societies "chiefs" were often leaders who did not have political power in hierarchal terms. Among the Guayaki people Pierre Clastres studied in the Panama jungle, a "chief" was a communicator, with responsibility to use language to sustain connections between members of a community and to communicate between the tribe and the external world. Within Guayaki social structure, individuals were fully self-determining, and if one or several members of a group did not like or agree with the direction the chief was leading, they would simply go another way.

I never saw the *toumu* exert authority over anyone. Amis society was not a "state" in which a discrete portion of the community is assigned the task of governance, to the absence of other responsibilities. The Chief worked and lived just like everyone else, but he was a connecting element. He was a repository of lore, not just as a holder of knowledge, but in his expression of it through singing. Part of the Chief's role was to lead the songs of the community, and he was considered to be the best singer in Dulan.

The role of *toumu* was created by the Qing Dynasty in aboriginal Taiwan beginning in 1877, in order to have a local "headman" through whom to communicate the will of the empire. It was a point of contact between non-state tribal communities and the state, and as such, an instrument of subjugation. However, like many externally imposed aspects of culture, the *toumu* had become an internally recognized institution—similar to the way that Amis and other aboriginals in Taiwan imbued Christianity with shamanistic and ecstatic elements, "indigenizing" the imported religion.

The *toumu* was elected by a vote among the elders. Voting probably was imported along with the role of *toumu* itself. An anthropologist friend of mine once said, "Voting is abolition of discussion and restrains emergence of collective ideas." Not a likely process among people for whom a leader was originally a communicator, and who made decisions by consensus.

The Chief had been chosen for his innate leadership qualities and the sense of wholeness of Amis culture he represented. But when the elders later elected a new chief, their choice was based on his Mandarin fluency—the new chief had worked outside Dulan for years, mostly on freighters, and the elders felt they needed a leader who could represent them more directly in dealing with Mandarin-speaking authorities.

"You are welcome in Dulan, and we wish all good things for you in your life here," the Chief said in Amis, with Siki translating. "Siki knows everything here. He will help you find a house."

"*Lai, lai, chi fan, chi fan*, come eat, come eat," shouted someone by the fire. We took the betel nut frond trays to be loaded with pork and taro roasted over the fire and sticky rice mounded in a broad woven basket. The Chief beamed and opened his arms to the food, inviting me to eat, then took a seat in the circle.

Yiming clapped an arm around my shoulders and took a swig from a bottle, then gave it to me to take a shot. Sweat ran down his face from tending the fire. "This is *shanzhu*," Yiming said, "wild boar. Have you ever had it?"

"Not yet."

"It's delicious, brother, the best meat there is," he said and belted out a line from a Puyuma hunting song. The Chief's *binlang* frond trays were loaded up and set on the table where everyone could get at them. With his fingers, Yiming picked out what he said was a choice morsel and handed it to me. It was a joint of bone with a strip of ragged meat stretched across it, stubbled with hair on the pale skin that remained on one side. I squinted at it dubiously in the flickering orange firelight.

"What are you doing? Eat it, that's the best part!" Yiming said.

I tore at it with my incisors, gnawing at the bone and gristle, more engaging it in some form of dental combat than success-fully masticating it, but found the taste gamey and unappetizing. I pretended to chew, working my jaw till Yiming turned to get a piece for himself, then chucked the unyielding knob into a potted plant. I decided to try the taro. It was nutty and rich, cooked crispy outside and flakey inside. "Have some more meat!" Yiming said with a grease-shining grin.

"I will in a minute," I said. I went over to get some *kugua* where Dou-dou was serving it from an enormous wok into disposable pink plastic bowls.

"What's wrong, you don't like *shanzhu*?" she asked me with a wink. I started to make some excuse for myself, but she said, "Shh, don't worry, it doesn't matter!"

Zhiming had found a guitar somewhere and sat on a concrete curb bent over it, fingering notes and trying out a melody, deaf to the shouts for him to come eat.

"*Ni jiao shenme mingzi?* What's your name?" someone said behind me in Mandarin that was stultified but lilting, typical of the aboriginal elders who did not speak Chinese with fluency but made a cadence of their own out of it anyway. An old Amis woman looked up at me from where she sat with a couple of others near the fire, her face imbued with a combination of pride and compassion that reminded me of my own grandmother, my father's mother.

I told her my name, and she turned it around in her mouth as if it were something intractable.

"This is the Chief's wife," Dou-dou said, stepping over to join us.

"What's his name?" the Chief's wife asked her, and Dou-dou tried to pronounce my name with a bit of an Amis inflection to help her get a handle on it. "Sca-tuh," she said, and alternated this with the Mandarin transliteration, *Shi-kao-te.*

The Chief's wife cocked her head, turned and spoke with her friends in arpeggiotic Amis that wandered in and out of falsetto. She clucked her tongue and shook her head as they all chuckled together.

"Rekal," she finally said to me, with a finalizing nod.

"What did she say?" I asked Dou-dou.

"Rekal, that's your name in Amis."

However, since the Chief's wife was the only one who ever called me Rekal, it may as well have been a personal nickname.

The Chief's wife held her hand out to me, as if, having ascertained or invented my name, she was finally able to greet me. She clasped my hand in hers, pressing and almost palpating it. Her hand was broad and warm as a beefsteak.

"*Ni shi shenme guojia*, Rekal?" she asked. "You are what country?"

When I told her, she and her friends nodded as if they'd suspected as much.

"We grew up in the Japanese time," she said. "We speak Japanese, but not American. Can you speak Japanese? It's too bad, we'll have to talk Chinese, but we don't speak it well."

She was handsome and broad shouldered, with thick, iron-gray hair, but despite her obvious strength of constitution and character she was marked by dissolution. Cataracts had turned her eyes milky and gray, which made her sight and strength seem scattered, unable to grasp and focus. And yet as she talked to me, the vast abstractions of colonialism, and the rise and fall of empires, became personalized and real. Things I'd only known as printed words took on life through her voice, the history of this place becoming real in the lines of her face and stiff gray hair, and in the sight draining from her eyes. When she spoke with her friends in Amis, I felt a layer of skin was being peeled away, the thin flesh of society yielding to a substratum of centuries, generations of community life in place. And I began to feel I might someday belong here when Amis, which had evolved for thousands of years, absorbing and reflecting this ocean, this shore, these hills and mountains, and had a name for every detail of this place on earth, now had a name for me.

. . .

Zhiming finally came and ate. The apprentices picked up the guitar but were too shy to play it. The fire burned down, and the gears of food and conversation began to slow as they meshed into each other. "*Toumu*, sing a song!" someone shouted. With the Chief's next breath he said, "Okay," and with the one after that he was singing.

The Chief's voice was so resonant and elemental that he seemed to simply open his mouth and let the songs bloom outward, as if they emerged from a reservoir at once integral to and beyond him. He sang without self-consciousness, as easily as breathing, and through him the songs, or the act of singing, became primary—not elevating him above others like a rock star, relegating an audience to passive receptivity, but rather a primacy that included those within hearing.

"The Chief has a good voice," said Siki, standing next to me, for the second time that day. I began to understand that in this community you spoke about a man's voice as you spoke of his character or heart, and that more admiration and respect were conveyed through these simple words than Siki could have expressed with heaped up superlatives.

Singing was a daily commerce among my friends in Dulan, whether it was Yiming bellowing out his Puyuma songs within the first three shots of wine, Zhiming always tinkering with a melody, or others who only sang in groups around a fire. However, no one under sixty ever professed to have a good voice; that would have been impudent, a kind of sacrilege. A man's voice, more than a woman's, was considered to be seasoned by the experience of his life—as well as, in most cases, by alcohol, tobacco, and betel nut. He was believed to reach a maturity of expression and range only late in years. How could a young man sing well? How could his songs please the ancestors? Even if his voice had a sonorous timbre, it couldn't have the resonance of age, of the long cultivation of humility and experience transmuted into depth of spirit.

DINNER WITH THE CHIEF

There were exceptions—rare individuals, cultural or spiritual mutants almost, who from a young age had a shamanistic ability to channel the spirit of their tribes through songs. Jie-xing (or Sangpuy, his Puyuma name) was such a person. A skinny young man in his early twenties, he sounded a hundred years old when he sang. Jie-xing came from Zhiben, Yiming's village, and inhabited the tribe's songs to an absolute degree. He was often referred to as "the youth who sings like an old man." Jie-xing performed one night in the music series that later started at the sugar factory. Pausing between songs, he said, "How could I be separated from the songs of my tribe? Can a fish be separated from water? Can a cloud be separated from the sky?"

Now, listening to the Chief, I heard the lambent beauty of the Amis songs emerging through centuries and blossoming from his mouth into this moment. I suddenly felt I must be insane to come here with a brain full of agendas, a plan to build a network of machines to capture and preserve music in fixed form, to then be commoditized, marketed, reproduced, and broadcast out into the world. Would I ever sing as gorgeously as the Chief, and if not, why bother recording what I composed? Shouldn't I instead devote my life to a relationship with a place and community, and to cultivating a wholeness as luminous as the Chief's when he began to sing?

The Chief stood up from his chair. His voice evoked the hills and ravines of Dulan, the undulating bluffs along the coast, the texture of the sea breaking blue-green over stones. The Amis songs had a rhythm and pulse that belonged to this place, passed down breath by breath through generations. The Chief stood at the center of the circle with his throat and chest opening outward, a union between two hemispheres that were already one, the landscape within him and the mountains and ocean that spread around us, a unity like a wave that spreads across the shore, then recedes back to the sea without ever having parted from it. There was joy in the Chief's face as he sang, or something precursive to joy, a simple wholeness, an inundation of song into life and life into song. No one could leave the Chief's songs untouched, unjoined. They wreathed around your lungs and bones like vines, you were implicated in the earth down to your marrow. The Chief's wife and the other elders stood up to join him. They linked arms and stepped with the Chief in synchronicity, the Chief's wife right behind him with her grave dignity and fading vision. Kala-OK howled like a happy beast as he threw out a line of harmony at the top of his range, raspy and wavering and yet prancing along the high wire of the song's upper register. The dozen elders shuffled forward in the dance, and everyone else got up and joined them, linking arms and forming a long line that the Chief led around the circle, hands joined in a crossover chain of bodies, with the back hand reaching to the person ahead and the front hand reaching behind, bodies shoulder to shoulder, a plait of arms.

Yiming pulled me into the mix. We grasped hands and joined the stepping rhythm, following the call-and-response songs in which the Chief sang out a line and the group answered as a chorus. The songs flowed back and forth, the rhythmic foot stomps like the slap and ebb of waves beneath it all. Nobody minded my wrong steps—it was better to have a stumbling fool dance along than to exclude him. The Chief led us around the compound, in and out of spirals, a wreath of voices and bodies, everyone shining with sweat and wine in the firelight, moving our feet along with these songs that had grown up out of the earth we stood upon. We stepped and swayed to melodies that rose and fell like Dulanshan in lovely curves against the sky, moving in a swell and resolution like waves washing up against the shore and subsiding to the sea, like the dilation and contraction of our beating hearts, moving blood through our bodies to raise our bones up from the earth to return to earth again, nourished by the soil to nourish it in turn, until all of us were moving and singing as easily as breathing, we became a spiral braid of songs and bodies rising and resolving in the night.

FOUR

A House at the End of the Road

After dinner at the Chief's, I slept in a guest room at the *tangchang* and in the morning headed out to hitchhike back to Jinzun. I turned left out the *tangchang* gate, waved hello to the smiling matrons of two *binlang* stands directly across the street, and ambled up the road past the shopfronts on the road through Dulan. They were sun-beaten and water-stained, some with doorways opening to mom-and-pop noodle shops consisting of a couple of tables and a few chairs, others with their wares spilling out into the street. The hardware store was practically barricaded by bins of screws and nails, stacks of paint cans, hoes and shovels, bottles of liquid fertilizer and pesticides, mops and brooms, angle grinder disks, and Japanese hand saws with reverse teeth that cut on the pull. A few old Hakka men always sat around on stools here, drinking tea or liquor in threadbare undershirts, a speckle of beard across their jaws. Right at the center of the village strip was a modern American convenience store, with a facade of slick plastic and fluorescent signs, the white tile floor always spotless except for once when an earthquake sent all the liquor bottles crashing down from the shelves behind the register. This corporate franchise sold all the same things as the local shops, but with the addition of imported ice cream and Japanese whiskey, and it was open twenty-four hours, thereby making it the only choice for A-cai's last stop at 4 a.m. a year and a half later on his way to the sea.

At the north end of Dulan, next door to the post office and the state-run Agricultural Co-op, the proprietor of a sundry shop hailed me and said hello. His store was a yowling chaos, with ten times too many things crammed on dusty shelves with no apparent organization, a mayhem of mercantile accumulation. I was in such good spirits from the pleasure of not owning a single key that instead of tossing out a greeting and continuing on, I stopped to chat.

"It's my good fortune to meet you," I said. "I see you've got everything here, barbeque skewers, plastic sandals, insecticide, bamboo hats, instant noodles, hacksaw blades. Just like a supermarket."

The man was surnamed Chen, and like any self-respecting patriarch he didn't work the counter—it was run by his wife and daughter. He was bone-thin, like a skeleton dipped in lard and wrapped in skin, with an avian presence about him, some quality of pigeon or turtle dove, an aspect of neutral observance and waiting. Chen had just come down from his hog farm up on the mountain and wore mud-spattered pants tucked into calf-length rubber boots. On a butcher's block by the cash register, slabs of pork lay for sale beneath a mesh dome, the wood scarred and concave from decades of chopping meat. A mechanical fly whisk turned above, a bit of plastic twine tied to a length of rotating coat hanger.

"If there's anything you need, just let us know, we'll help you," Chen said. "Wife! Come meet our new foreign friend."

Chen's wife was rotund, with short hair and small, round glasses, her face oily and pinkish. She smiled a wan greeting before locking her eyes back on a TV screen that was bolted to a metal rack almost directly above her. Apparently Chen didn't want to waste any valuable display space on keeping his wife entertained.

"Soap opera," Chen said blankly.

A HOUSE AT THE END OF THE ROAD

"I know how it goes," I said.

"My daughter works here in the afternoons. She goes to beauty school in the mornings."

"Nothing wrong with beauty," I said. "I'd pick up a little extra myself, if I could."

"You must be the American we heard was living out on the beach with the artists. How long you plan to stay? How come you don't want a house to live in?"

"Well, I never said I didn't want a house. I just haven't quite found one yet. My friends are helping, but I want to find something up on the mountain. Seems like there's nothing available."

"You want to live up on the mountain, huh? Well, I know of a place up there. Wouldn't suit you, though." Chen took a toothpick from his shirt pocket and stuck it between his teeth.

"What do you mean? Why not?"

"It's all the way up the mountain."

"What, up on top of the peak or something?"

"No, no, but it's at the end of the road, way up at the edge of the jungle. There's no one else around there. It's too far, takes twenty minutes just to drive there."

"But that's just what I'm looking for. I need solitude, a place with no neighbors near. I'm going to build a recording studio. I want to be at the end of the road, away from TVs and karaoke machines blasting through the night.

"A recording studio . . . I heard someone mention something about that . . . but don't you need a lot of expensive equipment? And don't they usually record music in cities? I've never heard of a recording studio in a place like this."

"Well, it might be the only one around here, but I've got all the gear. I'm tired of the way they make music in cities. I'm here to do things in my own way."

"Really . . ." Chen nodded and chewed his toothpick absently. Such bullish individualism would be downright misanthropic among people as community-oriented as most Taiwanese. Chen and his family were Hakka, part of the group that had moved down here en masse a few decades before, most of whom were connected by extended family relations. They had moved as a community, as a statelet, so they'd always have someone close by to count on. You can bet Chen had never had the idea of striking off alone into the wilderness like some Hakkanese John Muir. To him, what I was doing probably sounded as crazy as Columbus sailing off to find America in a one-man skiff.

"I can show you the place if you like, but I'm sure you won't want to live there."

"Where is it?"

"Up above Water Running Up, at the end of *Wu xian*, Line 5, where the gradual slope ends and Dulanshan lifts straight up at the sky. That's where the place is."

"Can I trouble you to show it to me some time?"

"I can take you right now. I got the hogs fed already. Why wait? Wife! I'm going to take our foreign friend up the mountain."

"Very happy to know you, Mrs. Chen," I said.

She turned to us long enough to wipe a tear from her eye, then craned her neck back upward at a contorted angle to the oblique face of the TV. *I'd make a fortune if I were a chiropractor around here*, I thought to myself.

Chen went down the street to where his car was parked and drove it over. It was an old hatchback with shot suspension, caked with mud from the door handles down. I climbed in the front seat. We drove south and turned at Water Running Up, but stayed right at a fork where Siki and I had gone left. We wound up along the edge of a ravine, through well-tended plum orchards, past corrugated metal farmhouses, past a backhoe parked in an empty field, and then began passing through rows of ragged betel nut trees, where the road ran like a trench through the woody green. The undergrowth had gone wild, with sprays of elephant grass reaching ten feet in the air. The betel nuts, which should have been harvested when they were thumb-sized and green, were yellow-orange and large as apricots. We drove into a thick mist, the air particulate and viscous. With the high growth of grasses we seemed to be navigating a gray-green maze. We bumped up the road, and Chen cranked the wheel left at a Y intersection. He gunned the engine hard to get us up a steep slope, veered off onto a cracked driveway, and cut the ignition.

We got out and slammed the doors. "Here we are," Chen said. "See how isolated it is? I told you you wouldn't want to live here."

We had arrived at a clearing in a drizzle that obscured the mountains above us and the sea below. A square, blockish house stood before us, its cement walls unpainted. Its straight edges and angles seemed extruded from the mist, its geometry a strange imposition on the swelling tangledness of this place where fog made everything amorphous. The dooryard was paved with an apron of rough concrete, the windows filled with frosted glass.

"No, not here!" said Chen as I started forward to have a closer look. "This is where the landlady stays when she comes down to visit. She's still got things stored inside. The empty house is up there."

We walked fifty yards up an incline, and another house came into view. "This is the one," Chen said.

This house seemed to sag and exhale there in the mist and green. It was a traditional Chinese design, a long rectangle facing forward with a double wooden door in the center, flanked by windows on each side, the roof an overlay of rounded ceramic tiles. A kitchen and bathing room were appended onto one end of the house, accessed by a separate door. A broad porch was created by extending the roof six feet beyond the front wall and supporting it with cylindrical pillars. The walls were whitewashed, and a chalky white substance came off where I touched them with my fingers. The bottom three feet were painted Grecian blue, as were the double doors. Vertical iron bars were embedded into the windowsills, and the wooden window frames were painted the same blue as the walls.

The bottoms of the window panes were frosted, the tops transparent. I looked inside, but there was nothing to see but a dim, dingy space and a few empty pesticide bottles. Chen said that Dulanshan rose straight up behind us, but in the fog nothing was visible. In front of the house was a grassy dooryard, and beyond that a patch of sugar cane, ragged and neglected like everything else on the property. I couldn't see anything further except the shaggy outline of betel nut trees— even the lower house was barely visible. Around the back of the house a tangle of wild raspberry vines grew over an earthen berm.

"See, it's just stuck out here at the edge of nothing, primitive. There's not even a toilet inside," Chen said. He pointed out a wooden outhouse twenty yards off to the right of the porch, next to a boulder the size of a small cottage, with a star fruit tree growing next to it. A power line ran to a corner of the roof from a telephone pole on the road, and a square concrete cistern sat on a rise on one side. Tall weeds and grasses grew out of control, walling in the house, as if the wilderness were pressing in on the space once tamed for human habitation.

"Can you see the sea from here?"

"Yes," Chen said, squinting ahead with his bird-like quality of observation. "The *binlang* trees break up the view . . . but yes, you can see the ocean through their trunks and leaves."

The atmosphere was shroud-like within the precipitation that enfolded us. I couldn't hear anything except the churring of a Taiwan five-color bird (black-browed barbet) and a muted rise and fall of cicada songs. We had left all farm and village sounds behind.

"It's gorgeous," I said, and took a deep breath of the wet clean air.

"There's no one within a mile of here. You'd have to fix the water line yourself. You want to give it a try?"

"Yes, yes. This is what I came here for. This is what I want."

"Okay. Then I'll help you. You're a long way from home. You know what we say in Chinese, *Zai jia kao jiaren, zai wai kao pengyou*, 'At home depend on family, outside depend on friends.' We'd better go down and see Mr. Huang. He'll be your nearest neighbor."

. . .

Farmer Huang poured us tea on the veranda of his metal siding house. We sat around his tea table made from the varnished root system of an extirpated tree, as he recounted the irrigation and construction projects his uncles and cousins had undertaken on this land over the past thirty years, the well his wife's third brother had started to dig before he went blind from drinking, and the time his wife was bitten by a cobra in her sleep.

"I always told him to save his money and build a catchment pond instead of a well. 'Course I didn't mind having the well after his widow sold the land to me. Look down the slope. See that row of windbreak bamboo? My land goes all the way down to there, and over to the edge of the ravine. A good-sized piece, eh? My wife, she was just sleeping, just right here where we're sitting right now, and that snake came up and bit her on the leg. I strapped her on my motorcycle and drove to the hospital in town. She couldn't even hold on, whole body rigid as a board. Shaking and rigid. I tied her to me with bungee cords. A cobra, it's a mean one, boy, only animal that will attack without provocation or hunger, just out of pure meanness."

"Except for a man," I said.

Huang cocked his head and sucked his teeth with a loud kissing sound, his flashing smile lit up at me. "That depends who your friends are!"

Like many rural Taiwanese, Huang's dental work consisted of metal dentures, so his mouth glinted silver when he smiled.

"Mr. Huang," Chen said, "this foreign friend wants to rent the old Tang place up the road. He's an artist."

Huang shuddered, as if he'd just heard a snippet of an insane mythology, but one that augured ill for his future and so couldn't be ignored.

"It's a damn shame," said Huang. He leaned back and sucked his teeth and frowned at fate, the evil bastard. "Everything about that place went wrong from the start. Old Tang drove over the edge of the ravine. The car crashed so deep in the undergrowth it took us two days to find him. We didn't know where to look . . . hell, we didn't even know if he'd crashed somewhere or just left his wife and run with his money to Macao. It happens. After the funeral we went up to help clean out the house. Lemme tell you, he liked his wine. There were hundreds of bottles up there, mostly Cognac xo. Nice bottles. I cleaned them out and put my homemade plum wine in them. I'll give you a taste one day.

"Tang was a dentist. Made a pile up in the north. He bought this place twenty years ago and came down whenever he could take a few days off. He always talked about moving here when he retired. They're Hakka too. His grandfather was the nephew of my great-aunt's adopted sister. You know how it is with a man like Tang, spent his whole life doing nothing much but making money . . . hell, anyone can pull a tooth. I've done it before. You ever have a tooth problem, just come on over. I'll take care of you, no charge. So he finally retires from the tooth-pulling racket and moves down here, and he wants to do something of substance for a change, carve something of himself on the land he owns. Not much glory in moving into someone else's field and collecting the fruit as it falls, see? Heh. So he came down here and spent his money tearing out that beautiful fruit orchard that was just in its prime, *shijia*, custard apples. Planted betel nut trees instead. He thought he'd catch the tail of the betel nut boom, thought they'd make him a fortune, get him proclaimed a genius. Waste of money, we all told him . . . all the betel nut farms are over on the west side of the central mountains. Even the *binlang* at the shops down in Dulan are brought over here from the west. Here we just grow a few, for our own use, but no one tries to make money off them. Sure enough, none of the wholesalers wanted to buy his crop. Wrong weather conditions, wrong soil, wrong everything. The taste just wasn't right.

"When they first moved down here, Tang and his wife lived in the upper house, the old house. Not a bad house. Originally built by Huangs, my father's sister's cousin-in-law. But Tang wanted a new house. Okay, nothing wrong with that. He built that new place, 'modern' I guess he would have called it, false ceilings and all. Problem was, when they brought the backhoes up and started digging the foundation, guess what they found? Sarcophagi! Two of 'em! Arranged in a T, one pointing east, the other north. Now, what does common sense tell you to do when you dig up a stone coffin from the past? That's right, you leave it in peace. Apologize. Light some incense, say a prayer. You go elsewhere. But what did Tang do? Paved 'em right the hell over and built on top of 'em. See, during the Japanese time, a lot of A-mei (Mandarin for Amis) were buried up in these mountains. The Japanese didn't let the tribes perform their ceremonies or rituals or whatever they do, so they brought their dead up here to bury them in secret. The land was wild then, unbroken. Take a walk, look around, you'll see. Old mounds of stone are still scattered through the orchards. You'll find long slabs of slate, cut into rectangles . . . that doesn't come from around here. There's no slate in the coastal range, only in the central mountains. Someone walked barefoot for a week with those stone slabs on his back to get them here. You'd better stay away from that place."

Huang leaned back, stretching his arms above his head as if in triumph. I looked over to Chen, to see if he was going to take up my cause, but he busied himself pouring tea into our half-empty cups.

"So Mrs. Tang moved back to the north after her husband died?"

"That's right. What else? You think she could stay in that house with her husband's ghost, not to mention whatever's buried there? She comes down once in a while to check in on things, but she left after the funeral."

I tried to infuse my gaze with resoluteness. Huang looked at me looking at him.

"What, you still want to live up there after what I just told you? If the ghosts don't get you, the cobras will. Snakes, wild boars, hunters discharging weapons in the night . . . we couldn't let you endanger yourself like that . . ."

Huang was king of the hill here, and as long as Tang's place was empty, its twenty acres of betel nut trees were part of his dominion. As an outsider, there was nothing I could do. In Chinese society you have to approach this kind of request through the proper channels. Chen was my channel, but he was a background presence. He didn't seem able or willing to exert an influence on the process.

". . . no, you can't rent that place. Look how far it is from everything, and she wouldn't rent it to you anyway . . . final resting place of her husband's drunken ghost, concrete and brick sarcophagus of failed dreams. It would be an insult to even ask. Women are emotional about those things, take my word for it. Hell, no one even has her phone number."

Huang rubbed his carefully shaved jaw with fingers stained dark from plant matter. He was about to stand up and dismiss us when the metal mesh door slid open with a crash, and his son stepped out, wearing only silk boxer shorts and plastic slippers. He was about my age, midthirties, with the look of a rural playboy about him. The son of an affluent farmer, he seemed to have been spared the crucible of hard work and had the smooth cheeks and ample belly of an epicure.

"What's wrong with giving it a try?" he said.

Huang senior was astonished. "Give what a try?"

"Give this foreigner a try! Let him give the house a try! What can it hurt?"

"But it's dangerous up there," Huang said. "And we have to respect Mrs. Tang."

Huang's authority had been capsized, not giving him time to do anything but wonder where it'd gone and try to stay afloat.

"Dangerous, shit. Why not get in touch with the old woman, see if she wants to rent the place? You don't have to worry about her. She's tough as a boar. Her husband was the soft one. You're not against the idea, are you?"

Chen nodded blandly. I didn't dare say a word.

"Me, no, of course I'm not against it. Personally I love Americans. But we don't have her phone number. We can't even write her a letter—we don't know her address."

"That's easy," Huang junior said. "Just stop by the Agricultural Co-op down in the village. They'll give you her address."

"I can do that," Chen interjected, starting to flow along with the momentum that had begun to swing my way.

Old Huang stood up, his mouth half-open, as if no longer sure what to do or say. Young Huang sat down, adjusted the crotch of his boxer shorts, and held out his hand to me.

"Welcome, neighbor," he said.

· · ·

Chen got the address and said he would write to Mrs. Tang on my behalf. The process was so tenuous and abstract that I had no faith in it—the co-op, the postal system, the whim of an aging widow. How could all these dice possibly come up in my favor? But a week later Chen called and told me Mrs. Tang had said yes, I could rent the house. She would come down the following week to give me a contract and show me around. I had the run of everything but the lower house, where she still stored a few things and stayed on her infrequent visits. With the advance from my record label, I paid for two years up front, and for the first time in years I didn't have to hustle and worry about how to pay the rent each month.

. . .

The house was isometric, with a boxy central room and single smaller rooms through doorways to each side. The ceiling was open-beamed, with long, thin betel nut trunks for cross-beams, one-by-fours laid laterally over these, then plywood, then the roof tiles. The roof was remarkably water-tight and only leaked in the heaviest typhoons. In fact, during periods of extended deluge, more water seeped up through cracks in the concrete floor than leaked in from above. Out on the porch, wasp and swallow nests lined the corners of the eaves.

The land was strewn with boulders that had tumbled down from the mountainside. A few fruit trees remained around the periphery of the dooryard, but the land was mostly covered with the betel nut groves that had reverted to a state of wildness. A one-inch PVC pipe ran a half-mile down the road behind the property, then high up a ravine, from where it carried spring water to the cistern. The water pipe required constant maintenance, and I often had to hike up with a machete and a can of epoxy to patch or unstop the line.

After I moved in, my guitars and boxes of books sat around the house like bored relatives. I entered a process of osmosis, sinking into this place particle by particle as it revealed itself to me. I had a few beat-up tatami mats that had belonged to Chinese poetry and sutra translator Red Pine when he'd lived on Yangmingshan, the mountain due north of Taipei, twenty years before, and I flopped them down on the floor. I patched the window screens and replaced the frosted panes with clear glass. A-sun, the self-appointed Open Circle Tribe handyman, came up one day with a welding torch to cut the iron security bars off the windows for me. "You sure your landlady won't mind?" A-sun asked, as he hauled the acetylene and oxygen tanks from his van into the yard.

"O man," I said, "I just don't care . . . I'll pay to put them back in later if I have to."

A-sun lit the torch and cut through the bars one by one,

and I twisted them out of the concrete sills with pliers. This theoretically left me vulnerable to theft, but the place was unlivable to me with bars on the windows. I couldn't stand the sense of incarceration. The only thing that was ever stolen from me here was a bottle of soy sauce from the unlocked kitchen a week after I moved in—by hunters, my friends said, who didn't mean any harm. But much later I discovered the thief had been a bearded man who lived in the river bottom and sometimes walked down the road at sunset with a mattock over his shoulder, appearing from nowhere and walking out of sight. He was filthy and wild, clearly either insane or a reclusive Taoist sage. I tended to believe the latter, but two years later he committed a horrific murder, killing an elderly couple with his mattock on another part of the mountain.

I found a discarded desk by the wall of tetrapods along the beach below Dulan. It was plastic laminate and particle board, ugly as hell but functional. I hauled it home and set it in the middle of the center room, and became commander-in-chief of four blank walls and twenty acres of brush. Dou-dou told me to always lift the toilet lid with a stick before sitting down in case a snake was concealed beneath it. I never encountered one there, but one winter morning I nearly stepped on a deadly krait coiled in the bathing room, black with coral-red markings. It remained motionless, lethargic from the cold, more hypnotically beautiful than threatening. I doubled a piece of wire and passed it through a three-foot section of PVC pipe so that it formed a noose. I looped it over the snake's head and pulled the wire tight from the other end, snaring the snake against the bore. I walked a quarter-mile with its lovely colors and curls dangling from the end of the pipe, and set it free among the betel nut trees. I never saw a cobra here, and all the poisonous snakes I encountered were brilliantly colored, sinuous, and docile, and never showed aggression.

In the coming months I lived between polarities of solitude and community. I dug into my farmhouse abode, carving out a space for my songs and poems, and every few days walked down the mountain and hitched north to Jinzun, to stay with the Open Circle Tribe. Before long my own driftwood infatuation was in full swing. I began collecting pieces and stacking them against the front wall of the house, creating a link between the two poles of my life, the mountain and the sea.

Night on the mountain was a lush symphony of insects, frogs, and night birds, singing, clicking, buzzing, and trilling. Geckos chirped as they hunted mosquitoes on the walls. Sometimes they fought each other upside-down on the ceiling; sometimes they fell with a soft plop to the floor. When the surf was large the sound of waves rose up from the coast, and I heard it as a distant hush and wash, diffuse but rhythmic as I sat at my desk typing poems and letters on a Japanese-made typewriter I'd bought used in Taipei. It was about three feet across and weighed half a ton, an enormous, beige office machine, which I painted green and blue with watercolors, and which hummed and clacked beautifully where I set it on my castoff desk. Down in my tent at Jinzun I slept dreamless white sleep, my mind blanketed in breaking waves, the "pop" and "ah" of ten trillion foamy bubbles.

One evening when I returned home at dusk I saw a hundred-pacer snake at the edge of the driveway, so-named because that's supposedly how far you can walk before you're dead if one bites you. It was coiled like a yellow, diamonded god, perfectly still against the concrete in the fading light. How strange to walk past it with the knowledge that if it chose to strike I would cease to exist in seconds—and yet I felt serenity in that heightened sense of mortality, in the acquiescence to a grand design containing me. The Bunun, Paiwan, and other mountain tribes worshipped the hundred-pacer, and to encounter one was considered a good omen.

FIVE

Beneath the Skin

One day a few months after I'd moved into my mountain abode, Yiming and I stripped off our shirts as we walked along the beach at Jinzun. Spring was ripening into summer, and a warm wind blew in thick and salty from the sea. We stepped through driftwood spilt like matchsticks across the sand, everything from logs three feet in diameter to twigs and shards of bark, hopping and skipping the way you navigate the scree and stones along a mountainside.

All the men in the Open Circle Tribe carried machete-length knives, with carved wooden sheaths and handles, that hung on their hips from leather belts. (The women too carried knives, but smaller, less obtrusive ones.) These had dozens of uses—to fillet a fish for sashimi, cut a trail through brush, whittle a bamboo spear, or peel a mango. And they were an essential element of style, not only because of the inherent charisma of the blade, but because they were an expression of one's own carving aesthetic, hanging right there from your hip. The sheaths and handles were lovingly designed and shaped, works of art in their own right that could be flourished and admired any time a task provided an opportunity.

Yiming drew his blade every time we came to a driftwood log he liked the look of, and cut a chip from its silvered skin to see what was concealed beneath the surface. Through this small eye-hole, a woodcarver could determine the type of wood and whether it was worth salvaging. Yiming generally wrought his sculptures from solid logs using chain saws, chisels, planers, and angle grinders, but allowing natural contours to guide the flow of the work. Others, such as Doudou, worked more with driftwood as found shapes, juxtaposing and interposing forms, as well as adding carved designs. For all the Open Circle Artists there was sanctity in the line, color, and grain of driftwood, in its expression of movement stretched between the mountains and the sea, a cycle vaster than anyone could capture or replicate, but carving was a way to partake of it. Driftwood was a love affair, and I soon became seduced by its myriad shape, texture, and scent, and with sawing, carving, sanding, lifting, and being surrounded by driftwood.

"Smell that," Yiming said after cutting a chip from a medium-sized log, about four feet long. "It's hinoki, the only wood they use in Japanese temples. It's good for carving."

Hinoki is the Japanese name of a local cypress. A rich cinnamon scent bloomed outward from a honey-colored grain, which had been sealed within the sun- and salt-bleached outer skin.

"Is that what you used to make your knife?" I asked.

"No, hinoki is good, but it's a soft wood, a conifer. I like harder woods, like *jumu* or *wuxinshi*. Not so easy to work with, but they're more durable and polish up beautifully. You can really make them shine."

Jumu is a dense, orange-colored hardwood, Shen-hui's favorite, and *wuxinshi*, "black-heart stone" in Mandarin, is so adamantine and heavy its name invokes "stone," just as American hornbeam is so hard it's called ironwood.

Yiming took out a plastic sack of *binlang*. We each took one, bit off the cap, chewed, then spit the red juice onto the sand. We turned toward the sea. Waves curled in against the rocky promontory at the end of the curving beach and crashed twenty feet into the air. Straight out from shore, Green Island sat like a lumpy crocodile head in the middle of the sea, and all around the sun glinted bright as welding sparks across the rippled ocean.

"Scott, is it like this in America?"

I thought of the driftwood shores of the Pacific Northwest, the same gorgeous ocean yawning out from beaches strewn with conifer logs, the Olympic Mountains rising up behind, the light all blue and silver across the sky and water—but I couldn't imagine moving there to live with a troupe of bacchanalian artists and their chain saws, cutting and carving logs on the beach and raising them up into sculpture, building bonfires to roast chickens and illuminate bottles of wine.

In the United States, authority and regulation have extended to the edges of the nation-state. There are more structures and regulations to follow, more taxes to pay. The internal colonialism of America was complete long ago, and the state has the financial and technological power to enforce its authority to the far reaches of its borders. Here in Taiwan the edges of the empire were still a bit frayed and loose, there was still a little space to wiggle and negotiate. On this remote stretch of coast, we were in the shatter zone, where fragments of various cultures remained, beyond the full embrace of the engulfment plan. Here it was still possible to live off the radar without consigning oneself to complete disengagement from the world.

The Republic of China had repressed cultural and ethnic diversity in Taiwan up through the late 1980s, but in the early 2000s indigenous expression began to be encouraged, as Taiwan sought a pluralistic identity, distinct from its colonial past. After all, the authorities could have shut down the Jinzun project at any time. Taiwanese identity was still plastic, up for grabs, while in America there is a firmly established cultural and political norm. Whether they are granted or denied permission to hunt whales, no one is asking the Makah Indians to help America define itself, to clarify what the United States is as a culture, history, or society. Indigenous American cultures' contribution to mainstream identity is mostly limited to the role of cultural relics, something to hang on display, like the Makah painted screens exhibited in museums. They are seen as windows to another time and way of being, not as a cultural presence to influence or inform the living interface between community and landscape.

How could I explain the strictures and bureaucracy of America to Yiming, who barely acknowledged time as a concrete phenomenon?

"It's the same sun, same sea, but with bigger mountains," I said.

"Ah, I'd like to see them one day. We'll go together, okay? Could we do a project on the beach just like this, with the aboriginal woodcarvers there? I've seen pictures. Some of their totem carvings are just like Chinese designs on bronze drums from four thousand years ago."

"Why not? I have some friends in art foundations. We can try to organize it."

"You're lucky, you know. I want to travel around the world like you, but there's always something holding me back. Did I ever tell you about the job I used to do up in the north? I worked in a karaoke bar in Taoyuan, singing with the customers. With the female customers, know what I mean? I was strong, the clients loved me . . . I made a lot of money. Sometimes I don't even know why I returned. Back in Zhiben, my home village, whenever I'm around the old men, my Puyuma elders, I feel like they're disappointed in me . . . like something's missing in me, something I'm supposed to have, that I have to have, but don't. Sometimes I hate the older generation for not teaching me, for not passing my own tradition on to me. Can you understand what I'm saying? Sometimes I hate the elders of my own tribe, my own ancestors. What does that make me?"

Two small tears trickled from the corners of Yiming's eyes. He was not ashamed of this. Here, there was no proscription against a man having a heart full of emotion and desire, or against these spilling from his eyes as salt.

Yiming's grandparents grew up as Japanese citizens, and he grew up in a time when it was virtually illegal to speak Puyuma and every other indigenous language. What chance did they have to effect a cultural transmission when he had no context to learn his own mother tongue? Many indigenous children in Taiwan could not communicate with their own grandparents. It was not the elders' fault, nor Yiming's, that their cultural lineage had been fissured. Maybe his anguish came from the general sense of alienation common to many indigenous peoples forced to assimilate to hegemonic rule, a displacement unfixable by any individual, unhealable within the arc of a single life.

"How'd you go from singing karaoke to becoming an artist anyway?"

"Aw man, I've had a million jobs. We all have. Let me tell you a story. From Taoyuan I went to Taipei and got a job delivering natural gas . . . there's only so much karaoke a man can sing. You know the big gas canisters for cooking stoves? You've seen them. We'd load them up on the back of our motorbikes and drive around the city, deliver them to people's kitchens. Fifty kilos per tank, and I'd heft them up on my shoulder and carry them up the stairs, fourth floor, sixth floor, wherever it was. Imagine doing that in the Taipei summer . . . a hundred degrees, 90 percent humidity, the air gritty and polluted with motorbike exhaust. Sweating and working twelve hours a day, I was nothing but muscle back then, hard as stone. One day after work the boss took me and the other workers out to drink beer, sitting out on the sidewalk at a street café. After a couple of hours we were all drunk, and the boss took us to a brothel. I went along, but when I went in and looked around, I saw that every single girl in there was aboriginal. Every one! Some of them about fifteen or sixteen years old. You can't imagine how sad that made me feel. It broke my heart. I didn't say anything to anyone, I just turned and left. A while after that, I quit my job and came back home. I wasn't making it in Taipei. I got a job as a lifeguard at one of the hot spring resorts in Zhiben. And at the same time I started an apprenticeship with a master woodcarver in our village. Just chainsawing, sanding, carving basic designs at first. But after a while, I started to have my own ideas, and one thing leads to another. That's how creativity works, right? You learn a technique from someone else, and that technique came from someone else before him. It's passed down hand to hand, but then you make it your own. You start to add something of yourself to it, and it becomes art."

Beyond the breaking waves, the ocean was rippled with iris and teal. The sky and sea were a blend of gray and green where they met at the horizon.

"What about you? You're so far from America, don't you miss your home?"

"I don't know, man. It's somewhere over there, across this ocean, but I've been away most of the last ten years. I don't have any home to return to. I don't have any place I belong to in America."

"You do, you just don't want to accept it," Yiming said.

What could I say? He was right. Every time I returned to the West Coast of America I felt the soil there was the stuff inside my bones. And yet something kept me roaming far away, pressing against some limit or restriction I felt I needed to surpass. The flip side of this yearning was sometimes isolation, displacement, alienation, the same kind of thing Yiming had just described, even including a sense of anger toward my own forebears, a sense of severance, of not having received some rite or ritual of initiation, which left me incomplete. I was bifurcated by the sea. I wondered if I would ever feel wholly at home in any place again. This is the conundrum of expatriatism—no matter where you go, some part of you will always be home someplace else.

This thought made me glum for a moment. But Yiming saw

my hangdog look and started laughing, and I couldn't help joining him. Yiming cupped his hands around his mouth and shouted "Whooo!" into the waves. I did the same. We howled and laughed at the sea and sky extending all around us.

"You and me, we're home here now," Yiming said.

. . .

We turned back toward the camp. Yiming rambled loose and easy, talking about the virtues of various woods, plans to go fishing, and his workshop in Zhiben, as he swung his knife around like a cutlass.

"Where do you get these knives?" I asked him.

"We buy the blades from Huang *shifu*, the blacksmith up in Chenggong, and we carve the sheathes and handles ourselves. You like this one?"

Yiming handed me his knife. The handle had a pleasant shape. The blade slipped easily from the sheath, with just enough resistance to keep it from falling out on its own. I took cuts at a couple of logs. I liked the heft and balance of the knife, the extension of my body into carved wood and a metal edge, and the revelation through these of what lay beneath the surface of the driftwood that surrounded us.

"Yeah, I like it. It feels good in my hand."

"That's good, 'cause it's yours."

I held it another moment, feeling the smooth grain of the wood against my fingers, absorbing the gift Yiming had offered me, then handed it back.

"Come on, man, I can't take this," I said. "I mean, you shaped it for yourself, to fit your own hand, right? But for sure I need a knife like this. If I buy a blade, would you carve a handle and sheath for me?"

Yiming grinned and placed a sliver of wood between his teeth.

"I'd be happy to carve a knife for you, brother. But wouldn't you rather carve your own?"

. . .

That was a good point. So the next afternoon I walked up the stairs to the highway to hitch the twenty miles up the coast to Chenggong. Yiming told me that once I had a blade, E-ki's workshop would be the best place to go to make a handle. "E-ki has plenty of tools and materials," Yiming said. "And besides, he's the best woodcarver we have."

I caught a ride with an ancient Taiwanese man selling sausages from a three-wheeled farm vehicle converted into a mobile barbeque. A brazier was mounted in back, and links of splotched meat swung between two upright metal bars. I squeezed next to him in the narrow cab. He smoked Long Life cigarettes, the government brand produced by the Taiwan Alcohol and Tobacco Monopoly, fitting them loosely into a gap where his front teeth must once have been, and offered me his pack. We drove on the shoulder of the road past fields of taro with leaves like broad drooping tongues, flooded paddies reflecting the sky. Beyond the fields the peaks of the coastal range rose up into clouds.

"Are you from around here?" I asked, lighting up a Long Life.

"Sure," he said. "I've never left, except when I was conscripted by the Japanese to fight in World War II. My whole village was taken away. All the men, that is. Not many of us came back. My brother was only fifteen."

"What did you do when you returned?"

"We're farmers. We were one of the earliest Han families here, from way back when the tribes were still headhunting. I can't work on the farm much anymore, but my children are in Taipei. I don't know who's going to grow our food in a few years. Only old people and small children are left in the countryside. Everyone else has gone to cities to work or study. My oldest grandson is studying to be a doctor there now. Where do you come from?"

"There," I said, pointing across the sea.

"Ah, America," he said.

We ran into a thundershower; a torrential cloudburst crashed down on us. The man grabbed a squeegee with a long red handle, leaned forward, and reached outside to swipe the water from the windshield with his left hand as he drove. Quite an acrobatic move for an octogenarian. We hit a pothole and jounced violently. He pitched forward and hit his face against the windshield. We careened across the road into the opposing lane and would have been creamed by any oncoming vehicle, but the road in both directions was empty. We passed out of the rain like it was a curtain drawn aside. Mist rose from the asphalt, and the vernal sun leapt out upon us hot and wet, like some jungle animal close and panting, blood on its lips and teeth.

When we got to Chenggong, the old man turned on a looped recording that barked news of his sausages out through a megaphone, and I stepped out into a potholed street still puddled from the rain. The blacksmith's shop stood between an overgrown dirt lot and an unfinished concrete building, with rebar sticking up from the roof. Inside the shop, shelves were stacked with all variety of knife blades, some almost as long as swords, some short and tapered like stilettos, as well as work tools such as hoes, axe heads, pickaxes, and spades.

"Huang *shifu*," I called out. "Master Huang! I'm here to buy a blade!"

Huang the blacksmith emerged from the forge behind the shop, in blackened overalls with a hammer in his hand. He was strong and simple as an ox, built like a furnace, and wore a smile of boyish astonishment.

"Well, listen to you talk," he said. "I've never heard an American talk Chinese before. You talk better than me!"

Huang was fulfilling the traditional Chinese etiquette of complimenting a guest. In addition, he was ethnic Taiwanese, and a "Taiwanese" accent carried a stigma of provincialism. A "standard" Mandarin accent (based on Beijing pronunciation) was considered to be more "civilized," even by many

Taiwanese, who in this sense had assumed the chauvinism of their colonizers.

"I don't speak well at all," I said, complying with the etiquette of a humble response to praise. "But I've been in Taipei some years, and now I'm staying with the woodcarvers down at Jinzun. Yiming told me I could buy a knife blade here."

"Ah, you must be an artist. What a good life! Not like me, sweating and dirty every day just to keep food in my family's mouth. As long as you're not hungry . . . but you must be all right," he said, winking at my belly. "What kind of blade are you looking for?"

"I want something strong, something durable. I think stainless steel is what I need."

"Look around, see what you like, you'll get a good price! And you can have stainless if you like, I've got it here. But look, these iron blades are what all your friends use. You can whet these down so sharp you can shave with them. You'll never get stainless as sharp as an iron blade. And if you keep it oiled, an iron blade will never rust!"

I looked through the shelves and picked out a blade about fourteen inches long, curved into a hook at the end, which I thought would have a useful sickle effect in cutting grass, the primary function I envisioned for my knife. It was a couple of inches broad, matte black but with a dull sheen along the sharpened edge. I tested the blade on my forearm, and sure enough it took the hair off clean. A narrow prong tapered down from the bottom, to which a handle would be affixed.

"That's for cutting bamboo," Huang said.

"Okay, I'll take it," I said. At the time I didn't know what he meant, but later I learned the curve was good for trimming the branches and leaves from a bamboo pole.

"You need anything else? Hoe? Mattock? Pitchfork? Any friend of Yiming is welcome here." Huang wrapped the blade up in a sheaf of newspaper and tied it with plastic twine. As I turned to leave he proffered one last ritual of Chinese etiquette, the perpetual invitation to eat. "Now listen, don't let yourself get hungry down there on the beach. Why don't you come in and eat with us before you go back?"

"Thank you, maybe next time. I just finished eating, I'm not hungry at all now," I lied.

"Are you sure? Don't say no just to be polite, we've got plenty . . . well then come back soon. My wife's a good cook. Come for dinner any time!"

· · ·

I walked to the edge of town to hitch back to Dulan. The Chenggong Mountains are the apex of the coastal range, at over 5,000 feet (Dulanshan is 4,220). They rose stark and severe behind the town, shard-like peaks jutting into bands of cloud. I stuck my thumb out as a car approached, a new Mercedes-Benz that streaked right by. At the same moment another car passed going the wrong way, but a hundred yards past me it braked hard and swung around. It was an off-duty cop in a charcoal-gray sedan, and he offered to drive me to Dulan, though it was the opposite direction he'd been heading. As I got in and shut the door, he squinted at me as if trying to decipher a code, with a mixture of suspicion and curiosity, then turned his eyes to the road and hit the gas.

"You are American?" he asked.

"Yes, yes." That was everyone's default guess. The large U.S. military presence in Taiwan from 1945 until 1979 had conflated "American" with "Westerner" in popular perception.

"But why are you here? This is a wasteland. There's nothing here."

He had a crew cut and wore a golf shirt with a pattern of dollar signs printed on it. He seemed like a man who distrusted everything but guns and money, as if any other valuation would bewilder him. He offered me an imported cigarette.

"Why am I here?" I repeated, as bewildered as he.

"Yes," he said. "America is advanced, developed, rich. These villagers are backward and poor. If I could get to America, fuck it, I'd be gone. The people here, they barely have language, they can't even write."

To me and my friends the allure of this gorgeous, singing landscape, where green mountains rose like waves above the sea, was self-evident. There was none of the stress and worry of city life, none of the compression and pollution of the metropolis—less of these anyway. To us this far corner of the world was a step away from industrial consciousness and economic reductivism. Down on Jinzun, eating wild greens and donated rice, we desired none of the things the cop seemed to think I was a fool not to possess. Residing in this blue-green world, on a lip of earth above the sea, I felt a space open in my mind that was primordial, raw, and free. I didn't feel I lacked anything.

For someone psychically, economically, or culturally invested in the system, this marginal landscape, far from the capital, might be a wasteland, a place of exile. But "margins" and cultural subversion are endemic to the larger arc of Chinese culture. All my favorite classical Chinese poets wrote their greatest poems from exile. As an aesthetic expression, this disconnection from worldly ambition, from the centers of power, is valued at the highest levels of Chinese literature and philosophy. It could be argued, therefore, that these "villagers" were not backward and uncouth, but were the most civilized of anyone in Taiwan—as civilized as Tao Yuan-ming, or Wang Wei, who lyricized a life of exile and wine, of letting go of ambition for worldly gain and sinking into the larger cycles of things.

But this evocation of natural beauty and simplicity, dissenting against the hierarchies of state power, exists only in literary memory, in abstract, textual consciousness. Try living like Wang Wei today, sitting around doing nothing, rhapsodizing about clouds rising from a valley, and your family will send you to dentistry school and threaten to disown you.

In the West, artists like van Gogh, James Joyce, or the Beat Generation existed on the periphery of their cultures but were such strong creative forces that they pulled the center to themselves, recalibrating it. But the corporations that pay a hundred million for a van Gogh today wouldn't give him a bed to sleep in if he showed up alive and hungry at their door.

Exile may be the only door to the pantheon, though you'll likely be dead before they let you in.

The cop drove fast and grim down the highway, squinting against his cigarette smoke and looking at me sideways. Our lexicons were so askew I couldn't think of a single word to say.

"So, where are you from?" I finally asked.

"Mainland," he said, folding a piece of chewing gum into his mouth. "We're from Shandong Province, in the northeast of China. My father was a soldier and came with Chiang Kai-shek in 1949. Before that we lived in the same village three hundred years. We still have relatives there."

"You have kids?" I asked.

"Yeah," he said as we pulled over in Dulan, and I unlatched the door. "I got a local wife."

SIX

Carving a Carving Knife

After the cop dropped me off I walked a half mile south and up a concrete ramp to E-ki's workshop. E-ki and his brother sat on the ground, reclining against a skinned log, wearing straw hats cocked forward, idle and patient as if waiting for a train. "Ho," said E-ki when he heard me approach, half-opening one eye.

The workshop was a compound of sagging sheds strewn with tools, wood scraps, and broken furniture. It belonged to a friend of E-ki's who planned to raze everything and sell the place, and in the interim E-ki had the run of it. Though E-ki was married, he stayed most of the time with his brother in a bachelor squalor of hammers, chisels, three-legged chairs, and chickens pecking through the yard.

E-ki's brother was simple-minded, with a slack grin perpetually hanging from his face. He was older than E-ki, but subordinate to him, competent to carry out assigned tasks but not to take initiative. E-ki embraced the world and embossed his desires, abilities, and vision upon the portion within his grasp. His brother was always a step behind, doing what was necessary to stay in E-ki's orbit but never establishing one of his own. He had never married. He was one of those derelict men whom it's impossible to consider in terms of romance. One night when I stopped by to say hello, E-ki was in town at his wife's apartment. E-ki's brother and I sat on plastic stools sipping *mijiu* from a bottle I'd brought. "Ah, Scott," he said to me, "have you got yourself a girlfriend? How good that would be . . ." He spoke these words as forlorn and wistfully as if he'd said, "Ah, how good it would be to win the Nobel Prize . . ."

As an elder of the local aboriginal woodcarving community, E-ki was often called E-*shifu*, "Master E." In this locution E-ki's *E* lengthened into a diphthong, and the pronunciation became similar to the name of the letter *A*, so it sounded like A-*shifu*. Riffing off this alphabetic pun, friends jokingly called E-ki's brother "B-*shifu*." But the name stuck, the suggestion that he was the *B* version of E-ki too close to the truth to be relinquished. E-ki simply called his brother *ge-ge*, Mandarin for "elder brother." By coincidence, the epoxy used by the woodcarvers was called A-B glue. Two compounds were mixed together, and formed an instant bond.

E-ki stretched lazily and motioned me to take a seat. "How's everything up on the mountain? You know, my father killed a bear up on Dulanshan. You seen any signs of bear up there?"

"Not yet."

"That's right, and you won't. They're almost gone from the coast range. There're a few up around Chenggong, but mostly they're only left in the central mountains."

"Did you used to eat them?"

"Bear, well, you can eat 'em, and we have eaten 'em, but we don't like to. We like to stay on good terms with 'em. It's not our tradition to hunt them. Truth is, they don't taste that good—not like wild boar or mountain goat, that's what we get if we can. The bears were hunted for the Han. Fifty years ago, after the Japanese left, Chiang Kai-shek showed up with two million mainland Chinese—suddenly there was a market for black bear. The Han tribe use 'em in medicine—their claws, their balls, who knows what. Meanwhile, we Amis were starving. We became professional hunters. All the tribes did, the ones who still could."

"Wild boars come down at night sometimes to eat the sug-arcane in front of my house."

"Sure they do, wouldn't you? A pig knows what's good. You call me next time they're out, we'll get us some meat. My brother can skin him for us, eh *ge-ge*?"

"Oh, I've skinned plenty of 'em. I got a knife just right for skinning pigs. I'll whet it up sharp."

"We'll have a feast, invite the whole village. Call me, and we'll get him together, unless you want to get him yourself. You've probably seen *feishu* up there too, flying squirrels."

"I hear them at night, and hunters drive through, shining lights up into the trees looking for them."

"That's right, they're nocturnal. The hunters look for the shine of their eyes, then shoot at them with crossbows. Guns are illegal for hunting *feishu*."

"Scott," said B-*shifu*, "what's in that package there? Did you get yourself a knife?"

I handed him my new blade. He took it from the newspaper in which it was wrapped and held it aloft by the stem. "Ah, this is good, this is a good one. I'd like to get a knife like this. How much did it cost?"

But E-ki took the blade and frowned, tracing his finger along the flat of its arc. "What made you choose this one?"

"I don't know, it looked good. I thought it'd be good for cutting grass."

"Shit, why'd old Huang let you buy this? When you're up there on the mountain, what are you going to do when that old boar charges in on you with his tusks? You need to be able to stick him before he sticks you. How you going to do that with this curved shit? It's got no force, no . . . what, no martial thrust to it. You'd have to swing this thing up around your head and chop it down like an axe before you'd do any damage, and what do you reckon would happen in the mean-time? Here, look at my blade. You ask Siki, Yiming, any of those guys. Their blades will all be the same."

He drew his knife, straight and long, broad at the bottom but tapered to a point at the tip.

"Now, tell me which you'd rather have. And hell, you think I've never cut any grass with this blade? I should be so lucky. Come on, I'll show you around, and then I'll get you started. I guess you want to make a handle for this thing. *Ge-ge*, what are you doing, going back to work?"

B-*shifu* laughed, "That's right, what should I do?"

"Better get that load of wood out of the truck and stack it against the front wall. We'll clean up that cedar log and work with it next."

E-ki led me along a dirt path between two sheds. We passed a garden of new greens planted rowlessly, simply broadcast across the plot. We came to an enclosure knocked together with scrap lumber and chicken wire. Inside were a couple dozen piglets, black and hairy. "These are mini-pigs," E-ki said.

"They're what?"

"Mini-pigs. Mini-*shanzhu*, mini–wild boars." He said "mini-pigs" in English; it sounded like "meeni-peegs." "You know *peeg*, don't you? That's your language."

"Mini" had crossed unchanged from English into Mandarin usage (for example, *qun* is Mandarin for "skirt," and "mini-skirt" is *mini qun*), and "pig" was part of E-ki's grab bag of English words from his job in the north.

"Yes, yes, I know *peeg*," I said. "What are you going to do with so many?"

"Make money! I got these two litters for a thousand *kuai*, a thousand NT, and once they're grown I can sell 'em for a thousand apiece. Think about it, twenty-four thousand, not bad for gathering up slop and throwing it to a few *peegs*, eh? I might come up to your place next week. We can cut some grass for them."

"Plenty of grass up there, sure."

We returned to the workshop. Two wood benches were abutted to each other at a loose angle, with a mesh of black nylon webbing suspended above for shade. Epoxy and chisels lay on the counters, along with grease-caked chains, nails, and screws.

"Now, let's make you a handle. You like hinoki?"

"Yeah, it's my favorite."

"Sure, the grain and color are beautiful. A lot of the guys like to use it for their sheathes, like Dafeng. That way, every time you pull out your blade, it releases that cinnamon scent. Plus, hinoki is easy to work with. It's a soft wood, a good place to begin."

E-ki found a piece of hinoki in the scrap pile and set it on the saw block. He picked up a chain saw, tested the tension of the chain, then grabbed the cord and ripped the motor into life. Smoke streamed out in thick clouds that clung to our clothes. He revved the engine and brought the blade down across the grain, holding the wood steady with his left foot, and bucked out an eight-inch section. He shut off the saw and set it down on the ground. He brushed the sawdust and grit from the block, inspected the grain for knots, then set it on end and trimmed it down by splitting along the grain with a hatchet.

"This is where you start," he said, "with a thick piece of wood. You can do anything with it. What it becomes is up to your intention and skill, not to mention patience."

E-ki went to his tool bench and returned with a small carving knife, a short triangular blade with a metal handle. He sat down and took a sharpening stone from a plastic basin filled with water. He whetted the blade, pushing it nearly horizontally across the stone, then flipped it over and repeated the motion, going back and forth.

"Sharpening's free the first time. Next time you got to do it yourself or pay me. Now, you want to carve away from yourself. Use long strokes, bring it down, shape it to fit your hand. Then we'll butt it onto your blade. Here, have a look at mine. See how that feels to you."

His knife handle tapered quickly in from the butt end, providing a smooth, solid grip, then broadened again where it met the base of the blade. The carved wood fit into my hand like they were latched together.

"Feels good."

"That's right, and when I head up the mountain I wrap some strips of inner tube around it. Wood gets slippery when it's wet. The inner tube helps your grip. Plus, how you going to start a fire in the rain?"

"I don't know."

"That inner tubing will burn when it's wet. So I just unwrap it from my knife, and I've got a start. Then you find a downed log, collect some dry duff and moss from beneath it—maybe even chop out some kindling from the underside of the log. You might have to cut away the bark and outer layer to get to the dry wood underneath. 'Course you want to start your fire in the shelter of a cliff or boulder, sometimes even next to a tree, so it doesn't get put out by the rain before you've got it going. Once it's kindled, you feed it small branches dry as you can find. The heat evaporates the surface moisture. Then you do the same thing with larger and larger branches. It's best to have one person tending the fire, protecting it, while another gets more wood. Of course, it's best if it's not raining too hard—hell, what am I talking about? It's best if it's not raining at all. See, no one would choose to start a fire in the rain, but sometimes you got no choice. But my father, he could walk into the forest with nothing but a bag of salt and a knife and walk out a month later whistling a tune. And no one from that generation came back from the forest empty-handed. They brought back food. They wouldn't show their faces without a deer or mountain goat around their shoulders. Those days weren't like now, when we just drive to the store and buy a piece of meat any time we want. In the old days when someone returned from the forest, there was a feast."

E-ki left me with the wood and the knife. I carved into the blonde and honey-colored grain, unpeeling the years of mountain sun and soil from before this tree was uprooted, washed down a river and out to sea, washed back up on the shore where E-ki and his brother loaded it up in their truck and drove it home. How many years from mountain to sea to shore? And now I carved this piece of tree to attach to a piece of iron to cut brush trails back up on the mountain. Wood shavings curled off the grain and fell around my feet, releasing a lush scent of cinnamon and cedar. The knife was a bar of sweat and metal curled within my fingers. The blade scratched and rasped as it cut along the grain. Cicadas anticipating the encroaching evening raised their cries into a swell of sound, and rays of sun slanted in from behind the mountain. Cars zoomed and whooshed by as they sped through the highway curves just below, between E-ki's workshop and the sea. E-ki returned from his workbench and looked down at my progress.

"Well, that's innovative," he said. "Never seen anyone make a handle quite like that before. The problem is, how you going to grip it?"

He was right. It was bulky and asymmetrical. I hadn't been able to accomplish the line and form that I'd envisioned.

"See, if you bring it down here, just above the butt, your hand would fold right around it. You want your fingers and the wood to fit right into each other . . . Now, look at mine again . . . if you're out in the woods and you got a wild boar charging at you, which would you rather have? See what's going to happen? The way you've got it, you stab that bastard in his gizzard, and your hand's going to go right up the blade of the knife, right as that tusk rips into your groin. Then what good are you? No more playing guitar for the pretty girls, and nothing to do with them if you could get 'em. Now, it's your choice, but if I were you I'd bring this down real slow. Don't gouge the wood, don't try to force it. There's no hurry. Just shave it down, caress it with the blade . . . Hold on now, not yet. Let me get a step away. You're wild with that motion. Save it for the *peeg*. I don't want to be your first victim—"

CARVING A CARVING KNIFE

E-ki's brother hollered something from across the yard. "Come on," E-ki said, "my brother has cooked a fish."

We walked across the lot and sat at a chainsawed log table stained with oil. We each had a bowl of rice and chopsticks, and shared a fried fish and a plate of greens.

"Know what this vegetable is?" E-ki asked me.

"Sure, sweet potato leaves."

"That's right. They grow like weeds. Throw a few stems in the dirt, and in a week you've got greens for dinner."

"I've heard that a lot of Taiwanese avoided starvation by eating sweet potato leaves when Chiang Kai-shek arrived and appropriated most of the economy for his army."

"Could be, could be . . . the Han only know how to eat what they grow. We didn't bother with sweet potato leaves back then. When times were lean we ate what we gathered from the wild."

"Scott, I didn't know you eat these in America," said B-*shifu*.

"No, not in America, but there's a big patch of sweet potato leaves up at my place on the mountain."

"Now you're one of us," B-*shifu* said with an open-mouthed grin. "In cities people have to spend their money in supermarkets. Here, we just go outside and pick what we need."

"Ho ho, there's still a few things to buy, still a few snares to catch you," E-ki said. "So far you can't walk out and pick a bottle of *mijiu* out of the weed patch. And too bad tobacco doesn't grow wild, eh? Speaking of which, brother, why don't you bring out that bottle so it's here when we need it?"

The filament glowed in a bulb hanging from a wire above the table. The sky shifted into evening, becoming grainy and gray-blue. Cool air flowed down from the mountain. Frogs and insects cooed, clicked, and trilled from beyond the edge of the lot. Fewer cars passed now, their whoosh and hum replaced by the hush of the night sea beyond the highway.

When we finished eating E-ki unscrewed the cap on the *mijiu* bottle and placed a small glass jar on the table for a cup. We took turns pouring and drinking.

"Do you have *mijiu* in America?" B-*shifu* asked me.

"*Mijiu*, hell," E-ki said, "who would drink *mijiu* when they could have whiskey? These Americans, they probably don't even feel this weak stuff, only 20 percent. Am I right?"

"We don't have much *mijiu*, but we've got plenty of everything else."

"Next time you come by we'll finish up your handle, then I'll show you how to make a sheath for your knife. Going to be hard with that curved thing of yours. All the old men have open-faced sheaths, the wood carved out and bound with copper wire. That was the only way to do it back in their day. Now we've got A-B glue, we can make solid wood sheathes. You carve out two halves and glue 'em together. You can choose which you want.

"Shit, my hands are stiff from using that carving knife today. I can barely uncurl my fingers."

"Ha, see? I told you woodcarving's no good if you want to play guitar. Every time I pick up that guitar . . . my fingers just don't do what I want them to. But what can I do? This is what I'm born to. Maybe in another life . . ."

"I'll bring some whiskey next time."

"Ho ho, now we're getting down to business. Come any time, but not Wednesdays. That's when I take the train up to Hualian to see my doctor."

"You sick?"

"No, nothing serious, just tests and pills. You know how doctors are. They got to make their dime. Lots of expenses for doctors, whooee, those nurses . . . and you'll never see a doc driving a crappy old truck, eh brother? Or drinking this cheap stuff."

I poured out a splash of *mijiu* for E-ki. He tapped the table next to the glass as I poured, a way of saying, *fill 'er up, please,* and *thank you, that's enough.*

"Ah, don't mind if I do," E-ki said. "Last one, then I'm heading into town to my wife's place. Come here, I want to introduce you to my mother before you go."

"To whom?"

"Just come on."

I followed E-ki to a small windowless room where an ancient woman sat on a bed bundled in cotton quilts. Her hair was pulled back into a thin bun, and her face looked like it was carved from a dried, shrunken apple. Her eyes were even more blurred and milky that those of the Chief's wife. E-ki spoke to her in Amis, and she said a few words in reply.

"She says welcome," E-ki said. I took her hand and bowed. "She likes Americans. Americans bombed Taiwan in the second war, but only the Japanese military. She says the Japanese were better than the KMT, but she doesn't blame you."

"She lives with you?" I asked, astonished. I could hardly believe she'd been sitting here alone in this darkened room while we moved through the arc of the day, or that she seemed at ease and self-contained in this isolation, as if some implicit self-knowledge or identity sustained her.

"Sure, where else would she go? Most of the Amis have sold their land. There were Japanese and KMT land allotments to the tribes, but they were our only resource. So, if someone got sick, the family would sell their land to pay the hospital bills. We kept our land, even when my father was dying. But now we've lost a court case. Another relative claimed our land, and we've got to fight to get it back. That's why we're here. This workshop isn't ours, it's just temporary. How 'bout that? What the Han tribe didn't get from us our own family is trying to take away." He spat in the dirt as we headed out again.

"Anyway, here we are. For now this is what we have."

SEVEN

Between the City and the Sea

Through the spring and early summer, people came and went from the Open Circle Tribe project on the beach at Jinzun. Feiyu became busy with his café, or with spearfishing and church meetings, and his teepee stood empty except for some tools and bits of rope. Siki was often occupied with work and responsibilities in Dulan. He was too central a figure to remain camped out at the beach for long, where there was only intermittent phone reception. Yiming was in perpetual motion, driving his pickup up and down the coast, between tribes and projects. He often worked with the internationally renowned Amis sculptor Laheizi, an hour up north in Dagangkou, and Yiming's own workshop was south of Taidong City in the Puyuma village of Zhiben. E-ki made almost honorary appearances and then seemed to drop out of circulation, as if he had stepped aside from the orbit of people and projects revolving between Dulan and Jinzun. Ha-na, an Amis weaving artist who was part of the Tribe, had put in her time at Jinzun before I arrived. I didn't see her once down on the beach, and her driftwood hut with its hanging tapestries was relegated to guest accommodation. Dafeng was a steady resident, and the three women artists—Shen-hui, Ai-qin, and Dou-dou—remained at the camp for weeks on end without leaving. They distilled into the enduring core of the project. Out-of-town and local visitors passed through, and I was peripatetic, moving between polarities of solitude and community, between Dulanshan and the sea.

. . .

There was always a guitar on hand at Jinzun, a communal beater left exposed to the sun and the salt breeze, available for whoever wanted to strum away the seconds and minutes as they rolled in with the waves. Sitting on the beach or around the fire, I'd pick it up and let my fingers move across the strings, my mind full of nothing but the color and texture of the ocean and the rolling topography of the coast.

The music that emerged was a confluence of visceralities—my own flesh and fluid corporeality, the bone and skin of my fingers as they touched the strings, the wood and steel instrument, and the liquid-and-tissue landscape, plus the "body" of the collective life of the community. Soon a set of instrumental songs began to take form and cohere. I called the collection *Ocean Hieroglyphics*, as the compositions were landscape paintings in music, a language of the ocean in pictures, without words.

These ambient guitar songs became a partial soundtrack for the Open Circle Tribe, the other part being the Amis songs everyone knew and sang. In the late spring a half-Amis filmmaker named Miyaw Biho came down from Taipei and began filming a documentary called *The Open Circle Tribe Drifts to Jinzun*. I was there plunking away on the beater guitar as he filmed everyone sitting around the fire, and later some of this guitar music became part of the film.

I was not exactly a fine hand with a chain saw. Still, I wanted to contribute a sculpture of my own to those that rose along the shore. By this time I was hopelessly in love with driftwood. Walking along the beach I probably spent more time looking down at it strewn across the sand than out at the waves and sky and sea. I loved the history implicit in driftwood—the weathered gray skin rasped by salt and sun, the golden fragrant grain within, the knots and twists of roots and branches. Often rocks were embedded in the still-intact roots, vestiges of the mountains that were embraced by trees and carried to the ocean. Driftwood washed down from the central mountains then out from the mouth of the Beinan River. During and after the heavy rains of typhoons, the river roiled and heaved, a driftwood birth canal, where logs were born into the waves, from the mountains to the sea, from where they'd return to earth again.

The concept for my "work-piece" was *Purification.* I found two tapered, gracefully curved pieces of driftwood, each twelve or fifteen feet long, with gnarled knobs at the end. They had once been small trees, and the knobs were the remainder of their root systems. I chose a spot at the north end of the beach, and dug a hole in the sand to implant them so they would bow outward and come together at the top, the knobbed ends fitting together like clasping hands. I planned to make a circle of white stones and to burn a pile of sticks and seaweed in the middle, which would char the bottom of the clasping pieces and leave a layer of ash, as if the arc they formed had risen up from the fire.

As I was digging, Zhiming ambled down the beach and asked me what I was doing.

"I'm working on my *zuopin,*" I said, and described what I wanted to do.

"What, you're just going to stick those things in the ground and hope they stay?"

"Well, yeah."

Zhiming burst into merry laughter, which, as usual here, held no trace of malice or scorn.

"Look," he said, "the sand won't hold those up, no matter how deep you dig. I'm not even talking about what will happen when a typhoon hits. Just wind, gravity, the moon, a pretty girl walking by, whatever, will pull them down. Don't worry, though, I'll give you a hand. I'll go grab some tools, and we can do it right."

Ever the individualist, I would have preferred to continue

working on my own and let the thing fall down five minutes after it was completed rather than accept help, even from a friend. But I didn't say anything, perhaps feeling I should acquiesce to the communal dynamic of the group, or maybe I realized Zhiming was right.

He returned with a hammer and nails and another shovel, and picked up a couple of thick driftwood sticks to use as struts. We built a framework to anchor my rib-shaped pieces, and set it three feet deep in a square hole. The two arms emerged together from the sand, arced away from each other, and reconverged, the roots knuckling together in an embrace at the top. Zhiming climbed on my shoulders to drive a nail through to hold them, though with some notion of purism, I'd been hoping to fit them together without any fastening agent.

The two convex pieces made a shape like a vertical eye, or a driftwood yoni, framing a slit of the horizon so that looking through you saw half sea, half sky, rising from a circle of stones.

"That's better," said Zhiming, grinning and wiping the sweat from his face. "It's not going anywhere now."

He was right, and ironically my sculpture was the last one standing after the enormous waves of a typhoon pounded the beach and washed all other traces of the project away.

. . .

At the end of June Miyaw began editing his documentary for public television and called from Taipei to ask if I had recordings of the Jinzun guitar songs. My full-scale analog studio was still a work in progress. I didn't have the machines connected and running, but I set up the simpler digital equipment I'd used to record demos in Taipei. The desk and living room floor become tangled with microphones and cables. I spent two weeks recording the songs, and Jie-ren offered to help me do the necessary postproduction processing at the Taiwan Colors Music studio. I decided to travel to Taipei, finish the music and hand it off to Miyaw, and see a few friends while I was there.

I took the eight-hour train to Taipei, chugging north along the coast, through mountain tunnels with vistas flashing open onto the sea of three blues and closing just as suddenly. The train turned inland, clacking over tracks between rice fields with high-tension power lines stretched across the sky. We rushed past small town stations and flag-waving conductors and left them behind like snapshots of a gone time.

We arrived in Taipei at dusk. I walked through the station as loudspeaker announcements clanged across oceans of floor tile, tides and currents of passengers swirling through. Outside, the street was an implosion of engines and electric light, the sky a million-eyed prism of advertising neon. The metropolis was tangled yet rectilinear, an inbred chaos spiraling upon itself, qualitatively different from the outwardly expansive chaos of mountains and forests and the sea. A pedestrian bridge crossed over Zhongxiao Dong Lu, a ten-lane road jammed with a solid river of buses and cars. Crippled beggars held out alms bowls to the crowds passing over. Motor scooters nosed between cars, their riders wearing dust masks over their faces like bandits. A long line of taxis snaked around the train station like an innumerably sectioned insect, and once they had their fares they shot off like yellow sharks through schools of traffic.

When I first arrived in Taiwan in the early 1990s, navigating through Taipei was a nightmarish undertaking. It took hours to get across town, and you'd feel you had to siphon off a pint of blood to feed like engine oil into the machinery. The surface streets were stultified with groaning, exhaust-belching buses packed to standing room only. You rode them sweating, with a layer of particulate grease blackening your skin. Then, as part of the process of turning their attention from "retaking the mainland" to improving life and infrastructure on Taiwan, the government began building the Mass Rapid Transit system (MRT). This project had been first proposed in 1968 but didn't get approval until 1986. Traffic and pollution got hopelessly worse as they dug up the center of the city, with construction teams and machinery blocking traffic and constricting flow. Then in 1997 the first major line was completed, followed by others. The construction tunnels were covered over, the streets repaved, the cranes and excavation machines moved elsewhere, as if the city had been given bypass surgery and now was sewn back together. Suddenly, to cross the city all you had to do was walk down the stairs into the metro system, step on an aluminum-colored train, and zip zip zip, half an hour of air-conditioning later you'd emerge on the other side of the city.

So after arriving at the train station, I took the MRT across town and met Jie-ren at Taiwan Colors Music, inside the vacuum-sealed silence of the studio, where we began the process of loading my recordings into the computer system.

"How's Taidong these days?" Jie-ren asked as the computers flashed and whirred.

"It's pretty good. Quiet. A bit different from Taipei," I said, my mind still spinning like a pinwheel from my arrival amid the conglomeration of lights and engines. "Are you still planning to move down and raise chickens at Tero's?"

Jie-ren coughed his habitual shallow cough and said, "Yeah, soon. As soon as I finish up a couple of projects here."

But this was Jie-ren's Sisyphean paradox—there was always one more album to do, always someone asking him for help, wanting the light but just right touch he brought to producing music. He was always almost ready to cut free and leave Taipei for good, but never quite able to do so.

"How'd you record the bird songs you've got on here?" he asked as we listened to one of the songs.

"You know how it is down there, man. I just opened the windows and rolled the tape."

"Oh yeah, I forgot. I've been stuck in the studio too long . . . if I want bird songs I have to buy them on a CD and mix them in separately."

"What album are you working on these days, anyway?"

"An Amis singer, Long-ge . . . do you know him? He's from Taidong."

"No, I haven't met him yet. Is he good?"

"Yeah, he's got the real stuff . . . writes his own songs and also sings traditional Amis songs. He's the opposite of a 'recording artist.' We had to get him drunk every time before we could drag him into the studio, and then once he was here he wouldn't do more than one take of a song. But he's so far off the map, I had to force the label to finish the album. Otherwise they would never have released it. We started working on it back when Jian-nian won the Golden Melody Award, when they thought they could sell anything aboriginal. Now that things have slowed down they didn't want to make the investment. It's taken two years already, but it'll be released soon."

We worked through the night, bouncing the music between formats, balancing levels and frequencies, playing it back, making final adjustments, then burning the songs onto a CD. We finished at 2 a.m. Jie-ren decided to sleep in the studio rather than going home to sleep, only to wake up and come back to work the next day.

I stepped out into the street with the mastered disk in my hands, the ocean songs that had emerged through my guitars and fingers, recorded in my mountain abode above the sea, now ready to broadcast through the air in Miyaw's film about the Open Circle Tribe. It was a miracle as always. The music that had begun as seeds within me had grown beyond me. To me the whole process was a form of sacredness, a ritual connecting my individual, corporeal life to something greater, as if breath itself had been captured on this plastic disk in 1s and 0s and could be moved place to place, over and over, to sustain a beating heart.

Walking through the dense quiet air of the city night, I felt high and free with a sense of completion and release, stoned with a rush of unfetteredness, as if the forces that normally kept me contained within my skin and skull had dissolved. I rose above the city, striding across its lights and boulevards ten blocks with every step, knocking my head against the sky that glowed orange like a pastel night light, reflecting the city's illumination.

The MRT only ran till midnight, so I took a cab across town to a party some friends had invited me to, in an old Japanese apartment building on the bank of the Danshui River. It was a sweaty, hirsute gathering of Western journalists and their local colleagues or friends, packed into a series of small rooms and connecting halls. The night churned against itself, exhausted and ready to topple over, beer bottles and hash pipes crowding every available surface. My newspaper friends were hanging around, shooting the shit, half-drunk and half-high.

"Welcome, come join us," Max said. "We're obliterating our minds. Try it, it's very nice."

"What's going on, man?"

"There's too much going on, the world is fucking itself as usual, and we're the ones who have to write it all down. Therefore we have to actually pay attention as it goes down the shitter. So, tonight we are in pursuit of nothingness, zero, void, *gefärtvergotten*, like the fucking snows of Sweden, infinitely blank and dead."

"You got to quit believing that shit you write, man," I said. "It's starting to tweak you."

"Did you see my article on the octogenarian prostitute last week? She was servicing a dozen clients a day, but the cops picked her up because she didn't have a permit. Cop report says she's eighty-four but with makeup could pass for seventy. As if that fucking explains anything. You see, they don't mind having an octogenarian sex worker, just so long as she keeps her dues paid up."

"Death and taxes, baby."

"Let me tell you, in this world grandma the happy hooker is a tame motherfucker," Dave, another journo friend, chimed in. "If you weren't writing about that, you'd have to start asking why they keep building nuclear power plants on this island nation . . . Like, where do they expect twenty million people to go if one of those babies blows? Swim back to the mainland? Get an airlift to Mongolia?"

"Careful, man, you're a journalist. You're not allowed to call Taiwan a nation, it's a province of China."

"Have you checked out the ROC map, man? Don't you know Taiwan's bigger than America? It not only includes all of China and Tibet, but all of Mongolia too . . . and there's a little note that says *Administered by the Republic of Mongolia*. Jesus H. Fucking Christ. As if by some act of benevolence the ROC is allowing the Mongolians to have their own government."

"Mongolia's no good anyway. That's where they're shipping the nuclear waste that doesn't fit on Orchid Island."

I half-listened to the banter, most of it glancing off my brain, too unreal to ingest. The weird vanity of the nation-state, the absurdity of political facades, the delusion of control. I felt caught in a crack between worlds, states of consciousness, between the seascape of Dulan and the petroleum embrace of Taipei. My interstitial dizziness was catalyzed by the jangly exhilaration of completing the film music. I picked up a half-drunk beer and swigged it down. The party was winding down, no one speaking or thinking coherently anymore, if they ever had. Across the room I saw a tall, slender girl, with long black hair and a mild, transparent smile. She was a pause of calm in the noisy room, even though she was laughing at something Max's girlfriend had just said.

"Hey, man, who's that?" I asked Max.

"Ah, that's Ming-sho, my girlfriend's best friend. She went traveling in Europe with us last summer. Want to meet her? Come here and say hello, you shaggy misanthrope. I'll introduce you."

Ming-sho and I stood looking at each other surrounded by the dregs of party conversation. She was so beautiful and

BETWEEN THE CITY AND THE SEA

serene I just wanted to invite her back to Taidong to live with me. It was self-evident to me that we could start a new life together from this moment forward. But my mind was empty of words, I couldn't think of a single suave or charming thing to say to impress a pretty girl. I stared at her like a deaf mute for what seemed like minutes.

"You want to get out of here and take a walk?" I finally asked her.

"Yes!" she said, as if she'd been waiting all night to leave.

We went down a dark stairway and through a doorway to the street. It was 4 a.m., the city quiet and brooding, no sound except the subbass rumble that never ceased, like the industrial soul of the city trying to rise up and speak. Orange light seeped from streetlamps through the particulate air. We walked along the edge of the vast, canted, concrete riverbank, still not talking, but here our silence was smooth and clean, a form of repose consonant with the surrounding quiet, not awkwardly juxtaposed against the ragged talk inside.

"This is a landscape built by drunken robots," I said as we looked across the river to clusters of twenty-story or hundred-story apartment buildings topped with antennae towers. I had no perspective to count such things.

"Built by robots for ant-people," she said.

"What are you doing in Taipei these days?"

"Today I had an exhibit of my drawings and photos. After it finished my friends brought me here."

"Where was the exhibit? At a gallery?"

"No, just at my apartment . . . I taped the images to the walls and bought some drinks and invited my friends. I just did it to share my mind with the people around me. Things are changing. My university classmates will get jobs and get married and move away soon. I just finished my degree, so I'm finally free to leave Taipei . . . I'm going to move to Taidong or Orchid Island."

"What are you going to do there?"

"Get a job working with children, maybe. I have friends in a social service organization, but I'm not sure . . . anyway, we come from the sea. From every point on Orchid Island you can see the ocean."

"Yeah, it's a different world. I moved down to Taidong six months ago."

"Really? What are you doing there?"

"Just playing guitar, carrying driftwood up and down the mountain, swimming in the sea."

"Next week I'm going traveling in China and Tibet. I don't know what will happen when I return. Of course, my family wants me to get a job in a city somewhere. I'll have to fight for my freedom . . ."

The river reflected the city lights like a current of shattered glass, moving in broad curves between the slanted riverbanks. Atop the girders of new skyscrapers, long, lean construction cranes reached across the horizon, mechanical beasts straining their necks into the air as pale bands of blue began to glow behind them in the sky.

Ming-sho and I walked back along the river to the party house. She went inside to find her friends, and I continued walking, past street markets preparing to open with the dawn, vendors unpacking fruit and vegetables from boxes. I walked to the nearest metro station, waited for it to open, and rode across town to pass the ocean music to Miyaw. Then I headed to a friend's house on Yangmingshan, where I collapsed exhausted into sleep.

• • •

Ming-sho and I met again after midnight two days later. We ate flakey almond pastries at an all-night breakfast place and took another walk through the empty city. We kissed in the middle of a neon-lit street with the taste of sugar and almonds on our lips. The next day I took the train back to Taidong, my toenails black with dust and grease from walking the city streets in my flip-flops. Ming-sho flew to Hong Kong to begin her travels in China.

And so our relationship began—a quite space surrounded by words, thoughts of the ocean within the city grid. Over the next two years we oscillated between togetherness and separation, but for now we were two silent wires drawing close to one another on the cusp of a departure.

EIGHT

Purification

July, the gut and groin of summer, the days sticky and thick with heat. Ducking out of the sun became a movement both primary and unconscious, an instinct like dodging a blow or swatting at the whine of a mosquito by your ear. The mountains that were sharp green in spring became drab and muted, as if their color was a blade hammered dull by heat. The ocean sank into a brooding blue, its currents and movements retreated beneath the surface, leaving a skin like old paint to absorb the crash and roar of the sun. The air hazed and thickened, the smell of decomposition climbing through like vines, rising up from the soil, from wilting leaves. Flowers shriveled, leaving seed pods that rattled as I moved through the brush up on the mountain. The sky yawned, blank and empty, a bored god, butane blue, serving no relationship to the steaming earth, to baking roads and concrete walls. But in the afternoons, tropic cumuli built above the islands off shore, Green Island straight out in the belly of the sea, and Orchid Island, a shadow on the horizon. Clouds erupted from nothingness into coronations of white rising five, ten, twenty thousand feet into the air, evaporation sculpted by currents of convection and turbulence, gleaming scrobiculations above the landmass of the islands anchored gray beneath. When Orchid Island was too faint to see, the cumuli above indicated its position. Along the flank of Dulanshan, the afternoons condensed into a layer of lead-bottomed cloud, a thick lid that blocked the sun but brought no relief because it held in the humidity and heat, compressing them, stifling the breeze. Standing in the yard, I was boxed in on all sides, by the overcast and the mountain and the earth. The only open space was out to sea.

. . .

Summer is typhoon season in the western Pacific. When one of these spiral storms approached far out at sea, the sky shone like a metal robin's egg, aluminum blue, hard and bright. Any clouds that remained were thin and elongated, like strips of zinc stretched out and welded to the sky.

Typhoons came heaving up from the Philippines, sometimes slamming straight into the east coast of Taiwan, sometimes veering off toward China or Japan. Some years there were no direct hits at all. There were a couple of near misses the summer of the Jinzun residency, including one that sent monstrous waves hissing up the sand all the way into the Open Circle camp. Most everyone evacuated during this time, though Shenhui sat calmly in her cave-mouth coffee bar and watched the tongues of water race into the clearing.

At the end of summer an enormous typhoon was headed straight toward us, a hard-slugging monster, a cetacean of a storm. As it approached, it sucked all the moisture and particulation from the air for a thousand miles. The sea and sky became blue mirrors, reflecting each other, each a looking glass to infinity.

There had been a closing ceremony a couple of weeks before, to officially end the Jinzun project, presided over by the Chief and the other Amis elders. Then the artists dispersed into different directions and orbits, waiting for the next collective project to converge again. After half a year of living and working together at Jinzun, we packed the cooking pans and sleeping bags and hauled them up the stairs, along with some of the moveable work-pieces—such as Ai-qin's paintings on driftwood boards, which she'd set against a cliff-face backdrop, juxtaposing the lines of the paintings with the patterns of cracks and crevices in the stone.

I hitched up to Jinzun and stood on the overlook above the cliffs. The open-air café here on the side of the highway had been a bland public works rest stop, with concrete benches and tables, and a roof supported by round concrete pillars. During the beach residency the Open Circle Tribe had spent a night bolting driftwood and carvings to every available surface, as if they could allow nothing within their orbit to remain untransformed by their aesthetic. Down below, work-pieces still lined the beach. Siki had driven his van up the sand at low tide to pick up his feather sculpture before the storm hit, since it was far to heavy to heft up the stairs. But others had left their pieces for the typhoon, either because they were site-specific installations or, as in Dafeng's case, because he had always expected to return it to the sea. His sculpture was a broad log split in half and opened into a V. A piece of thick mooring rope that had washed ashore ran through holes in the two sides as if stitching them together. Dou-dou's piece was an understated work of juxtapositions, seaweed and vines latticed across a kind of found totem, a hoary, deeply pitted piece of hollowed log, full of eye-hole notches and rounded burls, which she erected in the sand like a sentinel between earth and sea. Zhiming had created an expansive assemblage of abstract geometries, arcs and arrows all slotted into each other in a big embrace. It must've been twenty feet across and ten feet high, all compending upward toward the sky. And way down at the end of the beach stood *Purification*, just before the rocky spit extended into the sea, still surrounded by its circle of stones though the ashes from the fire had long blown away.

In the clarified air of the approaching typhoon, Green Island looked close enough to swim to, and even Orchid Island was palpable with mass and form. I trotted down the stairs to have a last look at our former campsite. All the huts were mildewed, overgrown with vines and grasses. Small trees had already begun to grow in the common area. The roof of Zhiming's toadstool cottage had crumpled inward. Shen-hui's cave-mouth coffee bar had gone completely wild, and weeds grew up through the chainsawed planks of Ai-qin's painting deck. Waves surged high up the beach and lapped at the stones of the former fire pits. In the fecund heat and wild growth the pulse and drone of cicadas rose and swirled, shrill and visceral, engulfing me like wormholes of sound. The artistry and energy invested in the days here had been subsumed by tropical entropy, swallowed by the life of grasses and leaves. This space of ritual and residence had reverted to the dominion of the monkeys that roamed the jungled cliffs above. After a couple of months, the residence of the Consciousness Tribe already looked like the ruins of a civilization that had disappeared centuries before.

In front of the main camp was a site-specific installation piece made by an artist who'd visited Jinzun while I was in Taipei. He'd dug a broad concavity in the sand just at the edge of the tide line, so that it filled with water like a shallow pond. Within this puddled depression he implanted a single row of long, slender branches, tufted with green leaves, that looked like saplings. The piece appeared as a weird seaside oasis, a meta-sea contiguous to the sea. The leaves had browned and crinkled in the sun, and the whole piece went through a temporal transformation. The "saplings" were now old and withered as the tide sloshed high across the sand, making the branches shudder. Having evolved with the seasons, this had become a time-specific as well as a site-specific installation.

Against the cliffs just north of the camp Feiyu had created a protest diorama of old oil barrels that had washed ashore, rusted waste metal he'd painted with radioactive danger symbols. This was an overt and angry statement against the nuclear waste dump duplicitously built and maintained on his home,

Orchid Island. Feiyu's rusted barrels, like everything else, would soon be washed back out to sea.

I walked the overgrown paths and paused at the central fire pit around which so many stories, bottles, and songs had revolved. Then I headed back to the stairs, and back up to the road, as the insects roared their drunken triumph in the heat.

. . .

The Open Circle Tribe began the Jinzun project fully cognizant the whole thing would be swept back to the sea. Driftwood came as a gift from the mountains and the sea, so maybe it was only appropriate to let it and the labor invested here return to where they came from.

The Open Circle artists maintained good spirits and lived with passion and good humor amid the real or perceived decay of their cultures and their displacement from their ancestral lands. They inhabited the earth, the changes in weather and seasons, and their own internal landscapes with little sense of rush or worry. Perhaps they were connected to something larger than their individual lives and concerns, larger even than the rise and fall of cultures and the world as we perceive it—the cycles and forces that created this landscape and the myriad expressions of humanity, the vast movements of migrations, of continental drift and evolution, the larger arc of being of which cultures and places are a part, never the whole. My father, a biologist, once said of those who believe human life begins at the moment of conception: "What do they think, that the sperm and egg were dead before they met? Life doesn't start and stop, it's a continuum." Whatever they rued of the past, or of lost elements of tradition, the Open Circle Tribe never lost sight of the fact that life is a perpetual unfolding, continually morphing and transforming. It can't be paused and held—the essence of life is movement and change.

No matter what we do on this earth, the only certainty is that we're going to die back into it. The Jinzun project was an analog for life as a whole, in which all we receive or become must be relinquished.

. . .

The gathering at Jinzun had been independent and autonomous, but it was not self-sustaining. There was simply not enough forageable food down on the beach, not to mention tobacco, *mijiu*, or chain saw fuel. There was no governmental funding or institutional support. The group was disconnected from markets at this time. No one was making anything to sell; their artwork had no immediate commodity value. As word spread locally and nationally, and even internationally, visitors came to have a look at what was going on. They came to see the "most beautiful bay in the world," as it was reported to be, and the fairytale houses in the clearing at the base of the cliffs. Most of all they probably came to see the people who had carried out such a concept, to see whether they were geniuses or insane, visionaries or crackpots, artists expressing a new Taiwanese indigenousness or just bums too lazy to get on the grid and get a job. Such visitors, whether families on vacation, highbrow professors, or luminaries from the art world, would invariably fold some bills together and pass them to Dou-dou, who served as docent and welcoming committee, before heading back up the stairs. Later, as the summer wore on, the heat falling like a cudgel from the sky and the cicadas pulsing madly, the flow of visitors slowed, and even many of the artists were busy elsewhere. Then donations trickled in from further afield, from friends or anonymous supporters in Taipei who did not have the time or freedom to drop out and undertake such a project themselves, but who sent cash so that the residence could sustain as what it was until it had run its course.

The Open Circle Tribe project at Jinzun was a turning point in contemporary Taiwanese art, something that had never been conceived before, and continues to resonate years later.

At the time, it sometimes existed with the day-to-day precariousness of having little more than wild greens to eat, or of being threatened by the encroaching waves of a storm. But this might be the nature of creativity, or of life itself—luminous and fragile moments, strung together like a string of pearls that could snap at any moment, become a whole, a subjectivity that inheres and remains, etched in memory, stories, and the arc of time. Or, maybe these delicate luminescences are themselves the arc of time.

. . .

The typhoon slammed in from the sea, pounding the coast range like a hammer against an anvil, and churned like a malevolent, bruise-gray deity above the coast. Some typhoons move sharp and fast, with a concentrated radius and extreme winds, and veer off quickly after they hit land. This one was sluggish and slow, hundreds of miles across, and disgorged unbelievable amounts of rain as it hung above the coast for three days. It was the hardest rain I had ever seen in my life, and never lessened or paused, like a thunderburst that became stuck and did not relent hour after hour. In my house, water ran down the inside edges of the ceiling, and seeped up from the floor, puddling in the living room. My recording gear and guitars sat on furniture or dry spots on the floor. Water collected in the yard and rose to the level of the doorstep. The rain was so hard, steady, and opaque that it seemed to have gone through a phase change and become a solid. My skin began to wrinkle and pucker as if I were in a bathtub. I was enclosed within the rain, buried, entombed in it. There were always landslides during such typhoons, and I wondered about the structural integrity of the mountain that rose behind me. There was nowhere to go. The rain fell every direction for a hundred miles, and you could not leave home during such a storm. Who knew when part of the ceiling would collapse or a window would blow in? You had to be on hand to deal with such eventualities. Anyway, the road might be washed out anywhere on the way down the mountain, or blocked by downed trees, and once you got out of the house you might never make it back. This was an incarceration by water, solitary confinement. In this isolation water began to leak into my mind, all thoughts, consciousness, sanity dissolving, till I felt I soon would surely wash away.

. . .

The rain stopped during the third night. In the morning the sky was scrubbed aluminum again, scintillant blue, not a cloud in sight. The smell of rotting vegetation rose in the clear bright sun. Debris was strewn everywhere, and freshets gushed out of the mountain face in spontaneous waterfalls. Toadstools grew from the tatami mats and along the betel nut tree ceiling beams.

I walked down the mountain, hopping through a few places where the soil of a slope had spilled down across the road. It was an emancipation to return to a world of motion and light. Everything moved slowly, and glistened as if just reborn. I caught a ride up to Jinzun and stood above the cliffs again. However they had survived the deluge, the monkeys were still there, chattering in the trees below. From the lookout point, the beach was clean and empty. It had returned to its original state, just as everyone had said it would from the start. The typhoon had washed everything away, with the exception of my sculpture, which somehow remained, though it was leaning over nearly horizontally, at the far end of the beach.

In the clean warm sun, reflected between the blue mirrors of the sea and sky, I ran down the stairs. At the bottom landing I stripped off my clothes and sprinted naked the half mile up the beach to where *Purification* listed in the sand, the two pieces still clasped at the top where Zhiming and I had nailed them together. The waves curled in, lustrous blue ribs rising up to crash upon the beach, but they no longer had the violent abandon of the typhoon's full force, when they had reached the base of the cliffs and left a residue of flotsam ten feet high.

I dug into the sand and heaved and pulled until my slitted driftwood eye came free. I dragged it down the sloping shore, the ocean swirling around my thighs. Salt and foam splashed across my skin, and I released my work-piece into the back-wash of the surf, to return to the waves that had washed us all ashore from somewhere out at sea.

NINE

Hinoki Studio

At the start of autumn I borrowed a sledgehammer from Siki and spent two days knocking out the brick partition that divided one of the side rooms into two, to make a larger space for my equipment and guitars. I hauled the debris load by load to the back of the house, where the wild raspberry vines grew over and enfolded the rubble.

Ming-sho and I kept in touch while she was in China, and she called from Hong Kong to tell me she would fly back to Taiwan soon. I bought a secondhand car, a crappy old hatchback with a rusted, buckled hood, to drive up and down the mountain, up and down the coast. The back seats folded down, making enough space to wedge in small logs and haul them home, secured with ropes and hanging halfway out the back. Soon the front wall of my house was lined with hinoki, as that was my favorite wood and the only one I could identify with certainty.

E-ki seemed to have disappeared, and I heard he was in Mainland China, where he'd been commissioned to do a sculpture project. Yiming and Ai-qin gave me a round, black and tan, ebullient puppy from some mongrel litter, to the disgust of my cat A-dong. By black spots on his tongue Yiming identified him as part indigenous hunting dog, which Yiming claimed was the fiercest and most loyal breed in the world. My dog, however, proved more of a canine epicurean than a pugilist. From his infancy he had a scruff of old-man whiskers on his chin, so I called him Mull, for the air of contemplation these gave him, and after "Stately, plump Buck Mulligan . . . ," the opening words of James Joyce's *Ulysses*. He would disappear yelping into the undergrowth several times higher than himself, and return panting and sneezing, but with a puppish swagger, a layer of seeds and burrs stuck to his coat like chain mail.

. . .

One day, as summer was turning the corner into autumn, I drove a few kilometers north from Dulan, and down a dirt access road to a beach with a long smooth break. Sometimes I saw Diva here, a Tao surfer girl from Orchid Island who rented a place in a village up the coast from Dulan. She stood like a deep sea goddess amid the waves, shining like a black pearl as the ocean bubbled blue and silver all around her. Diva was spunky and mischievous and gorgeous, like a nymph from a Greek myth. Every time I saw her I wanted to go out and perform some heroic and impossible labor.

The waves were empty, but I parked and ambled shirtless and hatless and barefoot through the driftwood along the shore, the tropical sun burning across my skin. In the course of the summer my hair had grown out long and tangled, lightened into streaks of blonde, the ends sun-bleached almost to transparency. A half mile up the beach I came across a thick, wishbone-shaped hinoki log, about six feet long, three feet wide at the broad end. The outside was splintered and silvered, as usual, but also as usual the grain inside was fresh and fragrant and golden, a magnificent piece of wood. It was love at first sight. The log was far too heavy to lift, though I tried, nearly dislocating my spine in the process. So I heaved and rolled it side over side down the sloping sand toward the water, then pushed it out into the whitewash of the waves till it began to float. The swells broke over the log and me as I swam it back the way I'd come, kicking and sputtering, struggling to hold it against the backwash, then pushed it ashore and up the sand. I backed the car down, hefted one end of the log up onto the back fender, then heaved and pushed until the balance shifted and it slid in and thumped against the back of the passenger seat.

I was sweating and coated with sand, my chest and arms scraped and abraded from the jagged edges of the log. Beads of blood were scratched across my belly like lines of tiny jewels. I was crusty with salt, half-naked, sunstruck beneath tropical light streaming amber and silver across the sea and me.

Just as I flopped into the driver's seat and started the engine, Diva turned off from the highway on her champagne-green motor scooter, her surfboard lashed to the side, and drove down the dirt road toward me. Her luminous body, tanned nearly black, pulled at me with the gravity of a dark and lovely star. But my driftwood infatuation, and the sweat and blood running together and staining the top of my shorts, made me impatient to continue on my trajectory without stopping to speak. I drove up the road, blew her a kiss as she flashed her flashing smile, and headed south toward Dulan.

• • •

Back home, I washed off my new wishbone hinoki log, turned the hose on myself, threw on a shirt, then wrestled the log back into the car and drove to the sawmill in town.

The Taidong sawmill had its heyday in the 1970s and 1980s, when clear-cutting was at its peak and the old-growth forests of the central range were mowed down and trucked away. By the time a moratorium against logging was enacted, in the late 1980s, there wasn't much original forest left to protect. With no local lumber supply, the mill now processed imported logs from Malaysia, straight, pulpy monsters, eighty feet long and six feet in diameter, which they cut and cut and cut on an enormous band saw down into one-by-ones or one-by-fours for light construction and shipping pallets.

The sawmill belonged to an ethnic Taiwanese family, and

they had done well enough during the lumber boom to send two of their daughters to college in America. As I pulled in to the compound, the boss jumped down from a forklift to greet me. He was tall and stringy, his belt cinched up so high and tight it looked like it should be attached to a leash. I backed my car into the saw area, and the boss motioned the sawyers to stop their work and unmount the log they were cutting. He did this every time I showed up with a hatchback full of driftwood, despite the fact that it was insignificant in comparison to the volume they processed, and that my logs were full of sand, which dulled the blades, and despite the fact that I looked rumpled and derelict as a vagabond. The boss refused to accept a single *kuai* for this service, a gesture of gratitude common among Taiwanese who'd been lifted out of poverty on the shoulders of the American economy.

Two old men worked the saw in a dim, vaulted warehouse space. They were gnarled and grizzled, grandfathers pushing seventy, their gray hair cropped close, revealing liver spots on their scalps. With a remote control they guided an automated block and tackle suspended from the roof to the back of my car. They looped a steel cable around my wishbone log, and lifted it to the saw sled. One man clamped it to the sled assembly with wedges and steel hooks, standing it on edge so that the saw would cut longitudinally through the broadest part of the log, preserving its Y shape.

The steel saw belt with its slanted inch-long teeth was looped between a drive shaft and spindle, about a seven-foot cutting edge from top to bottom. The man at the controls pushed a button and the sled glided forward. The blade bit into the wood, sawdust and a rush of sparks gushed from the cut. The boss stood behind me with his arms folded across his chest and said, "Those sparks, that's sand," but offered no further comment. They sawed the log into inch-thick boards, but toward the center, the thick heart of the wood, they cut it into two-inch slabs. Halfway through, the controller looked over and made a shut-off sign. The boss nodded and then strode back to his forklift to continue loading pallets as the sawyers shut off the motor and sat down to light cigarettes. After the whirring of the motor and blade slowed and stopped, they dropped their cigarettes into the gutter along the sled tracks, stepped into the machinery, loosened and unhooked the saw blade. The ends unclasped, and the blade became a fifteen-foot steel belt, which together they lifted onto a stack of blades waiting to be sharpened by a computerized machine. They picked up a fresh blade and fitted it onto the assembly; then they restarted the motor and continued cutting.

When my log was all sawed into amber-colored boards, the sawyers used the block and tackle to load them back into my car. As we tied the hatchback down with rope, I noticed each of them was missing the top joint of two or three fingers, amputations smooth and sealed as sausage ends. I thanked the old men, but they just looked bored and shuffled back to reload the Malaysian log and get back to work. The boss pulled up on his forklift and jumped down to make sure everything was all right. I tried to pay him something, but as always he waved me away as if I were a madman for even thinking such thoughts, and told me to come back any time he could help with anything.

• • •

Acts of generosity such as this, or drivers plying me with gifts of alcohol, tobacco, *binlang*, or all three when I was hitchhiking, were common gestures of thanks for the economic and military aid America had given Taiwan as the "Republic of China." Without the U.S. Seventh Fleet patrolling the Taiwan Strait, Taiwan probably would have been retaken by Mainland China in the 1950s or 1960s. The ROC would never have gone from one of the poorest countries in the world to one of the richest within a few decades without American support.

Yet in a concrete way, Taiwan's "economic miracle" was fueled by the U.S. war industry, from which I had no desire to benefit. In the early 1960s South Vietnam bought half of the steel produced in Taiwan and continued to be the largest consumer of Taiwanese manufacturing throughout the decade. In this triangular relationship of economic and military might, America pumped cash in from both sides—to Taiwan to develop industry and to Vietnam to funnel industry into an effort of war.

Much U.S. economic support in Taiwan came in the form of corporate investment in factories where wages were less than a dollar a day, and where labor representation was illegal. It was a form of internal colonialism for the government to create exploitative conditions favorable to American investment, and helped the KMT consolidate their rule, just as an anti-communist agenda, rather than altruism, motivated U.S. support of Taiwan. Meanwhile, the Chiang Kai-shek regime proclaimed itself "Free China" despite the fact that it was a dictatorship.

Taiwan was bombed by the United States during World War II when occupied by Japan. Tokyo was fire-bombed. Pacific atolls have been atomized by bombs. Taiwan made steel for Vietnam as Vietnam bombed and was bombed. Cambodia and Laos were bombed, but secretly. Destroying countries in order to save them. The American military machine moving like a buzz saw through Asian populations, spitting bone pulp, feeding dollars to vassal states. Sometimes I feel every landscape I've ever lived in has been bombed by my own country, including the West Coast of America.

This is the flip side of America, the dark side of the disco ball. The cop from Chenggong or the sawmill boss would never see this, only admiring from afar the sparkle and flash of power, technology, opportunity. It's a game of tiddlywinks, with nation-states flipping blood chips at targets of geopolitic agenda, playing regimes against each other while the paradigm tilts everyone's mind toward the technology hamster wheel the Chenggong cop thought I was mad not to leap onto.

For me this underbelly of American power is always present, integral to my experience of my self, my consciousness, and my native land. My native land is only "America" because the indigenous peoples of Turtle Island were displaced, "civilized," and exterminated nearly out of existence.

The Open Circle artists and I did our best to forge autonomous identities, authentic to our values, within a hegemon we could not change, and with which our lives were intertwined. None of us desired to cut off from humanity and trek into the wild, to turn our backs on the world as it is. My friends tried to piece together contemporary identities from fragments of former wholeness, while I tried to balance my sense of self and values with my American citizenship, and the privilege that came with it, as U.S. wars continued in Iraq and Afghanistan. Roots in my own life and experience connected me to the American war in Vietnam, and my own historical consciousness included the legacy of U.S.-backed assassinations and coups—and, more recently, drone strikes, shooting robot bombs into villages.

The woodcarvers were in love with their chain saws the way I was in love with my recording machines, both products of industrial society. The fuel to run them came from paradigms contrary to our organic being. Painting, poetry, driftwood sculpture, songs around a fire, would not bring down the Leviathan, nor had we any aspiration to do so. But maybe these were acts of subversion at the level of consciousness, that allowed us to define ourselves by our own terms, a way of sidestepping the machinery and letting it lumber by without us.

· · ·

I chose the widest, thickest slab from the heart of my wishbone hinoki log to make a new desk. I used an angle grinder to polish the top, and it emerged golden and smooth, undulated from the uneven pressure of the spinning disk. I didn't touch the edge but left the silver-gray outer skin intact, so my desk retained a rough and salted vestige of its driftwood days.

Beneath the plastic laminate, the drawers of the crappy desk I'd salvaged turned out to be hinoki. During the lumber boom, this gorgeous and valuable wood had been pissed away on shoddy factory goods, to my sorrow and boon. I would have preferred the forest to remain—but I also loved gathering and working with the boards, planks, and window frames that could be foraged from derelict buildings and roadside junk piles up and down the coast.

I hammered the desk apart, stripped the laminate from the column of drawers, and sanded them down, re-revealing their color and grain, re-introducing them to the light and air, and this became the support for one half of my new desk. For the other side, I had an almost talismanic piece of *wuxinshi*, which was the envy of Yiming, and which I'd promised to give him if I couldn't use it myself, a broad, bulky piece shaped like a whale's tail. The exterior was pocked like the skin of a puffer fish, scabbed and dun, but inside it was ochre, tan, and chocolate-colored, and so adamantine that when I used a chain saw to cut notches in the "flukes" to fit the desk top, the teeth became badly dulled. Siki laughed when I apologized for returning his saw in this worn state, and said his apprentices would sharpen it back up. Siki was one of the young guys E-ki said "use muscle to cut," so maybe he didn't care anyway.

I drilled all this together with self-tapping screws, and a two-inch slab of wishbone hinoki, suspended between a driftwood whale tail and a set of hinoki drawers, became my desk, where I worked on guitar songs or clacked away on my typewriter, with the songs of cicadas and five-color birds rising and falling across the mountain, and the sound of waves welling up from the coast at night, a soft and distant rhythm of the sea.

• • •

By the tetrapods on Dulan beach I found an eighteen-foot hinoki log that had been overlooked or disregarded by the woodcarvers. I called Yiming to ask for a hand, and we drove his four-wheel-drive pickup down onto the sand to salvage it. The log was so large and heavy it took us two hours of straining and heaving to get it in the truck. We had to dig out from under one end of it, then lever the other end up into the bed with smaller logs, and badly dented the tailgate in the process.

"Man, I never recognized Siki's genius before today," I said, as we drove to the sawmill. "We need to get us some apprentices to lift this heavy shit. Sorry about the damage to your truck. I'll take it somewhere to get fixed."

"Nah, you don't have to," Yiming said, offering me a betel nut.

"Then I'll give you some money to take care of it."

Maybe I really was Anglo, as I later told Vadsuku (not believing it myself at the time), and thereby felt it necessary to square all accounts as soon as they came up. But this whole concept of keeping things even slid by Yiming as naturally as a shot of *mijiu* down the gullet, gone without a trace.

"Don't worry," he said with casual dismissal, already forgotten, "I have a friend with an auto shop."

It was as if he had never assimilated the idea of obligations or debts between friends, so my offer to keep things even had no meaning. A kula-based belief system seemed to be in place instead, the knowledge that everything would revolve and balance in its own time and way, that whatever was given would eventually return, and with the accrued interest of having passed through others' hands. That was fine with me—I had no compunction or compulsion to count. I was happier to let things ride and resolve beyond me in a greater arc of movement. However, years later when Yiming and I met for an artist residency in New Caledonia, he was scrupulous about paying all bills fully and promptly. It wasn't that he didn't know how to pay debts; he just chose not to make them primary among his friends.

A week later the tailgate had been hammered back into approximate shape, and though the metal remained dented and wrinkled, Yiming obviously did not care—as if the driftwood, our friendship, and the effort of working together toward a common goal transcended quantitative accounting.

We had the log milled into three-inch-thick boards and the sides trimmed square, then returned to my place and stacked them against the front wall. Their honey-cinnamon smell sweetened the whole environment for days, a hundred years of soil and photosynthesis blossoming into the air.

From one end of the boards, damp cracks extended up the grain of the wood, then disappeared like rivers that run from mountains down to deserts and evaporate. The sea had seeped in toward the core of the wood here, and the cracks were filled with sand, which had caused hell for the saw blade and the sawyers. "See this?" Yiming said. "The wood is split. It won't have any strength, it's no good for us to use."

This was why none of the woodcarvers had picked up this log, but for my purposes it would function fine. Later, the sand in the creases of the grain became part of my studio, slowly sifting down as from an hourglass to the floor.

I stood looking at the rectangular concrete room, my studio-to-be, wondering how to best support the boards to make a counter for my mixing console and analog tape decks, these heavy, bulky machines from a former era.

"You should get Vadsuku to help you put this stuff together," Yiming said when he came in and noticed me pondering the space. He popped himself a beer he'd grabbed from the fridge, and handed one to me. "He's the best one to ask about interior installation . . . if you can find him sober."

. . .

I'd first met Vadsuku when he was in the midst of a three-day bender, striding around the *tangchang* shirtless and challenging everyone to arm-wrestle. (He beat everyone but Siki; Yiming was not there that night, though.) When he told me his name I didn't quite catch it, and asked him to say it again. He looked at me disappointedly and said, "It's easy, the first syllable is the same as voDka." This was not quite phonetically correct, though accurate on some psychological level.

Now I found Vadsuku in the yard in front of his house, wearing dark glasses and welding pieces of rebar into a metal lattice as cars whooshed by along the highway. When I told him I was working on my studio and had a big log already cut into boards, he stood up and answered cryptically, gesturing vaguely with the acetylene flame still roaring in his hand. I drove away, figuring it was hopeless to expect anything from him. But early the next morning, he showed up unannounced, saying, "What's this work you need to do?"

"Want some tea or something?" I asked, not feeling quite awake enough to discuss technical details of woodworking, hoping to stall a moment to get my head around the task and Vadsuku's insertion into it.

"No no no . . . just tell me, where's the job?"

"Okay, okay, come on in here . . . I've got to build a counter that can support these machines . . . I don't have much space, so I need to find the most efficient way to build the legs."

Vadsuku frowned at the space and the equipment, his face a mask of thought.

"It looks like heavy stuff," he said. "Not made of plastic."

"Yeah, it's old. From before everything was done with computers."

"Older is better for some things." Vadsuku considered a moment and then said, "You can do what you want, but if I were you, I'd bolt that counter right to the wall. No need to build legs that take up space. Get yourself some L-brackets."

"Some what brackets?"

"L, L. You know the alphabet, right? A-B-C, just keep going to number 12. You can get someone to make them for you at the industrial district in town. Bolt one side to the wall, the other to your wood."

He demonstrated a corner of metal, two inches on each side, with bolt holes machined into it.

"All right, I see. That's a good idea," I said.

As I thought through the details of this solution, Vadsuku turned and left as abruptly as he'd arrived. There was nothing more to explain, the whole thing was self-evident as soon as he described the concept, so he just turned and walked back to his truck with barely a grunt of farewell. I didn't know why he'd come at all, except that one afternoon I'd happened across him in an unused part of the *tangchang*, sitting on the ground with a *mijiu* bottle between his legs, and he asked, "Brother, tell me the truth, is your music good?"

"Nothing special," I said.

"Jie-ren told me it's good," Vadsuku said. "He was here last month, and I asked him about you. Jie-ren is my brother. He knows music. He said you're good, so you must be. Jie-ren knows. I know he knows, so I know."

I just shrugged and said, "I don't know." Which was true. I was just trying to carve music out of resonance, not so different from carving a driftwood log, following natural contours to see what would emerge. "You use a chain saw and chisels, I use a guitar and bamboo flutes. I don't know anything about good or bad."

"It doesn't matter," Vadsuku said. "You don't have to know. But I know, and if I know, we know."

• • •

I drove into town, custom-ordered a dozen L-brackets from the first machine shop I stopped at and picked them up two hours later. Back home, I bolted three of the boards together raft-like with two-by-twos, cut the ends square to fit the space, and fixed them with the brackets to the back and side walls at one end of the studio.

I sawed a square hole in the counter and set the transport deck of my eight-track tape machine flush with the wood, so the flow of magnetic tape from reel to reel was embedded within the shape and grain of the log Yiming and I had wrestled from the beach. I stacked the eight-track's *Star Trek*–looking preamps behind it, with their funky knobs and meters—it was an MCI, the brand used to record much of the great Motown music of the 1970s. I'd gotten this beautiful $20,000 machine for a hundred dollars when a TV station went digital and dumped all its old analog gear in a music store in Taipei.

I made a cover for the tape transport by caulking ten-millimeter glass onto a window frame I'd salvaged from the abandoned train depot in Hualian. Beneath the transport I built a soundproof cabinet to enclose the motors and power supply. I could barely lift the twenty-four-track mixing console I had on long-term loan from a friend in Taipei, but managed to wrest one corner up onto the counter and push it the rest of the way. The thirty-year-old gold plate reverb machine that I'd picked up with my tape machine fit perfectly underneath.

I left the brick seam broken and exposed where I'd knocked out the partition, but painted the rest of the studio walls blue and green—or rather, splashed blue and green paint across them—and within these colors of the sea added the gold and blonde of hinoki counters, tables, and shelves.

While I worked on the studio my hands became stiff and hard—no good for playing guitar, just like E-ki told me from the start. My record label called from time to time to ask how things were going. "Fine, fine, everything's going great," I said, though I hardly touched my guitars in those days. This was not just because my fingers were tired. My mind was in a different sphere, absorbed not with music but with driftwood, tools, and saws, and with the analog recording machines I was linking up and learning how to use.

One day I walked down to a stand of bamboo below the lower house and cut a pole to make a clothes rack. Walking back up the road, I absently trimmed the leafy branches with my knife, but cut too close to my hand and my left middle finger erupted with blood. I cried out in naked grief, mourning my lost guitar career, certain I'd lopped off the tip of my finger. I'd sliced off most of the nail and some flesh, but once I'd washed the blood away I saw the finger was intact, though I still have a scar on that knuckle.

Another time, as I shaped the edge of a board with a hand plane, the shoe of the plane slipped off the corner of the wood on the downstroke. As my hand continued forward, my right thumbnail caught on a spur of wood and was torn completely off. It took two months to grow back, and during this time I couldn't play my guitars at all, except to ruefully finger the fretboard with my left hand. But by mid-autumn, all the machines were connected and my fingers had healed, and when I started recording *Ocean Hieroglyphics* my hands were strong and hard, and my playing was better than it had ever been before.

TEN

Songs of the Amis

When the analog recording machines were linked up and ready to go, I invited Siki to bring the Dulan elders to my place to record their songs. A-sun came up in the afternoon to cut the overgrown grass, which I invariably neglected. Ethnically Taiwanese, A-sun had grown up in a partly Amis neighborhood and spoke some of their language. For no reason other than his innate good will, he assumed the role of self-appointed factotum for the Open Circle Tribe, lending his tools, his van, and his mechanical skills to whatever building task or broken-down car required them. He would think nothing of spending half a day on his back beneath Yiming's truck to fix an oil leak, or, as now, coming up to deliver a case of *mijiu* and clear out a space for the night's recording. A-sun unassumingly did things people needed help with before they even thought to ask him. He was a master metalworker and certified in underwater welding. He took on occasional jobs to make a living, and the rest of the time putted around in his tiny green and orange van full of greasy tools. He was one of those rare individuals who seemed never to require anything for himself, as if he not only were not only self-reliant but also didn't have the same desires and needs as the rest of us. He simply and solidly always did the right thing, without any intervening egotism or need for recognition, as when he'd hauled all his welding gear up to my house and cut the bars out of the windows just so I wouldn't feel like I lived in a jail.

A-sun swung the gas-powered grass cutter back and forth, the engine roaring and grass shooting everywhere, each muscle on his bowling ball physique bulging into roundness. When he finished, he unloaded some firewood and a case of *mijiu* from his van as I set up the machines and ran two microphones out the window on long cables.

"I only cleared out a small space," he said. "See? That way everyone will have to sit closer together, it will be better for the singing. The elders won't wander off, they'll be afraid of snakes in the tall grass in the night."

"Good thinking, man."

"Also, I brought you these." A-sun handed me two jumbo Kirin Ichiban beer cans, both empty.

"Empty?" I said.

"Yeah, these are great cans. If you fill them with water and put them in the fridge they'll get cold in no time. You've got that good spring water straight from the mountain. With these you can really enjoy it."

"Okay, I'll fill them up and stick them in right now."

. . .

Siki and Shen-hui each drove a van full of elders up to my place at dusk. I greeted them where they parked down by the lower house. "*Toumu*," I said, "Chief, thank you all for coming. It's my honor to record your songs."

"Yes, yes, thank you, thank you," the Chief smiled in return. The old men and women unfolded themselves stiffly from the vans, as if from a long journey.

"Ah, so this is where you live," Siki said. "Damn, I didn't think about this place when we were looking for a house for you."

"It doesn't matter, I'm here."

As we walked up the driveway in the twilight, the elders

turned and gestured at the landscape in all directions, speaking in the bubbling rise and fall of Amis.

"What are they saying?" I asked Siki.

He listened a moment and then said, "They're speaking the names of this place. These used to be our hills; this is Amis land. Every feature you can see from here has a name in Amis, all the peaks, ridges, ravines, even the boulders that stand above the trees. It's like coming home for them. Since the land was taken, or sold off to the Hakka, the only Amis who come up here are hunters, but these elders haven't hunted for a long time."

I had begun to feel at home in this house, on this mountain, on this stretch of coast, but this was another level of belonging. The roots of Amis language descended into this earth, as if their tongues and hearts grew directly from the soil. Still, the elders evinced no proprietary air, no bitterness that I was living on land that had been theirs, but over which they no longer held agency. They always welcomed me to join their community, honoring the etiquette of their residence in this place irrespective of the shifting titles and deeds of possession. Perhaps a deeper ownership lies in belonging to the land, rather than claiming land as a belonging.

The elders settled upon the plastic chairs Siki had brought. The apprentices fed the fire and started around the circle with the *mijiu*. I'd been taking a break from alcohol for a week or so, but accepted a shot when they passed by me.

"Hey, how come you're drinking tonight?" Siki asked me. "I was starting to think you'd quit."

"You always say drinking helps you sing better, right? Don't you know it helps you record better too?" That felled him completely, and he called for two shots so we could toast each other.

A-zai the apprentice shimmied up a betel nut tree and cut down a bunch of *binlang* that was not too overripe. The old women cut off the caps, folded them in leaves dabbed with lime paste, and passed them around in a woven basket. The elders cleared their throats and hummed to themselves as the *mijiu* made its way around the circle. The Open Circle artists and a few other locals arrived and sat around the yard. The elders looked uncertainly at each other and to Siki, waiting for whatever was supposed to happen. The whole idea of a performance, a musical expression for its own sake rather than as part of a larger context, did not fit their social or psychological makeup. They were used to singing at gatherings, not gathering to sing. Something unconscious and spontaneous was being plotted and organized here, taken out of a realm of elastic possibility and nailed down on a grid of time and space, with an aim toward preservation, a fixed and static form. Such documentation is qualitatively different from oral traditions and mythologies, which are passed from mouth to mouth, malleable and adaptable, and may be constantly refreshed and revivified. In a sense we were submitting the elders to what I had left Taipei to avoid, that is, the imposition of the terms of recording media upon the organic generation of music, upon the implicit relationship between songs and life. Even though they were sitting around a fire on their home mountain, there was a formality in this approach to singing that made them slightly wooden and self-conscious.

Still, as the elders began to sing, the songs bloomed into the night with the same magnificence they always had for me. The Chief cooed out his smooth falsetto, honey-sweet, ductile as warm gold, which seemed to wrap around and caress the moment. His throat, breath, and chest opened and resonated, spilling the old Amis songs into the evening, into the lush night sounds of Dulanshan, as the rest of the elders chimed in with harmony and countermelodies.

After an hour the Amis elders got tired of singing for abstract posterity. The songs became ragged and punctuated with laughter. "This is an old Japanese sailors' song," Kala-OK cackled. One of the old women slapped him on the shoulder as he started to sing—it was apparently pornographic. The songs moved around the circle, each person taking a turn to improvise, singing traditional melodies with extemporaneous words, describing the night or their state of being at the moment, saying anything from "Thanks to Scott for inviting us" to lampooning the lack of good looks or manners of someone across the circle.

Yiming, Ai-qin, Dou-dou, Ha-na, and Shen-hui had all remained in the background at the more formal start of the evening, but as things began to loosen up, they all joined in. Yiming knew some of the Amis songs almost as well as his own Puyuma songs. Ai-qin laughed so unrestrainedly that her laughter was louder than the singing, which when brought to her attention made her laugh all over again. Soon the whole notion of recording was forgotten, and everyone stood up and began the foot stomp dance, spiraling in the small space A-sun had cleared. Now nobody was thinking about how good or bad they sounded, though by this time the singing was wild and discordant, nothing held back or restrained. I joined in too, and let the tape machines roll on, the mics picking up whatever they could of this moving target, which was now beyond capture.

. . .

Later, when Siki and I listened to the songs, he frowned as if we had failed to secure an essence without which the recordings were meaningless. Whether this was a function of what we actually recorded, or due to the context of listening through electronic systems in a machine-filled room, rather than directly from mouths to ears in a night of friends and wine and firelight, I don't know. The music certainly sounded better to everyone when they weren't thinking about whether it sounded good or not. In listening to the recorded songs, and even in the objective of preserving them, we inserted a critical mind that never existed when they were sung for their own sake, with no motive beyond the time and place into which they emerged.

This happened again a year later when I went to Yiming and Ai-qin's place to record Tian Baba, who was considered the best Puyuma singer in Zhiben. Yiming was desperate to capture and preserve his voice, but after every session Yiming shook his head in frustration and said, "No, it didn't sound right, he never let go. He never reached his high point . . . we've got to record him at a festival, when all the elders are together. That's when they really open up, everything comes out. You should hear him then. The way he sang tonight, he was too subdued. It wasn't really him."

So I did attend an annual Puyuma festival, and sat with a portable recording system in a circle of elders, men and women in their seventies and eighties who spoke Puyuma as their mother tongue and were indeed emotionally "high." We were at a beach south of Taidong City, and the wind off the sea constantly distorted the recording. Shots of *mijiu* went around and around as the elders reveled in this pure plasma of their language and songs, which was becoming rarer year by year. The jubilation and expansiveness Yiming so desperately wished to record was here, but it was mixed with a sense of loss, the fact that their culture was waning, with no one to replace them as they passed away. They glowed in this gathering of the living remnants of their culture and memory, but it was not a sustainable candescence. Rather, it was burning out, a final flush of light that soon would be extinguished. These old men and women who were the last repositories of their heritage had to speak Chinese with their children and grandchildren. Tian Baba's voice was unrestrained and free that day. It was a thing of beauty, full of power, finesse, and personal expressiveness, but also now undercut with despair that deepened as the afternoon wore on. By the end of the day, as the sun descended beyond the peaks of the central range, and the wind cut cold through our clothes and blew sand into our eyes, the songs had become a gorgeous but heartbreaking threnody.

Years after this night recording the Dulan elders, Yiming and I attended an artist residency in New Caledonia, the former French colony, to explore the connections between Kanack Melanesian culture and aboriginal Taiwan. One week, while Yiming was busy with his chain saws and chisels, I traveled with a local music and dance group to an outlying island for a culture festival. During their many performances, both on stage and for rituals, I kept waiting for the moment when everyone would stand up and sing and join the dance, as always occurred in Dulan. But it never happened. There was a separation between performer and audience, as if the rituals and songs had been transformed from participatory ceremony into a spectacle. Perhaps in New Caledonia indigenous culture had been objectified by colonial influence and had become something to observe, like a musical recital or a painting exhibit, rather than to exchange or join in with. After all, you don't rush the stage, stomp your feet, and sing along with a Debussy piano recital.

Amis culture in Dulan was organic and deeply rooted, but it had also been influenced by colonialism. In the early twentieth century the Japanese banned the Amis *ilisin*, a ceremony for spirits connected to grain harvests and ritual headhunting. Japanese authorities allowed the ceremony to return after a few years, but in a simplified form and with Japanese gods rather than Amis spirits as the object of worship. More songs and dances were added, and a greater role was given to women. In the 1920s Amis hospitality practices were "Geisha-ized," such that tourists and local officials could choose a female dancer to eat and drink with them for the duration of an evening.

Amis spirits were reinstated in the harvest ceremony, and it became what is today called the *fengnianji*, or harvest festival, in Mandarin. Though it is considered an indigenous event, by both Amis and non-aboriginal Taiwanese, it has been altered from the original *ilisin*. For example, because of the state monopoly on the production of alcohol, the Amis could no longer brew their own rice wine, a process that was originally an integral part of the *ilisin*. Today they are allowed to perform rituals to their own spirits, but must do so with *mijiu* brewed by the KMT.

. . .

Siki and Shun-hui drove the elders back down the mountain in their vans, but for the rest of us the night was young. We sat down and the song circle recohered, everyone taking a turn, singing whatever he or she wanted. Siki's ex-wife Ming-ling sang a Mandarin pop song, but at everyone's insistence followed it with an Amis song. Her voice was like an iridescent insect wing, fragile and shimmering in the night. Dou-dou sang so softly and beautifully that the whole world became silent, except for the fire that crackled, blowing her sparks and kisses. No one wanted to sing after she finished. Frowning to cover her abashedness, Dou-dou finally said, "Scott, what are you waiting for? Can't you put on some music we can dance to?"

I ran to the studio, turned the speakers out into the yard and cranked the volume high. Michael Jackson sang "1-2-3, A-B-C," the rhythm thumping in the night.

"Aha," Zhiming laughed, "now I know why you don't want neighbors!"

We began dancing wildly. We became a plasmic mass of bodies. The *mijiu* ran out. Yiming drove down the mountain and returned with a case of beer. Shen-hui reappeared from her taxi duties with a whoop. The dancers surrounded her, and she threw down a few moves. Then the circle broke up, everybody shaking off on their own.

Ming-ling wore a tight opalescent skirt and matching blouse. She looked ravishing, and kicked off her shoes to dance, ruining her stockings. I went down low, shimmying with my knees bent ninety degrees so we'd be face to face. We grinned like drunken moons. She jumped up on one of the plastic chairs and shouted, "Now you're not so tall!" She looked up to the few stars bristling through the haze, and her flesh rose above me, her thighs, ribs, collarbone, and throat filled the sky. She jumped down and fell into my arms, almost knocking me over, and we continued dancing. Was she simply acting out in the freedom of Siki's absence? Or was she emerging, like a butterfly from a chrysalis, to reclaim the self-determination of her body and her being?

Yiming swiveled his hips like a cowboy and danced up bowlegged to Dou-dou, she laughed and whipped her hair around like a lariat. Someone had brought a bottle of whiskey. It made its way hand to hand and mouth to mouth with no intervening formality of cups or glasses. I danced like a man with his chest cut open, waiting for someone to reach in and grab his heart.

Plasma, ganglia, blood and bone, sweat, gelatin, grease—this was physical exhilaration unspooling into the night, the sovereignty of all the skin contains, which needs no justification or explanation, like Walt Whitman singing his body out into the air and centuries around him, "what I assume you assume . . ." And when you assume freedom and self-determination for yourself, you're happy to encourage and allow these in others, there's no need to force their dance steps into your rhythm. "The love of the body of man or woman balks account, the body itself balks account . . ." No ledgers, no accounting, no tax or census, an illegible scrawl of corpuscles and marrow, autonomous, anarchic, self-contained and self-realized from the start, every corporeal body begins unfettered and free. Even A-sun was moving and shuffling to the music in a sort of syncopated movement, as if his body were a fly whisk swatting at the music, while bumping into everyone like a bowling ball in a crate full of pins.

Ming-ling went to check on her daughter, who was sleeping on the tatamis in the living room despite the blast of funk into the night. She paused and flipped through my book of van Gogh's paintings on the driftwood coffee table in the living room. I recalled van Gogh's advice to painters to live like a monk but with a visit to the brothel every two weeks. I went to the kitchen to grab a beer. While there I ducked into the shower room and took a piss down the drain, as there was no toilet here and I didn't feel like wading through the dark to the outhouse. I stepped back outside and intercepted Ming-ling as she emerged from the living room. I leaned against the wall and stared at her but said nothing. Yiming was dancing with his wife now, he and Ai-qin locked in a gyrating embrace. Ming-ling looked at me solemnly as if about to speak, then giggled and returned to continue dancing. The phone rang on my desk. It looked like something from Mars, strange white rounded plastic, the receiver like conjoined twin ears. I ignored it and rejoined the dancing bodies.

The dancing slowed. I turned down the music. One by one everyone wandered away to their cars and trucks and drove away. The fire burned low, till only coals remained. The music finished, and the silence of the mountain descended again. Yiming, Ai-qin, and Ming-ling were the only ones left. We were sweat-stained, barefoot, with grass cuttings between our toes, exhaling the jangly but exhausted energy of the party back into the cool quiet air.

"Did the recording go okay?" Ai-qin asked.

"I think so . . . we captured the sound of your laughter perfectly," I said. "I'm not so sure about the songs."

This of course elicited more laughter from her, but it was 3 a.m. We were tired, there was nothing left to think or say. Yiming and Ai-qin headed down the incline to his truck.

"Help me carry my daughter to my car," Ming-ling said to me. "I don't want her to wake up."

I went into the living room where the girl was asleep, covered by a quilt. I cradled her in my arms and carried her to the car, while Ming-ling rounded up her shoes and walked down to her car in her ruined stockings.

"It's late, maybe you should stay here," I said.

"My daughter would catch cold," she said. "She tosses and turns all night, and always kicks off the covers."

"So what do you do at home?" ·

"We sleep in the same bed together."

Sleeping with Ming-ling and her daughter in one big bed had a strange and lovely allure, a collectivity of blankets and bodies and warmth and dreams. This struck me like a revelation, something I'd never conceived before but suddenly desired. But it was new and ungainly. I had no place then to fit it within myself.

"I guess it would be strange for us all to sleep together," I said hollowly.

"Would it?" Ming-ling said, looking briefly in my eyes. But then she put her daughter in the back seat and got in behind the wheel, the spell was broken.

"By the way," I said, "what's your Amis name?"

She laughed. "Why do you want to know?"

"No reason. What the hell, you're not Chinese, I'm not Chinese. Why use a Chinese name?"

"Okay, you win. It's Hadec."

"What does it mean?"

"No one remembers the actual meaning of Hadec, it's just a name. But if you pronounce it just a little differently it means delicious."

I could only silently, hungrily agree.

She started her engine and backed out, bumped into several betel nut trees as she maneuvered back and forth, and drove away.

I walked back up the slope to the house. Empty beer cans were strewn in the yard, cut grass had been tracked everywhere. I grabbed my guitar and absently strummed some chords. The glow of the coals in the fire pit subsided, and the sound of the sea came washing up the mountain.

The night was over. The beer and *mijiu* were drunk, the dancing was finished, everything was a mess, but the Dulan

Amis songs were down on tape, including the Chief's voice. This part was easy; all I'd had to do was set up the microphones and press the record button. Next would be the full recording of my ocean songs. I wondered if I would be able to play and record them as I heard them in my mind, or if the process would end up just the same as in the Taipei studios to which I proclaimed ideological opposition.

I also wondered whether there was anything I could've said to make Ming-ling stay. And if so, if I had some magic words, I wondered whether I wished I'd said them. I couldn't answer. Life is blind—you don't know what's behind the curtain till you step through it, you never know if you want what's there until you've crossed the threshold, until it's too late to go back. The coals were almost dark; a dull orange pulsed within the burnt wood. The phone rang. I went inside and answered it.

"Hello?"

It was Ming-ling, calling from her place down in the village.

"It's because of my daughter," she said.

"I know," I said. "I understand."

The phone clicked on the other end of the line.

I took one of A-sun's Kirin cans from the fridge. It was perfect, a cylinder of cold spring water in my hand, A-sun was right as usual. In the living room my van Gogh book was still open on the table. I went into the studio, rewound the tape, and listened back to the songs we'd sung.

ELEVEN

Big and Small Things

Ming-sho returned from traveling and came down to see me in Dulan. She stayed a few days, then went to visit her family. After a couple of weeks Ming-sho came back to Dulan and moved in to live with me.

We painted the living room ochre and blue, sloshing and spattering color everywhere. I made driftwood shelves for the kitchen, and we carried buckets of water from a spring when the pipe ran dry. We drove up and down the coast and swam together in the sea. At night Ming-sho drew in her sketch pad and translated Pablo Neruda's poems while I played my guitars.

When I first moved in, the frosted kitchen windows had been smeared with grease to the point of opacity. After A-sun cut out the window bars, I simply removed the frames and glass and stacked them outside—so after sundown the kitchen windows became gaping mouths, with all the lovely sounds of the dark pressing in. "Volunteer" pumpkins grew wild here and there across the mountain, Ming-sho and I picked them from the side of the road when we drove home. With her long slender limbs, Ming-sho was willowy and fawn-like and moved with dreamy slowness. At night she stood at the stove cooking pumpkin soup, performing the simple actions of cutting and stirring as if under water, a mermaid with a swirling current of hair, or a strand of kelp swaying with the rhythm of the sea. Onion peels fluttered from her hands and scattered across the floor.

In the afternoons Ming-sho walked up a hill behind the house, the autumn grasses pale yellow and tan, full of thistles and seeds, and set up an easel to paint on, or just sat cross-legged with a sketch pad on her lap, as eagles turned circles against the sky. Mull the dog loved to accompany her, proudly serving as her escort, happily sprawling on his back at her feet. But if I ever started down the mountain, Mull would hear the car engine and howl as if heartbroken, hurtling himself down the hill into the thick growth of grasses five times his height, yipping and whimpering as he crashed through the brush in desperation not to be left behind, finally emerging matted with seeds and burrs like a second coat of fur. I'd comb some of the tangles from his beard and let him lick my face—then I'd wave to Ming-sho where she stood atop the hill amid golden sun and grasses, and continue down.

Ming-sho and I often drove down the mountain, across the highway, and along the dirt road to Dulanbi, Dulan Point, where the earth pushed out into the sea as a series of cliffs. Large, aloe-like succulents grew up from among the stiff shore bushes and thrust long stems topped with seed pods twenty feet into the air. We walked down a rocky path as waves came breaking in across boulders and the pebbled shore. Mull and I wandered among the rocks and sand and driftwood, while Ming-sho sat down with her sketch pad, drawing the lime-stone boulders that had eroded to reveal harder rounded stones embedded within them. The waves splashed up against boulders stranded out in the surf, strange conglomerations of geologic material striated and lumped together, miniature monadnocks off the shore. Then we'd drive back up the mountain, through acres of plum orchards always changing with the seasons, making new leaves and flowers, budding into fruit, or standing with naked branches reaching to the sky. The plum trees

BIG AND SMALL THINGS

blossomed all across the mountain with billions of tiny white flowers, tinted with a hint of purple, so that when we drove through the orchards with the windows open, the scent was sweet and wild as the taste of wine. Then the tiny round petals fell, and for a few days they carpeted the earth like a layer of faintly blushing snow, until the wind blew them away.

I salvaged a stack of thin-planed camphor boards from the abandoned train depot in Hualian, built by the Japanese in 1911, and one day began to saw them into lengths to make a set of bookshelves. The boards were ancient, grayed, weathered, light as dried bones. The depot had been built by a government no longer in existence, by carpenters whose flesh was gone, their planes and chisels turned to rust—but inside, the boards had a coarse gold grain, and a drunken, urgent camphor smell bloomed out from them, a mineral exuberance of roots and leaves sealed within almost a hundred years.

This happened every time I sawed open the old faded skin of some piece of wood, but still I couldn't believe it. I ran to where Ming-sho was reading in the living room. She leaned over and closed her eyes, smelled the camphor wood, and then just smiled at me, like I was a fool to be surprised by breath, delicious and alive, in any time, in anything.

During the dry season when the water pipe was empty, or when it was blocked and I was too lazy to go up and fix it, we bathed at a spring in a *shijia* orchard to the north of us on the slope. Light and water flowed across Ming-sho's skin, her hair black and luminous as coal oil streaming down her back. Temple bells tolled across the acres of plum trees, and wild cranes passed by overhead. These were days of hammers, nails, pots and pans, carrying water, sweeping the floor, as trees, grasses, flowers, and clouds swirled across the mountain. Far below waves curled in to embrace the shore, a hush from the sea at night as we slept together beneath the sheets and sky we shared.

Though we met in Taipei, Ming-sho was originally from Tainan, on the southwest coast of Taiwan, where the first colonial outpost on Taiwan was established by the Dutch in 1624. Only after the Dutch arrived did significant migration from China begin. Before 1624 an estimated 1,500 Chinese lived in Taiwan—seasonal fishermen, traders with aboriginal hunters, and pirates. The Dutch East India Company recruited Chinese immigrants to work on sugar and rice plantations, and within a few decades there were a hundred thousand Chinese residents in Taiwan. Most of these immigrants were from southern Fujian Province, directly across the Taiwan Strait, and spoke Minnanyu, "southern Fujianese." This seventeenth-century migration was the beginning of "Taiwanese" identity and language, which are of a body with those of southern Fujian, but with localized variation.

Fujian was historically on the margin of China, separated from the geographic and political center by a range of mountains. The people turned for trade and sustenance to the sea, such that historically most Chinese merchants and immigrants to other regions of Asia have been from Fujian. Because of their position and maritime excursions, the Minnan people have had a disproportionate influence on the exchange between China and the West. The first Western outpost in Mainland China was that of the Portuguese in Xiamen (known as Amoy in the West), in Fujian. The word *tea* is derived from its Minnanyu pronunciation *te*, though it is more commonly known in China by the Mandarin word *cha*, which in India became *chai*. Many Taiwanese have told me that classical Chinese poems are pronounced more correctly and sonorously in Minnanyu than in Mandarin, because the former is closer to the court language spoken in the Tang Dynasty, and preserves the original musicality of the poems—while Mandarin is a language that spread from the far north more recently. (The Cantonese, another southern people, make the same claim of their language.)

The west of Taiwan is now an agricultural and industrial zone, crowded with a series of major urban centers from north to south. But according to Dutch records, in the seventeenth century the western plains were forested and home to herds of thousands of deer. Trade in deer products was one of the earliest industries in Taiwan. Even before the establishment of the Dutch base, western plains aboriginals traded deer products to merchants from Japan and China in exchange for iron and salt. Over a hundred thousand deer skins were exported annually to Japan through the seventeenth century, where they were used to make samurai armor. The continual civil wars in Japan kept demand high—then as now war was good for business.

Indigenous peoples hunted deer with snares and arrows. As social and economic structures expanded in the mid-1600s, Chinese hunters began taking over the deer trade, leasing the rights to aboriginal hunting grounds from the Dutch administration. The Chinese hunted with pitfalls, which could kill hundreds of deer at a time. The Dutch outlawed pitfalls in an attempt to preserve a sustainable deer trade, but populations were eradicated within a hundred years anyway.

Zheng Chenggong, known as Koxinga in the West, was a Ming Dynasty loyalist who opposed the Qing Dynasty. The Qing leaders were from Manchuria, the northeast corner of China, and overthrew the Ming Dynasty in 1644—*Mandarin* comes from the term for Manchu administrator, *man da ren*. Koxinga refused to submit to the Qing emperor and ousted the Dutch from Taiwan in 1661 to establish a military base from which he hoped to overthrow the Qing. (Three hundred years later, Chiang Kai-shek followed the same strategy of using Taiwan as a base to retake the mainland.) But Koxinga died the next year, and soon Taiwan belonged to China. The Qing emperor didn't want Taiwan and almost pulled all Chinese settlers back to the mainland—historically the Chinese have been culturally, economically, and politically disinclined toward overseas colonization—but advisers convinced the emperor to keep control of Taiwan as a buffer against foreign powers, and to deprive pirates of its use. As Chinese settlement of Taiwan expanded, western plains aboriginals, or *pingpu zu* (literally "flatland tribes"), were ethnically and culturally assimilated into "Taiwanese" society and identity, to the point that these tribes no longer exist as discrete groups. However, it could be said that they did not disappear but still remain, as some studies estimate that 80 percent of ethnic Taiwanese have *pingpu* genes.

Originally called Zeelandia by the Dutch, Tainan is the oldest city in Taiwan and remains the center of Taiwanese language and folk culture. Ming-sho's family spoke Taiwanese at home, and this was her mother tongue. But she had been sent to boarding schools starting in middle school, where Mandarin was the dominant language, and her Taiwanese language fluency had declined. She had been in a Mandarin language environment for over ten years, through high school and then for five years of college in Taipei, and like many people in Taiwan she was in a continual process of reconnecting with her roots. This process was ongoing because identity and society were constantly shifting, and at the same time individual migrations like Ming-sho's, between regions and cultural milieus, kept one's position with respect to "tradition" in a state of flux.

The broad flat plains of the southwest are now intensely industrialized, with flaming smokestacks rising above enormous refineries, massive spherical autoclaves, and chemical tanks lined up row after row in a sea of effluent mist. The western cities are paved over and congested, densely populated, and polluted; the whole fifty-mile stretch between Tainan and Gaoxiong is a corridor of factories.

Having been shuttled between cities and educational institutions since adolescence, Ming-sho had come to the east coast, this least developed part of Taiwan, for more direct contact with an open, breathing landscape. Tainan offered access to a cultural history of almost four hundred years. But in the east there was freedom and space to develop her own path and sense of self, to paint and draw in a place where time was slow and malleable, contrary to the urban grid in which everything moved with increasing speed and rigidity.

In other words, Ming-sho was drawn to this place for the same reasons I was—and even for the same reasons as Yiming, E-ki, and most of my other friends here, who had left "home" to work within the mainstream economy but had returned with a desire to reinhabit, rediscover, or create an identity more genuine to them. The marginal regions of eastern Taiwan held the possibility of self-determination that was difficult to cultivate elsewhere in contemporary Taiwan.

There was an implicit synchronicity between Ming-sho and me, in our desire to step away from mainstream social expectations and live according to our own values. But over the course of months, Ming-sho couldn't feel she belonged in this house at the end of the road, that it was her home as well as mine. This place and way of being was a life I'd conceived in one-pointed solitude. I didn't know how to share it, or share myself, or how to open my own space and time to include another. I was engrossed in ever-expanding projects and plans and could not then appreciate how she helped balance these abstractions with her interior focus, her calm engagement with ordinary things, the fineness of her drawings about small facets of emotion and experience. Ming-sho would spend hours shading and cross-hatching the lines and details of a stone or piece of driftwood while I was working on *Ocean Hieroglyphics*, a set of wordless songs with titles such as "Sun Sets on All I've Left Undone" or "Throwing Questions to the Sea," with my wild hunger to embrace a totality of human experience and expression. There was no scaling down for me, as if every time I took a shot at things I had to encompass an infinite unity.

Our relationship stalled again and again, never quite cohering into a subjectivity with its own mass and essence. We loved each other like two live wires that had the potential to arc and surge with current, but which never quite clasped and held. Our life remained a closed orbit, never expanding to include others, maybe not even broad enough to include the two of us.

"I never feel you're really here with me," she said. "It's like I'm living alone in this house that belongs to you."

"I'm trying," I said.

"You keep spinning around and around in your own mind. What is it you really want?"

"How can I explain? I don't have a plan, I'm just acting with animal instinct. I'm trying to survive as what I am. I have to put everything I am into this. I'm afraid I'll fail if I don't."

"Then why did you invite me to stay with you?" she asked.

There was no uncowardly answer to this except, "Because I love you." These were words we spoke to each other, but in that moment I could not say them. No doubt opening my heart and life to Ming-sho would have made me stronger rather than weaker, and would have augmented and deepened my creative effort, as well as other aspects of my life, but I was afraid of becoming diluted, of having my intention or energy dissipated by obligations.

"I just need to feel free," I said.

"You are! You always are! You always do exactly what you want. You can't think about anyone else."

"I can't help it. It's just my nature."

• • •

So when Ming-sho was offered a job as a social worker on Orchid Island, the tiny tropic garden of coral and taro fields that rises from the Pacific Ocean fifty miles southeast from Dulan, she accepted it. She packed up her things, including her paintings and drawings, both of us glum and dismayed, and I drove her down to the ferry pier north of Taidong. A one-eyed, three-legged dog watched us cross the concrete quay, then scratched himself against a jag of iron rebar sticking up from an unfinished piling. The sun fell dazzling and metallic across the water. The tropical air was thick liquid with smells of sea rot and diesel. We walked together up the gangplank to the passenger cabin.

"Take care of yourself out there, okay?"

"I will . . . and I'll come back to see Mull soon . . . and you."

I felt bereft, but she smiled serenely as usual, without a trace of sadness. After all, she was heading to a new beginning, a new incarnation, and had not yet arrived, so the possibilities were still infinite. The engines started up, and I returned to the dock. Sunlight rippled across the ocean like a crust of jewels, diamonds and sapphires that blinded me. The enormous weather-beaten ferry idled in a wash of diesel exhaust. Ming-sho waved from the stern and held her arms out to me, then she raised them above her head, stretching to the sun, as the engines bellowed and the boat pulled out to the open sea.

. . .

After Ming-sho was gone, the house still resonated with her presence, in the paint on the walls, the pots we'd cooked with, in the way Mull sometimes looked at me forlorn, as if something integral to life here had been dissolved from within our midst, and in the faint shadow of Orchid Island on the horizon, which oscillated between presence and absence according to the weather and the clarity of the air. Sometimes when the phone rang I lifted it to my ear to hear her voice from across the sea. But Ming-sho and I had little to say to each other through disembodied voices transmitted by electric signals. Face to face and skin to skin, whole continents of wordless communication were possible, spaces of silence in which weather, sunlight, breath, music, bird songs were a shared experience, a form of communion with each other and with the world that did not require spoken articulation. After all, there was little I could say about my music arranging and recording—to anyone who asked, all I could say was that it was going well, or slowly, or poorly, the only real way to communicate about it was to play it back when anyone stopped by. So even when Ming-sho and

I called each other, we sometimes did little more than word-lessly keep the line open for minutes at a time.

In the wake of Ming-sho's absence, my guitars became strangers in my hands. I had built a recording studio to record my songs the way I wanted them recorded, but this meant I recorded them alone, playing my guitar into microphones and a spool of magnetic tape, and there was a hollowness to play-ing music to machines.

I drove up and down the mountain, to and from the green and blue waves of the sea, the sea I was trying to express as a physical and metaphorical body through music. I was lost to what I was supposed to be doing here, until I slowly settled back into my desk, my studio, rediscovering myself in this place, reimagining the trajectory of my work and grappling to make it real in this farmhouse at the end of the road. From my stu-dio I would put my guitar down and walk out into the yard, where Dulanshan rose up behind me, and look to the ocean spreading blue to the horizon. On the clearest days, through the ragged crowns of the betel nut trees, I saw Orchid Island at the extremity of vision. Then I would go back inside to try to capture this vast concreteness and vast abstraction with my fingers and my mind, with guitars and flutes, typewriter and pens, with music and poems about the color and texture of the ocean, a love song painted in green and blue.

TWELVE

A Woodcarver

Vadsuku stood drunken in my doorway, snot and spit hanging from his moustache, the morning sun streaming in behind him, a plastic *mijiu* bottle in his hand. Mull was still barking at the sound of his truck, which he had parked next to the lower house. His dog appeared, a monstrous, black, almost ursine beast, limping around with a plastic vet's shield encircling one paw. Vadsuku wore army pants with a cigarette hole burned in the crotch and a dirty T-shirt that said, *hang ten, founded 1960, san diego, california.*

Vadsuku was from the Paiwan tribe, at the southern end of Taiwan's central mountain range, but had a workshop here on the coast highway between Dulan and Taidong. He rented a half-built vanity mansion from a rich businessman at pennies on the dollar. It was a castle of dirt-colored bricks, complete with spiral staircases and crenellated towers, which locals called the "ghost house." The place was a desolation of crumbling walls and broken windows, but Vadsuku had transformed it into a work of art as honest and transcendent as a van Gogh painting. He gutted the interior but left jagged edges of cracked brick and tile in the corners, and across this derelict foundation he laid thick slabs of driftwood, retaining the original shape of the wood but polishing out hidden contours and lines. He didn't alter the rough concrete and exposed rebar of the ceiling, but twined it with flowers and vines. He knocked out all the window frames, and built wrought iron balconies extending above the sea, where you could sit and sip a cup of tea, suspended amid the sound of waves.

Vadsuku smiled fraternally and held out a rough, callused hand. "My brother," he said. I shook his hand, expecting to regret it. I hadn't seen Vadsuku much recently, except for brief glimpses of him chainsawing logs in the dooryard of his house. Everybody had been avoiding him. His dipsomania had been out of control, and when he lost control he veered into violence and self-destruction. To be around his drunkenness was like watching someone rush headfirst at a stone wall, charging toward death without caring, like the projection of a film you could not halt. I saw punches swung like clumsy axes, dishes thrown and shattered, shouted insults that cut like blades.

A few weeks before, he'd shown up at my house, the entire bed of his pickup filled with stinking fish. "Look at this!" he said. "These washed up on the beach by my house. Someone dynamited them out at sea but couldn't net them. They would have rotted and gone to waste, so I collected them to give to all my friends." That day Vadsuku had just come off a bender in which he'd offended everyone. This was his post-binge, cheery-helpful-friendly mode, which was almost worse than his drunkenness. It was his form of apology, but a truck full of reeking fish only repulsed me, and anyway the anger of the community could not be assuaged through me.

. . .

Before assimilation, the Paiwan were one of the most stratified tribes of Taiwan. They developed an elaborate culture of carved wooden doorposts, which served as prestige objects for their aristocracy. The Paiwan were a "house society," a term coined by Claude Levi-Strauss to indicate that clans and lineages were collected and concentrated in houses that acted as "moral persons." These houses transcended generations and were repositories of both material and non-material wealth. In this respect the Paiwan were similar to the extinct Lapita cultures of the South Pacific, who were also Austronesian language-speaking house societies.

The Paiwan were originally a mountain tribe. They lived in small settlements that encouraged a self-reliant identity. By contrast, pre-assimilation settlements of plains tribes like the Amis reached populations of five hundred to a thousand people, probably contributing to their more communal orientation. The Paiwan, like all indigenous peoples of Taiwan with the exception of the Tao on Orchid Island, were headhunters and were among the most fiercely resistant to subjugation by the Qing and Japanese. In the nineteenth century many ships ran aground in the dangerous waters off the southern peninsula of Taiwan. Shipwrecked crews were often attacked by what would later be known as the "Paiwan" tribe. At the time, Taiwan's indigenous peoples had no social identity beyond the village level—the macro-identities of "tribes" did not exist until Japanese ethnographers created these classifications in the early twentieth century. In 1871 the crew of a Ryukyu Island shipwreck was massacred by warriors from a "Paiwan" village. The Qing government claimed to have no authority over this part of Taiwan, so in 1874 Japan mounted a military expedition to subdue the "savages" responsible for the killings. This Japanese incursion prompted the Qing Dynasty to extend their sovereignty over all of Taiwan. Before then, parts of western and northern Taiwan were settled and administered, but the central mountains and east coast remained beyond state control.

The Paiwan's fierce independence remained in Vadsuku's character. He exuded frustration that he had been born into a world where he and his culture were subject to an alien value system. Vadsuku was a supreme craftsman, with an innately rich and innovative vision. He may have seen himself as the bearer of the Paiwan woodcarving tradition, which once held social prestige, but which was now subsumed within the commoditized economy of the Republic of China.

Vadsuku often remained aloof from the *tangchang* community. And yet he was, at least sometimes, personable, down to earth, contemplative, with many qualities you would welcome in a friend or colleague. He was always available to help anyone who braved his gruffness to ask for it. His Malaysian-Chinese wife also veered away from intimate community connection. I never learned how they met or how he wooed her. This wasn't the kind of question you ever felt you had an opening to ask Vadsuku, and even if you did, and even if he answered, it would more likely be some cryptic red herring than anything pointing inward to himself. She was kind and gentle, and was always accepted by the community here, but she remained somehow alien, as if she were walking through the atmosphere of a world in which she was not adapted to breathe. Maybe this alien quality is something Vadsuku felt in himself, and by linking with his wife he may have felt some resonance or harmony between his subjective experience and its outward manifestation. On the occasions when he joined a project of the Open Circle Tribe, he worked furiously, tirelessly, perfectly, expressing innate leadership and yet fitting his skills into the greater communal effort.

Except when drunk, Vadsuku said little and existed in self-enclosed solitude, a married bachelor like E-ki, despite the fact that his wife lived with him in the ghost house. Conceptually and in terms of execution his work had the quality of genius. It came from a different state of being, beyond the plane of everyday transactions and perceptions. As an artist, he did things no one else here could do. Because of this, and because of the non-judgmentalism of the Open Circle Tribe, his self-indulgence was condoned. In addition, as long as Vadsuku acted out the role of hellion in the community, everyone else's excesses seemed mild in comparison. But forgiveness allowed him to continue his self-destruction and the wounding of his friends.

. . .

Now, with sunlight streaming in behind him, Vadsuku let go of my hand and sat down on my porch, the *mijiu* bottle hanging loosely at his side.

"Want a cup of coffee?" I asked.

"I don't understand coffee," he said.

"How about some tea?"

"This," he said, sitting down on the front step and lifting the *mijiu* to his lips.

I went to the kitchen. In the middle of the floor was a half-eaten field rat my cat A-dong had caught the night before, its entrails spilling out and staining the concrete. I put some water on to boil and stepped back outside.

"Let me tell you a story," Vadsuku said. "When my father had cancer we went to see him in the hospital. What can you do with a dog in a hospital? Nothing. So we left the dog at home. When we came back the next day the dog was gone. Who knew where? We drove around the mountain to look for him. Well, the dog knows the sound of my engine, so he came running. But with his front paw up like this—"

Vadsuku glared at me and held an arm up to shoulder height with the hand hanging slackly from the wrist, like a position in a kung fu move.

"He was dragging a trap. The jaws were locked around his foot, with the steel cable trailing behind. He came running up like this, look! He pulled that motherfuck trap right up out of the ground with a broken foot. Do you see? Do you know what that trap was? His medal. That trap was his valor, the symbol of his heart. Running up like this, goddammit. His medal, like a soldier's, you know? And I tell you, everybody's got a medal like that, stuck to their chest, that they press out at the world. Chiang Kai-shek had one. Mao Zedong had one. Stalin had one. And my dog had one, the teeth of a steel trap, hanging from his broken foot like this. Everybody's got one. What's yours?"

I heard a voice from the direction of Vadsuku's truck, and his wife appeared. She was tall and slim, with voluptuous curves, a mild, oval face, and straight black hair flowing to her waist. She was gorgeous, actually, but her face was tainted with sourness, compressed and drained like a lemon that's been through the juicer. Her sheen and color had been squeezed dry, with only a few tendrils of vitality still inhering. I made my coffee and a cup of tea for her, and offered her a chair, but she stroked A-dong and squatted in the shade of a jackfruit tree across the yard instead.

Vadsuku raised the bottle to his lips, but before he could suck down a single drop his head slumped forward on his chest. The tropical sun was sweet and liquid, pouring straight in across the sea, and a pair of eagles keened and turned in circles high above. Vadsuku jerked awake and looked at me as from far away.

"You are American. But where are your fathers from? England? But are you Anglo or Saxon?"

The words were faint, unresonant echoes in my head. *Saxon* linked up with *Anglo* fifteen centuries ago, Old High German romping through the Celtic hills and vales of England. My genealogy fades beyond my great-grandparents. Conquest, pilgrimage, defeat, assimilation—how far, how distant from the freeways and shopping malls of America's West Coast.

"Anglo," I said for no reason except that it came first.

"Ah, good," he said, "I'm glad you're not a Saxon. Now, if you were from Ireland I could really talk to you, Ireland or Scotland. By the way, where does your name come from? Is it because of Scotland, or your father, who or what actually are you?"

Vadsuku seemed to lose some inner balance, to totter and fade, and he mumbled in English, "How are you, my brother, what, how, why?" Then he regained control, and continued in Mandarin, "Where's your guitar? Go get it and play me a song. No, wait, I'll sing one. I know only one song. My brother taught it to me. It goes like this."

He sang, and his voice was like his hands, rough and cracked, but self-assured, possessing autonomy at least within a certain sphere of things. In the dappled shade of the jackfruit tree his wife's face was still sour, but as she stared down at the ground she patted the rhythm of the song out on her thigh.

Mull growled at his dog as it hobbled over to sit by Vadsuku's feet.

"Dog! Goddammit, that's your brother. Say hello, don't fight. You're a lucky dog, your father is white, he can do anything, what he wants he gets, not like us ab-O-riginals . . . Listen . . . listen to the eagles' song, can you hear? I can sing it, listen . . ."

Vadsuku whistled the dry sharp cry of the eagles through his teeth.

"Twenty-five years ago I knew what would happen when I came down from the mountains. I knew before it happened. The eagles told me. I heard it in their song. How long have the eagles been here? Count the years, give it a number. See them fly—but they are gone. There are no eagles."

Vadsuku began to sob. Tears and mucus ran down his face. "I knew," he said, "the eagles told me."

I had no consolation to offer. I could only watch and listen. Vadsuku seemed to retreat to some abject sadness in his personal history or psyche, beyond the possibility of change or redemption, some place unreachable by words or others.

"Here, drink some tea," I said, when he finally quieted and reemerged into this place of time and sun. He stood up and gulped from the cup, but the liquid exploded from his mouth.

"Goddamn that's hot!"

His wife rose from the grass and moved forward, floating mirage-like against the ocean in the distance. "Can we go now?" she asked.

"Yes, yes," Vadsuku said. But he lingered, looking up at the eagles, now specks in the sky, as if not wanting to leave. He leaned over and blew his nose on the knee of his camo pants, saying, "Sorry, sorry, 'scuse me . . ."

He straightened and shook my hand again, a boyish grin now framed beneath his snot-glossed moustache. His brow was dark and furrowed as with the anguish of some ancient innocence, some old, tired hope, something worn and half-abandoned, but still twinkling at the corners of his eyes.

"It's okay, it's okay. We're going to the river now to catch some fish. You know me, I know you, we are brothers, we are the same. You know where I am. Whenever you are lonely, I am there."

He stepped off the porch into his half-broken, army-leftover strut-2-3-4, beneath the belly-flop sun falling golden all around us, his wife following behind, his dog bringing up the limping rear. I heard the engine catch and rev, Vadsuku let out an inarticulate holler of farewell, and the thrum of the engine receded down the mountain into the rise and fall of cicada songs, leaving only a faint scent of exhaust and the cry of the eagles spiraling unseen high above.

. . .

That afternoon I hiked up the ravine to fix the water pipe, chopping forward with my knife in one hand, a can of epoxy in the other, a few strips of inner tube in my pocket to tie like tourniquets around the splices in the pipe. Soft, sluggish gnats and whining mosquito fighter planes swarmed along the stream. The current gurgled over rounded stones, a water song descending from a cleft in the mountain, the ravine enclosed by branches dense and myriad as bone marrow sponge.

Spiders broad as my hands hung suspended by silver threads between the tops of trees, their fluorescent green and yellow stripes lit up by gelatinous sun that ran dappling through the canopy. The rise and fall of insect sounds droned through the heat. Brittle flecks of shell and wing arced out into air and

A WOODCARVER

light to buzz and click and chirr, then flaked back into earth and rot again.

I found the place where the line was blocked, and pulled two sections of pipe apart. A tangled root ball clogged the line. When I pulled it out, water began to flow again. I cleaned out the pipe and split one end of it with my pocketknife. I crammed it into the other opening, then wrapped and tied the joint with strips of inner tube.

Heading down the streambed, I froze at a stab of movement in the brush—a fruit fox was snared by a strand of steel wire, a hunter's trap. Silver fur shimmered on its twisting back. Behind its thin snout wildness pooled like mercury in its eyes. The fox flashed and bristled with raw energy, like a burning fuse leading through millennia to a naked state of being. It was a vision like a mirror with the metal scraped off its back, half-transparent and half-reflecting, half-opening to reveal the other side.

I moved forward to release the fox from its impending death, from the hunter on the way to collect his bounty, today, tomorrow, next week, somewhere in the continuum of time—but the animal retreated beneath a shelf of rock and snarled at me, protected from my mercy by its instinct to be free.

THIRTEEN

Hunting with the Bunun

A Gift of the Spirits

Nabu stroked the braids of his hair and smoothed his lycra tights. His hands were enormous, almost caricatures of hands, meaty sprawls of finger, but they had a quality of softness and were lined with wrinkles like those around his eyes, the fine eye-wrinkles of squinting to see far or to keep out dust. Across the lawns of the Bunong Culture Village, at the foot of the central mountains, the smell of mowed grass spread through the November air. A half dozen of us filled our trekking packs with rice, noodles, and dehydrated pork, as local tourists milled around, waiting for the culture performance to begin. Big looms hummed and clacked in shops abutted to the stage, worked by women in dark blue tunics and long skirts embroidered with red and gold diamonds enclosing diamonds down to a center point. The looms were a success as a cottage industry—all the tourists wanted something from the Bunong Culture Village, even if this was only one of many half-hour stops off the tour bus along the rift valley. Nabu was the cultural director of the Culture Village and had called me a month before to invite me on this two-week trek of "cultural re-establishment," a phrase he spoke in English.

"Sixty-five years ago the Japanese moved us down from our villages in the high mountains to reservations in the valley," he told me on the phone that day. "Now we're starting to move back up. It will take another sixty-five years to get back, at least that's how we're planning it. We want to rebuild the old trails and villages, so we have a place to go home to, a place for our children. You know, we're a hunting tribe, a mountain tribe. We don't belong down here in the valley growing pineapples."

"So what can I do?" I asked.

"You don't have to do anything, just come along. Last year we received a government grant to locate our old village sites and airlifted a group of elders up the mountains in a helicopter. We're going to keep going up, year after year, and establish a base. We're gathering a group of artists to come on the trek next month. We want creative expression to be part of the movement home. We have to re-create our culture from what remains."

"Who else is coming?"

"Vadsuku the woodcarver, a writer from Taipei, plus a couple of others."

"What should I bring?"

"Nothing, we'll take care of everything. You just bring yourself."

· · ·

The Bunun had been seminomadic hunter-gatherers and were one of the last tribes to be relocated by the Japanese in their program of assimilating indigenous peoples. As late as the early twentieth century there are records of Bunun hunting Amis heads. So, when moved down to reservations in the rift valley, the Bunun were relocated next door to their traditional enemies. Unlike the Paiwan, Vadsuku's tribe from further south in the central mountains, the Bunun had no social stratification and no centralized leadership except during war or hunting expeditions, when a temporary leader would be chosen based on past success. The Bunun developed a unique notation for keeping track of the lunar calendar, a writing system independent of outside influence, which they carved in wood. Recently the Bunun have been best known for their eight-part polyphonic singing, which they have performed internationally.

The Bunun have a sense of origin in a physical landscape, which is in turn connected to a concrete sense of culture, identity, and means of livelihood. My own native place was virtually accidental, determined by my parents' careers and resultant moves—jobs and migration, the two primary forces of American identity. I agreed to join the Bunun trek as a way to see how the Bunun related to the concept of "old village," or "home," and to consider my own sense of indigenousness, or relationship to place.

. . .

Now, at the Bunong Culture Village, we finished packing for the trek as the tour buses idled, their engines grumbling like bellies. The tourists gathered in the small amphitheater around the stage to see the performance of Bunun songs and dance. The MC for the show, a mustachioed man wearing a leather vest and safari hat, ascended the stage, thumbs hooked in his belt.

"Some people ask why we're called the Bunong tribe," he said into the mic.

Bunun, the tribe's name, which means "human" in their own language, is transliterated into Mandarin as *Bunong* 布 農. These characters mean "cloth" and "agriculture" but form no syntactic meaning. Now the MC toggled *Bunong* into a pun by pronouncing *nong* as *neng*, forming the Mandarin grammatical construction *bu neng* 不能, meaning "can't do," or "incapable."

"I'll tell you why we're called the *Buneng* tribe," he drawled. "It's because we 'can't do' anything." The crowd chuckled comfortably.

"Come on," said Nabu, not looking at the stage, "it's time to go." In addition to Nabu and myself, our group included Ishi-gaki, a Japanese anthropologist, Su-zhen, a young woman from

Taipei volunteering at the Culture Village, Deqing, a nineteen-year-old who'd just finished his compulsory military service, and a nine-year-old Bunun boy, A-liang. Just as we stood up to go, a lean, thin-haired man in an army jacket slipped in and crammed the last portion of food and gear into a pack.

"This is Biung," Nabu said.

Biung glanced up to briefly nod at me as he stuffed his pack. He looked like an old tent stake, so weathered and worn I wondered if he was really coming with us.

"Where are the other artists?" I asked Nabu.

"They all canceled. You're the only one who actually came," he said, grunting as he lifted his grotesquely large pack. Chanted songs and barefoot stomps resonated on the wood boards of the stage behind us, where the culture show had begun. We walked through the cut lawns toward the gate where a four-wheel drive van dented like an old beer can was parked. Our driver stood waiting by the van, smiling through a cleft lip.

But before we could pass through the gate, a cluster of Bunun elders intercepted us to bless our journey. These elders were the last of those who had been born in the old villages up in the mountains and had been part of the forced march down to internment camps in the 1930s. Some had been infants and remembered nothing about it, but the oldest had been eight or ten at the time of the relocation and had helped direct the previous year's helicopter expedition.

The elders grasped our hands two-handedly, tears streaming from eyes like pits in stone, overcome by the fact that we were on our way to the home that they might never see again. Between their accents and emotion it was hard to understand them, but Nabu translated their Mandarin into Mandarin for me, standing stoic amid the melee. "They're thanking you," Nabu said, "and saying they wish they could go too."

"Shush," an old woman said fiercely. "I have to say a prayer."

"That's my mother. She was born in the mountains," Nabu whispered. She was large and powerful, larger even than Nabu, wore iron-framed glasses, and had a rope of gray hair down her back. We shuffled into a circle and bowed our heads as she spoke in Bunun, then gave a brief translation in clipped Mandarin, asking God to protect us and make sure we returned safely.

The Bunun traditionally worshipped the sun and moon, and social conduct was based on a strict set of rituals and taboos. Almost all aboriginal peoples in Taiwan adopted Christianity in the course of the twentieth century, including the Bunun, largely as a form of empowerment during their mass disenfranchisement as they were engulfed by the nation-state. Christianity and other global or "immigrant" religions locate holiness outside the world, while for indigenous religions, sacredness usually exists in the land, in this world, not separate from material existence. Despite importing an exotic mythology, Catholic and Presbyterian missionaries provided an administrative structure for indigenous communities to resist government policies of assimilation. Missionaries helped aboriginal peoples fight for autonomy and recognition and built schools and hospitals at a time when the KMT saw them as little more than another resource to exploit. Among most indigenous Taiwanese, religion was now a mélange of Christian and animist beliefs, though the younger generations, like Nabu and my friends in Dulan, generally took to Christianity with less alacrity, and some had begun to search for the roots of their tribal belief systems.

"Amen," we said, and headed out the gate.

One of the administrative assistants ran up to ask Nabu some final question; then we piled into the dented van, and the door slammed shut. We drove out of the parking lot and stopped a half mile down the road at the real Bunun village, a collection of concrete and plywood shacks, where children played in the street and dogs snoozed in the dust. Biung and the driver got out and walked down the street while the rest of us sat sweating in the van.

They returned ten minutes later, flanked by two old men

with faces like sides of beef left out in the sun too long, beginning to sag and fade. Biung carried a homemade gun—a single barrel, bolt-action rifle, the stock hand-carved from pine, with plumber's tape wrapped around the butt. He sighted along the barrel and shook his head, dissatisfied with the line. The breech and stainless steel bore were joined with a thick weld seam, the safety was a piece of plastic stuck between the bolt and firing cap.

"The barrel's bent. The sight's all off," Biung said. "How you going to shoot straight with this thing?" He frowned at the gun but looked up and grinned at me, as if to say a crooked gun is better than no gun, and put two plastic sacks on the floor by my feet, one of homemade bullets and one of firing caps. Biung offered betel nuts all around and laid the rifle lovingly in the back of the van. The old men clasped our hands and smiled with half-extinguished envy, wishing us luck but still wishing they could come too, their few remaining teeth like wounded sentinels over the loose hang of their lips and cheeks.

We drove along the valley floor through the late afternoon, then turned up a road of gravel switchbacks west into the central mountains. I looked across the rift valley to the back side of Dulanshan. Its silhouette was dark and graceful, backdropped by speckled light across the sea as we drove up higher than its peak. Biung became animated, answering Su-zhen's questions about where we were and where we were going, telling stories of how the road was built, of the trail that had existed before, who had worked here, the wild animals he had encountered, and the forest that had been hauled away. I still had no idea who he was, and leaned my head against the chill of the windowpane, thinking about my notebooks and guitars on the other side of Dulanshan, the downslope to the sea.

It was dark by the time we pulled into a clearing rutted by machine tracks. We stepped out of the van and into a cold fog. Biung strode off into the blur. Whoops of greeting came from somewhere nearby, and the smell of wood smoke mixed with the wet air. I walked toward a triangular shadow in the fog, a crude lean-to, sheets of corrugated siding propped into an A-frame. Biung squatted on his heels at a fire along with three other men talking fast and loud in a mix of Mandarin and Bunun—the others were on their way down from working on the old forestry road, rebuilding it to be put to use again. Biung had a *mijiu* bottle in his hand that he flourished and splashed into his mouth.

"Look here," he said when I approached. "This is our American friend. We're taking him into the mountains." He turned to me and said, "We're taking you to our home, to our old village. You don't have to pay me, but one day you take me to your home, to your mountains—then we'll be even. It's a brotherhood to be in the mountains together. Look, this is Hushong. He's been up in the mountains two weeks already, but he's not going down. No! He's coming with us, to help show you the way. His father and my father were great friends. They hunted together."

The other men grinned and nodded, deferring to Biung's appropriation of the bottle. Hushong looked on serenely.

"Hushong here, his father sent him to school," Biung continued. "He's a great scholar . . ." At this everyone laughed and held their bellies. Biung glanced around but didn't crack a smile, squinting hard at me. "But my father kept me with him in the forest. I worked hauling loads starting when I was twelve, working for the forest department—whoo, that tumpline, twelve years old and fifty kilos on my forehead. See, this Hushong, he's a philosopher, but that rope across my brow was the only teacher I had—so I only know what it knew, the trails, the deer, the trees."

Now Biung couldn't stop his laughter. It burst forth from his body and churned with the others' laughter. Biung spilled *mijiu* into his mouth and handed the bottle to Hushong.

If there's a man on earth with a physique more like a hog's I'd like to see the proof. Hushong's belly didn't hang down, but swelled straight out from sternum to pubis. A *Dulan Art Festival* T-shirt was stretched over his body, smeared with grime and muck. He had a beardless, boyish face, plump and smooth, and wore a baseball cap turned backward. Hushong said nothing, but in spite or because of this he radiated competence. He swigged from the bottle and offered it to me.

"No thanks," I said, "I'm taking a break from drinking."

Everywhere I went in Dulan someone handed me a beer as if it were the word for hello. Sometimes I felt I needed to step away from the social lubrication of alcohol, to make sure it wasn't dissolving me. This trek was a good opportunity to do so, as the limitations of portage meant we would be dry anyway.

The crew paused for a moment and looked at me in consternation, but Biung said something in Bunun, restarting their laughter, and Hushong handed him the bottle.

I wandered to the edge of the clearing, where a backhoe was parked. The machine was incongruous with the fog and the mountain, but completely consonant with the gashed-out feel of the clearing and the rutted mud. Nabu walked over and stood next to me. He looked strangely sleek and refined in his name-brand mountain gear, his long hair plaited into two neat braids.

"The other tribes used to call us 'dirty ghosts,'" he said. "We were a fearsome people. We hunted and raided, dressed in animal hides. Biung, he's the last real hunter we have left."

"What about you?" I asked. "Did you go hunting when you were growing up?"

Nabu smiled his trademark smile, a sad, kind, patient smile, and stroked his moustache where it overflowed from the corners of his mouth.

"I was ruined completely," he said. "I went to school in Taipei. I was sent to the city young, not like these guys, not like the boy A-liang here. I learned how to live in the modern world, but I lost something that can't be taught."

"Do you speak your mother tongue?"

"Some."

But in the coming days I saw that he had learned Bunun as a foreign language and knew only isolated words and phrases.

"Let's unload the van and then I'll make some tea," Nabu said. "Looks like we'll sleep here tonight and start out on the trail in the morning."

. . .

We slept in the grease and muck of the A-frame, a shelter for the backhoe drivers and trail workers, with cardboard on the ground for padding. Water dripped in, condensed from the fog, the space was filled with the smell of kerosene and smoke. Biung, Hushong, and the trail crew stayed up all night singing and telling stories, laughing around the fire, everybody stepping on everyone on their way to piss throughout the night.

In the morning, my sleeping bag was damp, my bones felt cold and wet. Breakfast was rice gruel cooked over the fire, little different in complexion than the fog that hung over everything. But Nabu presided over a mini-sultanate of gas stoves and windscreens, and soon a pot of coffee was snorting and steaming in the fragile morning air.

"Why do you come up here when it's so cold?" I asked him as he poured me a cup. "Wouldn't summer be better?"

"There are too many snakes in the summer," he said. "Now they're all underground. And in the summer it's too hot for trekking. Wait till you see what's ahead. Then you'll know why we don't do this in the heat."

I could not help but regard my gruel with a bit of dismay. But Nabu pulled a piece of smoked cheese from his pocket, winked, and offered me a bite. I couldn't have dreamed a more epicurean breakfast than coffee and smoked cheese, seasoned with fog blowing through the pines in the high mountain air.

As we prepared to head out on the trail, Biung strode to the edge of the clearing and siphoned diesel from the backhoe into a *mijiu* bottle. "The boss won't mind," he said. "In this weather we might need a little help to start our fires." He grinned, seeming to glory in every movement and action in the mountains. Hushong put his arm around A-liang's shoulders, his nephew at several degrees of remove. The boy almost skipped with anticipation in his baseball cap and rubber boots. He was a full-blood Bunun, nine years old, and though he went to a public school and spoke Mandarin as his primary language, he came along on every excursion into the mountains.

"What's your name?" I asked him.

He looked at Hushong and Biung, but they returned his gaze silently.

"A-liang," he said, and shrugged.

"Tell him your other name," Biung said gently.

He looked at the ground and mumbled, "Li-an," his Bunun name. Hushong rubbed the boy's shoulder and helped him with the day pack that carried his clothes and sleeping bag.

Deqing's pack swayed on his back like an evil spirit. He staggered drunkenly till Hushong tightened up his strap system, but he still reeled beneath its weight. Deqing was half-Bunun, half-Chinese, and this was his first time in the high mountains. His father, a Nationalist soldier who came to Taiwan in 1949, had just died in the army hospital in Taipei. When Deqing came back from the funeral two days before, he spontaneously decided to join this trek. Biung and Hushong had designated him to carry the ammunition and a car battery that they hooked up to a powerful headlamp for night hunting, in addition to his share of the food and his own gear.

Ishigaki was slim, bespeckled, rosy-cheeked, and his academic career was laid out before him like a map. In their fifty years of rule the Japanese had done extensive surveys of indigenous tribes in Taiwan, and Ishigaki's PhD dissertation would be a matter of researching and synthesizing data collected in the early twentieth century. He had already spent time with Bunun communities on the other side of the central range and cheerfully described this trek as part of his "field work."

Su-zhen had worked some years in an office in Taipei before

deciding that lifestyle wasn't for her. The rushed, crowded commute to work every morning, the cramped office with nowhere to go, physically or professionally, the gray rain that fell in every season, as if it too were unable to escape Taipei, that basin city ringed by mountains. She had relinquished everything and moved here to volunteer in the culture center while she figured out her next step.

Ishigaki lifted his pack and his eyes bugged out. Su-zhen did a breathing exercise to prepare for the path ahead. The driver started up the van and ground its gears. The trail crew, catching a ride down the mountain, waved to us from the windows like we or they were a ship pulling away from shore. Biung stepped onto the old logging road with the rifle in his hand, and we followed him down the trail.

· · ·

We walked through a misting rain. Pink-white flowers grew along the road through the second-growth forest. After half an hour we came upon a dead *shanqiang* (barking deer, or muntjac), curled dead in the middle of the trail. Biung whooped triumphantly—this was a gift from the spirits, he declared, and a good omen for the beginning of the journey. He and Hushong laid down a bed of branches and grasses, and Hushong began to butcher it on the spot. The deer had russet, tawny fur, thick and soft across its back and ribs, its ears spotted with ticks. It had stubby antlers, and long, protruding canine teeth—fangs on a deer, which looked ridiculous, but there they were.

Hushong sawed through the neck flesh with his machete. He twisted the head to snap the vertebrae, and set the head aside to make a hat for Li-an later. He flayed off the skin with a curved hunting knife and severed the legs at the hip joints. He slit open the belly, and the intestines spilled out. Hushong reached in and pulled out the liver, cut it into pieces on a flap of skin, and offered it to us. Biung took a pouch of salt from his pack and passed it around, and we ate the liver off the wet hide of the animal. Nabu chewed with a rather thin version

of his usual smile. Ishigaki seemed to grow profoundly intro-
spective as he contemplated this high mountain sashimi. The
liver was like fibrous, mushy, dark purple jello, and it stained
my fingers with blood. Green-yellow shit had spilled from the
deer's intestines into the body cavity, and its fetid smell per-
meated the act of eating. Hushong offered me a second piece,
holding it out on the flat of his knife, ochre shit mixed with
blood on the metal blade.

Biung cut off the *shanqiang*'s balls, smacked his lips, and put
them in a pocket of his pack, saying he'd eat them with liquor
later. "Someone else shot this deer," he said, lighting a cigarette. "But it got away, then died of its wounds." He wrapped
the legs in grass and leaves and strapped them beneath the
hood of his pack. Hushong put the ribs and back in plastic
bags and gave them to Deqing to carry, adding to the already
terrible weight of his pack, and gave the head to Li-an. We
threw the hide and viscera into the bushes for foxes and rats.

• • •

After two hours the fog burned off, giving way to a clear
bright morning, mist still drifting through the few old conifers left standing along the ridges above us. We walked all day
on the regraded road, with new log bridges laid down where
landslides had carried the hillside away. At dusk we stopped
at a listing, broken-down forestry shack, abandoned twenty
years. The corrugated metal roof was rusted and full of holes.
Half-burned planks were scattered amid the ash of a fire pit,
left by a previous hunter who had torn them from the walls
rather than forage for firewood. "Han tribe," Biung said with
a glance at the trash in the corners and pornographic pictures
drawn in charcoal on the walls.

"Just down the slope from here is a grove of thirteen camphor trees," Hushong said to me. "Old ones, at least five hundred years old, and each tree as thick as fifty of you. Not many
like that remain. But last year they were all cut down. The
stumps of those old camphors grow a certain fungus, which is

a delicacy, extremely rare and expensive. So these guys came out and found these ancient trees, cut them down, then came back a year later to harvest the fungus and get rich."

Camphor was a major industry in Taiwan starting in the eighteenth century, and in the early 1890s Taiwan exported 30 percent more camphor than the rest of the world combined, much of it to the United States. Early efforts at pacification of the mountain tribes were aimed at making the forests safe for Hakka camphor workers.

"But how did they know where to find those trees?" I asked.

"They bribed the forestry officials to get a copy of the logging maps. All the forests of the central range were surveyed by the Japanese. All you need is the map, and you can find whatever you want, whatever is left, anyway. We know exactly who did this, but there's nothing we can do about it."

"Why not? Why can't you report them?"

"Because what we're doing here is illegal too. If we report them, they'll report us. But once those trees are cut down, they're gone forever. The ancient ones will never come again."

Biung returned with an armful of dead branches. He started a fire and added the half-burnt planks once it was burning strong. We ate a dinner of roasted *shanqiang* and rice; then Nabu set up his system of pots and windscreens to make tea. Hushong broke the jaw off the deer head. Li-an ate the brain out of the upturned skull, scooping out the gray-white tissue with an oxidized tin spoon. When he finished, Hushong placed the head with its grin of lipless teeth to dry above the fire, the bone slowly darkening with smoke.

The next morning, striding along the overgrown two-track, Nabu and Biung talked and laughed about the old logging days, and all their friends and relatives who'd worked here, but there was a grimness to their risibility, as if it were being pushed through gritted teeth. Maybe because all they had depended on for a sense of home and identity was razed along with the forest. Hushong walked along next to them but said nothing.

"Why did they cut down the trees?" the boy Li-an asked.

"Hmm, good question, I don't know," Biung said, cocking his head in mock contemplation. "But one thing I do know is your uncle was one of the hatchet men!"

The uncle, a cousin of Hushong's, had worked driving a logging truck on this very road until the trees were gone.

We cooked lunch on the trail, noodles with dehydrated pork. Afterward Nabu pointed to the ridge above us, where a single ancient tree stood against the sky, towering above a straggle of second-growth it dwarfed.

"See that?" Nabu said to me. "If it could, that tree would commit suicide. That's a thousand-year-old hinoki. It stood and watched while they cut the forest down. It only survived because they anchored a cable through its trunk to choker the others down the slope. That's the tree that helped all its brothers die."

After lunch, I walked up the slope through foot-deep duff, and sure enough, a rectangular four-by-two-foot hole was cut vertically into the trunk of the tree. A thick steel cable was looped through it, but the tree was still alive, still lifting from roots and soil into the sky despite the square hole carved in its heart.

That night we camped at another forestry shelter, a corrugated hut on the side of a ravine, the forest angling down the slope beside us. After dinner I walked out into the swirl of mist rising up the mountainside. I saw a flick of movement along the trunk of a snag, followed by a long thin tail, and had a moment to think *feishu*, flying squirrel, before it snapped open its flaps of webbed skin and soared off down the slope like a bat with a whole body of wings.

When I returned to camp I mentioned the flying squirrel to Biung, where he reclined looking into the fire.

Deqing leapt up and said, "Let's go shoot it!"

Biung didn't move a muscle, didn't even look up from the fire.

"We never shoot anything on such a steep slope," he said. "It's impossible to recover. Come here, have a seat by the fire," Biung said, motioning to me. "Listen, hear all the noise the fire's making, the crackles and pops? That's telling us we're going to have good hunting tomorrow. It's the spirits talking to us. They'll tell you everything if you know how to listen. Did Nabu tell you not to sneeze? Never sneeze in the mountains, it brings bad spirits. Well, it probably doesn't matter for you, you're a guest here. But we Bunun, we never sneeze in the mountains."

Darkness and cold settled in, the fire flickered orange. Smoke passed up into the mist and the sharp dry bark of *shanqiang* came from all directions in the night.

. . .

Small trees began to grow up between the tracks as we walked the next morning, then the logging road disappeared. We turned onto a faint trail through a stunted forest and began switchbacking up and down ravines, sweating and straining to climb fins of earth, blades of stone, then descending with thigh muscles burning. The landscape was like a broad, rolling terrain that had been embraced by giant arms and compressed, wrinkling and buckling into mountains.

We crossed a slant of forested earth between two valleys and at midday arrived at a grove of old-growth hinoki. This was the tiniest fraction of the forest that once blanketed these mountains, but still it seemed vast, miraculous, immortal. A single thousand-year-old tree is an entire history, an ecosphere unto itself, a citadel of brachiation, leaves, epiphytes, insect trails, funguses, and birds. We dropped our packs, stunned by the ancient trees, walking around them and touching their bark, faces uplifted as to a revelation. It took me more than twenty steps to walk the circumference of one tree. I breathed the scent of photosynthesis and lichen as sunlight filtered through the canopy and spottled the forest floor.

Within this grove, all remembrance of destruction, degradation, pollution, or fracturization faded. It was a node of wholeness that approached divinity, at least to me.

"Scott, what do you think?" Nabu asked me. The braids of his hair were beginning to untwist and tangle. Smudges of dirt had appeared on his face, but there was less reserve in his smile than I'd ever seen down in the valley.

"It's like coming home," I said. It felt just like the old-growth redwood forests in California, but when I said "home" I wasn't talking about geography. Here was a physical sense of unity and belonging, nothing to aspire to, nowhere left to go.

"There are a few groves like this left," Biung said. "We could find them."

"I'd like to come back with a guitar, spend a month here recording music in the forest."

"Why not? Tell you what, we'll come up together," Biung said. "We can stay as long as you like. There's good hunting around here. We'll never have to worry about food."

I was honored, and yet the thought of gunshots ringing through this cathedral-like light and silence confounded me. Maybe I was stuck in the romance and distance of aesthetic apprehension, detached from basic questions of sustenance, of how to eat, while Biung fronted the wilderness on a more primary level, in which there was no perspective to say, "This is beautiful," just as moment to moment we don't perceive our muscles and nerve pathways or the sculpture of our skeletons as beautiful—they are just the physical terms of being.

. . .

After a lunch of plain noodles, Biung said, "Hurry up, we've got a long way to go," cutting short our usual postprandial rest. We all moved lazily in the slow spell of the old-growth canopies spread above us. But Biung hefted up his pack and started forward with the gun in his hand, and the rest of us hurried to catch up, Hushong bringing up the rear.

We passed into a forest of dull, dun trees, their trunks like overcooked noodles, stringy and bent. The whole area was filled with a smell of dry rot. We trudged lethargically beneath a sky the color of paste, same color as our diet of white rice and white noodles with a thin veneer of protein. Even Biung walked grim and silent, the rifle slung wearily from his hand.

We emerged into a clearing atop a rounded hill. Biung signaled us to stop and put our packs down. From up ahead, the sound of a river washed over us. At the far side of the clearing, a crude shrine sat amid the exposed roots of a sinewy tree—a few piled stones, a plastic cup, some old food wrappers.

"We have to be quiet here," Biung said in a whisper, "and offer something to the spirits. Hushong, get the *mijiu*."

Hushong took a bottle from his pack. Leaves rustled in the wind, mist began to swirl around us. Biung walked across the clearing to the shrine, head bowed. He kneeled and poured *mijiu* into the cup, dribbled a few drops onto the ground, murmuring, and tossed the rest down his throat. He returned and passed the bottle to Hushong, and we took turns making the spirit offering, including Li-an, though his was without *mijiu*.

"Thank the spirits for protecting us so far, and ask their permission to pass," Biung said when it was my turn.

I performed the ritual, thinking about the cycle the *mijiu* had taken—it emerged from the earth as grain, was fertilized, cultivated, harvested, fermented, and distilled; then it traveled up these mountains in Hushong's pack to be spilled into the earth again. I dripped out three drops with a finger, wet my lips with *mijiu* as a ritual libation, and spilled the rest back into the ground before the altar.

Biung and Hushong filled the cup and left a few bits of food for the spirits. We set off silently, packs heavy and legs stiff after the pause. The mist turned to rain; the trail angled down into a valley and then disappeared—or rather, fragmented into many almost-trails through underbrush and briars. Biung lit a cigarette and called Hushong to take the lead. Hushong's bowl cut lay lank across his forehead as he hacked forward with his machete, his belly pressing forward, pulling us along. Branches scratched my arms and face; the ground became muddy and slippery. We stumbled down in a ragged formation. Rain ran into my eyes and blurred my vision. We emerged at a broad freshet rushing down a tumble of marble boulders. We crossed over the crashing stream on rocks just beneath the surface, stepping into the skin of the current, then continued down the other bank. Biung took the lead again, sheltering the gun the best he could with his body.

I was last in line and stopped a moment to look down to the floor of the ravine a thousand feet below. Back across the stream, atop a large slab of marble, a mountain goat appeared, golden-bronze, majestic, bristling into the space around it, with curled horns and a powerful, protuberant chest. At that moment Hushong stepped up next to me. We watched for a few moments till with no precursor of movement the animal sprang and vanished into the brush. Hushong looked at me and nodded. "*Shidee*," he said, the Bunun name for Taiwan's indigenous mountain goat.

The rain came down harder. The bank along the stream became impassable. We diverted into a patch of nettles. Nabu pulled on a pair of cotton gloves to protect his hands. The ground fell away, we slipped and bumped down a steep embankment, grasping at branches and grasses, my hands and arms swelled up scratched and red. The sky darkened as the sun went down beyond the rim of the valley. We reemerged at the stream, now a gray roar, and descended half-falling down a vertical scar of mud and stones, holding onto hairy tree roots that jutted into the air. My pack hung like a load of regrets on my back, trying to pull me down. We intersected a gravelly wash and stumbled down the last hundred yards to the valley bottom.

The gray-black river arched and buckled over stones. Broken branches were washed up along the banks. We crossed over a small subsidiary stream, its surface currents weaving like braids, water spilled in over the tops of my boots.

Biung and Hushong threw down their packs and rushed to set up a shelter between two cottage-sized boulders. They chopped branches into stakes, drove them into the sand for the guylines, and propped a tarp with poles of river driftwood. The rest of us moved so slowly from fatigue and disorientation in the rain that the tarp was erected before we could help. We dropped our packs and paused in the shelter a moment, but it was nearly dark, so we immediately got to work spreading groundcovers and gathering firewood from beneath the overhang of boulders, where it was still dry.

"Look at all the deer tracks in the sand," Biung said as he started a fire and set a pot of silty river water to boil for rice. "We'll get something tonight for sure."

We laid our sleeping bags out, clustered close together to keep away from the edges of the tarp where strings of rain streamed down. After eating, Nabu fired up his stove to make tea, but Ishigaki, Su-zhen, and Li-an were already asleep. Evincing no fatigue, Biung and Hushong took their sleeping gear, the gun, and the battery headlamp a hundred yards downstream to a low cave that formed a bunker to shoot from. I fell into a sleep too shallow to be removed or insulated from the cold and wet or the need to piss out Nabu's tea. The night was punctured by gunshots whose intervals I could not measure, five minutes or five hours between shots, I could not tell. The rain poured through these punctures in my sleep, and my dreams were indistinguishable from waking.

· · ·

"Ho there," Biung said when he saw me moving, "breakfast is ready."

The rain had stopped some time before the dawn. I had not so much wakened as reached the end of the time to sleep. Biung and Hushong squatted by the fire. Breakfast was reheated dinner, the thought of which made me vaguely ill, but Biung grinned and took the lid from a smaller pot on the edge of the fire. It was cowboy coffee he'd brewed especially for me, as everyone else drank tea in the morning. The rich coffee steam and kind gesture made me smile.

"What did you get last night?" I asked.

"Ah, didn't you hear that woodpecker knocking as we came down the slope yesterday?" Biung said. "He was telling us to save our bullets. No, we were up all night, but the spirits didn't give us anything. Good thing, though. You'll see once we get started this morning." I followed his gaze to where a thousand-foot talus slope rose almost straight up from the other side of the river.

After breakfast we rolled our pants up above our knees and slung our boots around our necks, and stepped into the river. The cold was sharp as the edge of a blade, the river stones round and slippery. The current rushed against my legs, my feet instantly too numb to feel out footholds. We lurched and staggered across, then sat on the opposite bank putting our socks and boots on. Everyone's feet were red and swollen, but Ishigaki's were badly blistered as well, and his steel-rimmed glasses were smeared with dirt and grease. He looked to be having serious second thoughts about his chosen field of study. Dirty ghosts indeed.

We began to toil straight up, Biung and Hushong leading

the way. The slope was sand and broken stone, each footstep had to be dug out of the shifting scree as it filled your boots. Everybody paused and looked up after about thirty seconds, as if collectively thinking, *You cannot be serious.* Nabu squinted upward and said, "This used to be a forest with a switchback trail, but five years ago a landslide wiped it all out . . ."

Cold comfort, baby, to be five years older and five years late.

Biung and Hushong put their heads down and plowed forward. We followed in the trail they half-broke, trying to step in the blunt divots of their footprints. We staggered and bellowed like escapees from a lunatic asylum, cursing the slope and our burning thighs. My muscles felt exactly the texture of what we'd been eating for five days, bland sticky paste.

Down below, a thin trail of mist flowed up the river. I looked up from the sand runneling around my feet and saw a rock outcropping halfway up the incline. I decided to make for it, and headed directly up the slope. I got to the solid stone outcropping just as Nabu cried out. He'd loosened a large stone that tumbled and bounced down the slope toward Ishigaki. It seemed improbable that in all that empty space the stone would actually hit him. He stood still, awkwardly balanced, until at the last moment it was clear the thing was going straight for his head. Su-zhen screamed. Ishigaki reacted too slowly, not accounting for the weight of his pack, but he wrenched his torso just enough that the rock only grazed his chin, giving him a shave he didn't need. But the torque of his movement threw him off balance, and he fell like a corpse, arms straight out, and slid back down to the riverbed along with a minilandslide of sand and stones. Su-zhen stumbled back down to where he lay to see if he was hurt.

Hushong and Biung had already reached the tree line and were sitting on the roots of a stunted hemlock. Hushong grabbed something from his pack and launched himself like Japhy Ryder down the Matterhorn in Jack Kerouac's *The Dharma Bums*, ten feet per stride, and was at the base of the slope with Ishigaki and Su-zhen in two minutes. Ishigaki was scraped up but uninjured, though he looked around as if heartbroken and confused. Hushong hefted up both Ishigaki's and Su-zhen's packs and tied a rope around his waist, giving the free end to them. He then began his second ascent, this time pulling Ishigaki and Su-zhen along and carrying their packs as well.

Meanwhile, Nabu moved so slowly he seemed to be crucified to the incline, a moose of a man set to a donkey's work, unsuited to it—but here and throughout the trek he never complained, never did anything but smile and help with what he could, deferring to Biung's and Hushong's authority. Maybe he took the arduousness of the trek as a spiritual necessity, a penance to expiate his administrator's sins, to scrub his bureaucratic softness away against the hardness of the mountains.

I made it to the hemlock tree and collapsed in exhaustion. Deqing joined me, then Li-an, then Nabu. We reclined in positions like we'd been deboned, and watched Hushong labor upward. The wind cut through and chilled me in my wet shirt, but no one made a move for a jacket. Hushong heaved up the last few feet of the slope and dropped the packs. Ishigaki flopped face-first on the ground, his legs twitching, his lips smeared in dust. Su-zhen lay down on her back and began to snore. Everyone looked lugubrious and defeated, except for Hushong, who wore the same calm look he always had.

We're sunk, we can't go on, I thought, but I didn't think it. It was dumb bestial certainty of the kind that allows goats to chew their cud while tethered beneath the carcass of a sibling.

Biung had gone ahead to check the trail. Hushong coiled the rope and returned it to his pack, then pulled out a plastic sack of sesame-molasses bars and passed them around. It was incredible to me that a) he had packed these in to share with everyone—I, for example, had done everything but drill out my toothbrush to reduce the weight of my pack; and b) he had not stolen off some night to wolf them down after days of eating rice and noodles with dehydrated pork, a bit of *shanqiang* meat the only variant. The rush and taste of sugar when I bit down must be what junkies feel when a shot hits a vein. It was nothing short of resurrection. Deqing waved a bar beneath Ishigaki's nose, he spasmed and jerked upright, spitting dust and snot. Su-zhen woke up with an "Are we there yet?" expression on her face and wordlessly took a sesame bar, smiling as if this were the very thing she'd been dreaming of.

Biung returned, whistling a tune between his teeth. "This is a forest I worked on with my father," he said, ignoring or oblivious of the oscillation in our collective mood. "I hauled in seedlings on my back, now they're trees, look at 'em. See how far we've come these several days? That used to be half a day's journey. Load up, pack in, unload, and get back home all in one day." He finished his cigarette and ground it beneath his boot. "This is a good forest, well planted. We had a smart foreman. Measured out a line and planted the seedlings along the line. You can look a mile down these rows of trees. They go straight. A whole mountainside of cedars, fast growers. They can come harvest these trees any time, that's why they're rebuilding the road. Yep, I planted these trees with my father, thirty years ago."

· · ·

We continued ahead into the monocrop silviculture. A pointillist monochrome, brain wrinkles stretched taut and nailed in place. A monotony of space, height, bark, bore. A grid of wood, a field of trees.

We stopped for lunch at some generic point, then moved laterally across another landslide. Dry earth puffed up from the trail and clogged the pores of my skin. In the late afternoon we descended into a spectral forest with green moss hanging web-like from gnarled trees. Evening settled in as gray light faded, filtering through the leaves. We raced the dark, tripping forward through muted birdcalls, stumbling over roots and stones, faces clawed by branches in the half-light. Biung was way ahead and let out whoops to guide us, all thoughts of the trail gone. I stumbled forward, groping with my hands to protect my eyes as a rush of river roar built and sustained around the crash of footsteps through the brush. We broke out of the forest into a clearing along the river. Biung stood with his arms upraised, a half-moon in the sky behind him. "We're home, boys," he shouted, "we're home, we're home!"

We woke on beds of pine boughs in a clearing along the river-bank. Sunlight illuminated bright thin blood in an aluminum pan. Deer back and thigh meat smoked on a wood rack above a fire. Biung had shot two *shanqiang* in the night, and now we ate their livers and kidneys for breakfast, roasting them on sticks over the fire, the outside burned to a black crust, the inside pulpy with blood. The taste was rich and buttery, a flavor of char and flesh that peeled open on my tongue, as if the wilderness were nourishing my body and brain directly.

Takivahlas, "place where two rivers meet," was the old village from which Nabu and the others came, the place their parents were removed from in 1937. From here it was a short day's trek to Shou, the end of our journey in.

Everyone was lighthearted and sad, like they couldn't believe they were home, but also couldn't believe they didn't live here. Jubilation in a sumo wrestling hold with mourning. Home had become a place you had to fight your way back to, a place you needed permission to enter. During Taiwan's period of martial law, ROC citizens needed reentry permits to return home from abroad, and any with dissenting political opinions were denied. How anathema such restriction seems to America's values of freedom and self-determination. Then again, during the Cold War, American scientist Linus Pauling was denied a passport because of his pacifist beliefs and was only granted one when he was invited to Sweden to receive the Nobel Prize for Chemistry in 1954.

I walked downstream to bathe in the freezing river despite the cold, and washed off a layer or two of dirt, squatting naked on a stone amid the current. Returning to camp, I passed Hushong heading down with a towel and toothbrush. When he returned, Ishigaki saw our wet hair and asked, "What were you guys doing down there?"

"Nothing, just having a soak in the hot spring," Hushong said, nodding to where a layer of mist floated above the river. "See the steam there? Didn't Nabu tell you?"

Ishigaki couldn't have looked more stunned if we'd told him there was a geisha with a cup of hot sake waiting for him by the river. I nodded blandly, my lips twitching, and turned my deer liver on the fire. Ishigaki gazed at the mist rising from the river, then stood up and walked downstream with a gait between a saunter and a barely reined-in gallop. Hushong winked at me with the faintest smile the world has ever known.

· · ·

Takivahlas sat on a wedge of land between the two rivers that converged here. We crossed over from our camp at a place where the river was broad and shallow, sixty feet across, hopping over stones. The village site was blanketed with crinkled golden grasses, wild meadows overgrown with thistles and their thorny purple blossoms. A shaggy walnut tree bushed up next to a low slate wall.

"Look at that," Nabu said to me. "That's how we used to build—flat stones stacked into walls. We're coming to my uncle's house, my mother's brother. My grandfather is still buried there. Each house had a courtyard, and we buried our ancestors right there in the yard. Not laid out horizontal, like the Christians, but upright, in a fetal position. The houses had wood walls and roofs atop stone foundations. The Japanese burned them so we wouldn't have anything to return to, so no one would try to escape the internment camps. But the stones remain."

"These were millet fields," Biung said, pointing downstream. "Men cleared the land and women harvested. Ha, we hardly ate the grain. We grew it for wine! Want to know how we fermented it? Women chewed the grain to a pulp and spat it out into a jar. We left it overnight and then added it to a whole pot of cooked millet, and in a few days it turned to wine. You could leave it longer, and it'd turn to liquor, knock you over, boy. Sometimes we let it age for years—that was the best stuff. Look at these trees. Plums and nuts. Some other tribes kept bees for honey, but we didn't. We raised pigs and goats, though, and grew our own tobacco."

"Professor-san," I asked Ishigaki, drawing him aside, "did they really drink up all their millet, like Biung says?"

"Yes Mr. Scott. According to what I've read it seems millet was mainly grown to ferment into wine. The Bunun were semi-nomadic, but in addition to hunting and gathering, they grew maize, sorghum, beans, peanuts, sweet potato, taro, radish, plums, peaches, bananas, ginger, and sugarcane."

"Sounds better than what we've been living on this week," I said.

"There it is," cried Nabu, "my family's house!"

A slate wall enclosed a courtyard. The foundation of the house was a stone wall that rose two feet off the ground, wobbly and crooked now, with a doorway gap. "Deqing," Nabu said, "your uncle's house is just beyond this."

We stood quietly in the courtyard, the earth feeling heavy with ghosts, or maybe we were the ghosts, transparent and soon to pass away.

"You know, when they moved us down to the valley they fed us Japanese rice," Nabu said. "They believed if they just gave us their rice we'd become 'civilized' and would become Japanese."

"Plus they were afraid of us," Deqing said.

"Yes, that too."

"All the years I worked these mountains, I never knew I was so close to home till we came up last year," Biung said. "Say, did you hear about the elders during World War II? The Japanese had us living in camps down in the valley. Don't worry,

Ishigaki, we don't blame you, at least not too much. They told us the American planes were no good, that they were coming to kill us. See, the Americans were bombing the Japanese military." Ishigaki and I looked at each other and shrugged. "When the planes came in flying low the men turned to fight them, but of course they didn't have guns, so they turned and drew their knives, like this . . ." Biung pantomimed drawing a machete to face a fighter plane.

Nabu pulled a few of the most egregious weeds from along the edges of the stone walls and dusted the dirt from the doorstep of the home where his grandfather remained. I wandered off alone through the old village, between stone walls like arthritic fingers. Down an embankment I came upon two large sambar deer (*shui lu* in Mandarin, literally "water deer") grazing on wild daffodils. They seemed unconcerned by me, but slowly moved away, keeping a safe distance. There was a feeling of suspended time here, of something preserved, even though time had clearly come romping through, coolly sucking away all that had been before. Somehow the life of the village lingered, like it was a held breath rather than a severed breath.

In a grove of pines a wobble of movement caught my eye. I followed it through the green sap smell of the pines, where orange toadstools stemmed up from the needle duff. It was a mikado pheasant, nicknamed "king of the mist," a large round bird, blue-black and shimmering with purple iridescence. The red circle of a large false eye surrounded its true eye. Its tail feathers were splayed out, banded with white lines. It waddled along the forest floor and out of sight, disdaining flight or haste, like a spirit presence animating the stone and water here.

I rejoined Nabu and the others as they wandered through the ruins.

"Look here," Nabu said, standing next to a crumpled pile of stones. "An old cistern. You know, when they took my mother down the mountain she cried the whole way down."

We crossed back over the river, broke camp, and started toward Shou, the Bunun village set up as an administrative center by the Japanese. We walked along the remains of the military road, originally two yards wide, hacked from stone to accommodate carts, horses, soldiers, whatever the Japanese hauled up here. "Shou" is the Mandarin pronunciation of the Japanese name for the village, the character for "long life," 壽. Nabu and the others always called Takivahlas "Takivahlas" but said "Shou" instead of the Bunun place-name Kutuvuki.

We waded into the river where the road had been washed away. Thigh-deep in water, Biung stopped, the current bunching like a drawn curtain around his hips. He raised the rifle to his shoulder, fired up a wooded slope, then turned and shouted to Hushong. They rushed across to the other shore, raising rails of water in their wake, shed their packs, and ran up the hill. Biung shouted for Deqing, who splashed across like a drunken horse and jogged uncertainly after them. The rest of us crossed over, sat on our packs, and waited. Another shot echoed across the ridges; shouts receded into the trees. I imagined Biung furiously jamming the charge and bullet down the rifle bore, Deqing standing by helplessly, wishing for something to carry or purvey, and Hushong charging through the underbrush with knife drawn, a force of nature unto himself.

The river swirled around an outcropped stone lip, and the current deepened around the curve, taking on a deep blue tint as the morning fog burned off. When the hunters returned empty-handed, Biung was flushed and angry for the first time.

"Goddammit, I shot that sonofabitch twice, and it still got away from us," he panted. "Got away just to die and feed the crows. I got him once in the thigh and once low down on the belly. Big deer, big rack, but he wouldn't give up, wouldn't fall. Strong one. This gun barrel is bent. Fuck, if they'd only let us hunt legally, we could get a decent rifle. This homemade shit, what can you do?"

Biung sat down and rolled a cigarette, and this action restored a bit of philosophy to his mien. Deqing sat with legs crossed and pulled his cap down over his eyes. Biung lit his cigarette and his eyes flicked over us like he was holding court. "So you're a singer," he said to me.

I didn't want to say yes, but it would have sounded like false humility to deny it. "Well, I try," I said.

"I used to be a singer too. When I was eighteen I was discovered. A producer took me to Taipei to sing on TV. I used to sing old Taiwanese songs, listen—"

Biung closed his eyes and softly crooned a verse of a wistful Taiwanese folksong, the melody probably something that traveled here from mainland China three hundred years ago, filled in with new place-names. I was astonished by the sweet, supple timbre of his voice. The song sat like a jewel within the river sounds enfolding us.

"How do you like that?" he asked me when he finished.

"It's . . . it's lovely."

"You didn't believe I could sing—ha! I can sing old Japanese songs too. That producer, he told me I'd be famous, I'd be rich, and on the show I was a hit, the audience loved me. But the next day I waited at the hotel, and the producer didn't come back to get me. Never even paid me for that show. I didn't have a copper in my pocket. There was nothing I could do. I had to come home. I snuck aboard a freight train to ride home from Taipei. But I was good, and back then a singer could really sing! Not like the pop stuff you hear these days, all polished with machines. You know Biung, right?"

"Sure, I know him," I said. He was speaking of his namesake, the Bunun folk-pop singer Biung, a friend of mine from Taipei. We'd performed at a few festivals together, and I played harmonica on his second album, which won a Golden Melody Award. He was a pan-aboriginal idol up and down the coast. I'd even seen Amis boys and girls in Dulan use his first album of heavily chanted Bunun songs to practice their own traditional dances.

"We have lots of Biungs," Nabu explained. "It's a common name."

"Well," Biung the hunter said, "he's talented, sure. But hell, some of the stuff he sings, I just can't get over it . . . *hei-ya hei-ya hei-ya, hei-ya hei-ya hei-ya* . . ." he sang, pastiching one of Biung's famous songs. The light-hearted, pseudo-tribal chant sounded so ridiculous in this context that Nabu lost his administrative composure, slapped his knee, and fell over laughing, and even Hushong couldn't keep from grinning.

"See, in this song he claims he's singing a hunting song as he skips down the mountain with a wild boar slung over his shoulders. You've seen us here, you see anyone skipping down the trail? You save your breath up here in the mountains if you're wise. That boy's never been hunting in his life, and look at him, skinny as a fishhook. How's he going to lift a four-hundred-pound boar and sing a song too?"

"Why don't you sing one of your songs, a Bunun song?" I said. "I'd like to hear it."

Biung ground his cigarette beneath his boot and shook his head.

"Sure, I could sing one. But see, we Bunun, we don't just sing our songs any old time. Our songs are for rituals, ceremonies, gatherings. We sing them on special occasions, and we have to get them right, because the spirits and ancestors listen when we sing."

"But you sing the songs at the Culture Village every day."

"Well," Biung said, winking at Nabu, "some people do."

Biung stood up, and we prepared to continue. "It'll be all right," he said. "Our ancestors will take care of us."

At first I thought he meant the ancestors would help preserve the old songs, the culture, the tribe. But then I saw he was scanning the slopes, and I realized he meant the spirits would provide us with game.

. . .

We continued along the course of the river, detouring into the forest when the banks were impassable. We ascended a high stone ridge and looked down hundreds of feet to the blue blur of the current, where tangles of driftwood were piled up at nodes and bends in the river. I had always assumed that driftwood was stripped and bleached by its time at sea, but now I saw that it takes years for a log or branch to make it down from the mountains, caught in the river like a bone in the throat till the big rains come and wash it further down, mile by mile, a digestion of years.

We followed a ledge of the old Japanese road, walking over gone footprints that had left no trace, all their ambitions gone. We arrived at two stone posts etched with Japanese characters, the gateway to Shou, the former administrative center, now a wooded bluff.

"Deqing," Nabu said, "you should have seen your grandmother here last year. She was so young when she left that she couldn't recognize the place, even though she knew she knew it. She kept turning circles, trying to find some memory to latch onto. She was frantic, almost hysterical—she couldn't match the landscape to her memory. Of course, it was a village when she left, not a forest. Then she came to these gateposts here, and everything snapped into place. She fell down weeping and couldn't move. They had to carry her back to the helicopter."

Deqing scratched the side of his face and looked up through the trees. Parallel stone borders ran ahead, the remains of a raised roadbed, into an open forest of hardwoods and pines. Shou was a plateau bordered by rivers, the sound of flowing water rose from all directions. We stood hypnotized for a minute, as if caught in a mesh of time, entranced by the image of what this place must once have been—a military post full of soldiers, horses, uniforms, now peeled back to what it had been before. Brown leaves drifted down and settled on the forest floor.

"Let's go," Biung said, "we've got a lot of work to do."

. . .

At the center of Shou, we strung up the tarps like blue bat wings. Biung and Hushong built a series of wooden racks for drying meat. The first night in they shot two *shanqiang* and a *shui lu*, returning at dawn with the *shanqiang* over Biung's shoulders and the much larger *shui lu* hanging between Hushong and Deqing on a wooden pole. Then there was the happy butchering, blood and shit smeared on knives and arms. Biung passed raw heart around the fire to the rest of us to share as a communion with the hunt, though we were still groggy in the dawn, and raw meat would not have been my first choice for breakfast on a cold November morning.

For Biung and Hushong, "nature" was not a dumb mineral objectivity, but a medium of communication between human and spirit worlds, a border area between natural and supernatural. Hunting was not simply a matter of skill and luck, but a venture into a zone where spirits made contact with humans, bestowing or withholding game. The hunters entered the mountains to the depth of shit and blood, a depth beyond comfort or convenience. Cold, rain, sleeplessness, exhaustion were not factors for consideration. The wild mountains were home to Biung, and there is no romanticization of home, no aesthetic distance from home. It is the place where you work and live, exist and subsist, where you do what's necessary to sustain as what you are.

Along this trek I had often wished for time to reflect and ruminate, to scribble in my notebook—to enter the kind of contemplative relationship with this place and journey that I had imagined when Nabu said they wanted "creative expression" to be part of their movement home. Now we had a day of rest and would stay a second night before heading back down the mountains. For the first time in a week we would not spend

HUNTING WITH THE BUNUN

all the daylight hours on the trail, then rush to pitch the tarps and dig out rain gutters and collect firewood.

I strolled through the forest, past the stone walls of a food cache that had imploded in slow motion over decades, past a structure Nabu said had been a stockade, collapsed to the earth as if exhausted. These vestiges of colonial authority were broken, crumbled; they had yielded to entropy completely and seemed to belong more to wilderness than to any human effort or design.

The Bunun had been removed from their native lands, confined to reservations, and marginalized within the society that had subsumed them—essentially the same thing that happened to Native Americans in the United States, and to most indigenous peoples in nation-states across the world.

In the process of returning to their "old village," the Bunun knew exactly where it was located, where they had come from, and when they had left. The Bunun were semi-nomadic and may not have settled in Takivahlas for long, but it was the place where their autonomy had ended, where they were driven from the continuum of their self-determined past. It was the beginning of their forced migration, the point of departure from the place to which they were indigenous.

America is a blur of migrations and distant origins, where a thousand cultures assimilate to an ideal of progress and opportunity. The United States is an immigrant society, with the overarching mythology that everything will be better at the next stop on the road, the horizon is always bright. So, when European-Americans reached the West Coast, the end of a continent, we did not stop our migrations but continued cycling through, always moving on to the next place, choosing the opportunity behind the blind curtain over that which is already known—perhaps because where and what we are has never been well known by most. Our mythology of open roads and bright futures has always ignored those who were buried and paved over.

. . .

Shou's flatness buckled at the far edge of the plateau, dipping into a wide hollow then rising into stone ridges. The valley cut straight down hundreds of yards to rivers on three sides. On the eastern edge the remains of a suspension bridge spanned the chasm, rusting cables and rotted planks extended to the opposite wall and toward the high peaks beyond, the heart of the central range.

I hiked up the escarpment above the bridge, where twisted steel cables were bolted into slabs of stone. My feet sank into powdery soil as I climbed between shelves of rock and dwarf conifers to a wedge of stone at the peak of the hill. I looked down the deep cleft of the valley onto the confluence of two rivers, two blue rushing gods that blended into one. Beyond the valley, ridges of forest receded, line after line of green. A black moth with splotches of sunflower yellow fluttered through space and landed on my hand. It walked across my knuckles, turned, and the wind swept it out into the void.

I filled my lungs with the high thin air and let out a whoop of delight, forgiveness, defeat, triumph, laughter, release, whatever had accumulated in this week of accompanying the Bunun on their journey home. This startled a *shanqiang* from a hidden hollow just below me. It leapt out into the sunlight with its small, knotted horns and comic fangs, and soared down the face of the slope. Three bounds, and it was even with the bridge, and it kept on going, a silver-tawny flash, a twanging spring that gulped large arcs of space. The *shanqiang* disappeared down the nearly vertical valley wall, descending toward the rivers where they conjoined in a wishbone of currents, and was gone before my voice had ceased to echo.

. . .

The night before we began the return journey, Hushong broke the thigh bone of a *shuilu* open on a rock and passed the pieces around. Nabu handed one to me along with a spoon. The marrow was a cylinder of milk-white grease within the femur, packed in like congealed bacon fat. It looked crude and gamey, with an edge of broken bone, but it melted rich and delicious on my lips and tongue, like a butter made for kings, rare as uranium or poetry, a single gram refined from a thousand tons of earth.

Staring at the racks of meat in the firelight, here at our furthest point into the wilderness, it seemed to me that "civilization" means removal from the food chain, and is therefore very temporary, because we all are ultimately food.

Dried meat was piled in neat mounds on a tarp in the morning sun. Long loops of intestines hung over the wood rack to dry.

"What are you going to do with this?" I asked Biung as he adjusted the lengths of intestine above the fire.

"Look here," he said. "At this end it's grass. On this end it's pellets of shit, and in the middle it's halfway in between. The elders love this halfway stuff. They make soup out of it. I'm taking it to give to them, along with all these organs packed in blood. See, we're smoking the back and thigh meat as much as we can before we pack it out. But the livers, hearts, kidneys, gall bladders, I'm keeping these fresh. This is what you have to bring back to the village if you're a hunter. We'll have a big party when we get back, and this is what everyone will want. Your pile of meat there, that's yours. It's for you. We have enough for everyone. You can share it with your Amis friends in Dulan, you can throw a big party over there with all this meat. Your friends will love it. You can give some to the Chief, too."

Each of us had a pile of meat to pack out. Despite the fact that this flesh had nourished and sustained me, I had no desire to take it with me. I felt oversaturated with hunting and gunshots, with too much meat and death along these trails. These days sometimes felt like a mash of flesh and ash, skin stripped from the world of rivers and mountains, peeled back to raw tissue and bone.

"Why don't we take a break from hunting on the way back?" I said to Biung. "We've already got more meat than we can carry."

Biung grinned and looked at the fire. "Well, sure . . . but you know how it is. If the spirits send something our way, it's a gift. What would they think if we refused it? How would you feel if you brought me a gift and I ignored it, left it just sitting on the ground? You might feel a little angry, right? We don't want to make the spirits angry, see. If we don't take what's offered, they might think twice about giving us anything again."

• • •

We buried a cache of rice and noodles for future use, packed our gear and meat, and set out midmorning to head down the mountain.

Biung's pack had become so heavy it took two people to lift it. Every pocket and compartment was expanded to maximum capacity, bags and tools were lashed to the outside. We passed Takivahlas but this time didn't stop. Biung carried the gun in one hand and the cooking pots, which no longer fit in anyone's pack, in the other. The internal organs of several deer sloshed within plastic sacks inside his pack. On uphill slopes he could only take twenty steps before stopping to rest. Each time he stopped he dispensed some brief story or insight related to where we were—which mountains we could see, which rivers flowed beneath us, the history of the trail. We only half-listened, because of our own weariness, but Li-an was rapt and wide-eyed, absorbing all the stories whole, preserving them as indissoluble units. Maybe it was to the boy Biung was speaking anyway, standing on the trail with a cigarette burning between his fingers, raising it to point to the horizons all around us. Then he turned and looped his arms through the straps of his pack, Deqing and Nabu helped him raise it to his back, grunting as the weight bit into his shoulders. A thin smile, lazy and postcoital, never left Biung's lips on the way down, despite the stomp of weight on his spine and the crookedness of the trail.

• • •

Slog on, baby, slog on. That load on your back is your virtue and your vice and your survival too, nowhere to go but down. We passed through valleys and across the scars of land-slides, up through bush and brambles, through the forest flats of ferns and cool green shade, barely looking up to acknowl-edge the ancient trees. We walked for three days, my flesh and our food and the landscape all blending together as one, till it began to feel impossible to pull my flesh feet out of the flesh trail, or to eat deer flesh lunch, pork flesh dinner, and the rice gruel that was not like my flesh so much as my mind, white and diluted and lumpy. Everything slid by in a scrim of monochrome exhaustion. We were ghost pirates, our bones and coins tossed overboard, sunk to the bottom of the sea.

On the third day, halfway down, the trail bisected a spiny ridge, atop which there was a tiny radius of cell phone recep-tion. Nabu turned on his phone and climbed to the highest outcrop of the ridge to call the Culture Village and inform them we were alive and would need a ride back down the mountain in two days. Apparently this call was anticipated, because Nabu talked to his assistants, then to his mother, and then he motioned Li-an up to talk to his parents. The boy answered in the monosyllabic manner of children—"fine," "good," "yes," "no," inexpressive as a sea urchin. Nabu took the phone back, listened a moment, then waved to Hu-shong, who pretended not to notice. Nabu covered the mouth-piece and half shouted, "Hushong, dammit, it's your wife!" Hushong looked around with an expression like, "Wife? Whose wife?" but then scrambled up the incline, his belly jig-gling. His half of the conversation was of an even lower order of speech than Li-an's—inarticulate grunts with occasional "Okays" like reluctant capitulations. He handed the phone back to Nabu.

"Come up and meet us," Nabu implored someone on the other end of the line. "We're out of food. We need you to pack in and meet us on the trail. I don't know if we can make it. Get a pen, I'm going to tell you what we need, ready? Five pounds of pork belly—no make it ten pounds, you know, the kind that grills up real nice . . . yeah, ten pounds at least . . . and a bottle of xo. What? No, don't worry, I'm paying for it. Make it the good stuff. We need something to lift our spirits. Bring us some sausages, a couple of chickens. We'll drive a spit through 'em and roast 'em, and cigarettes, about twenty packs, just in case. So it's settled, you'll drive up tomorrow, pack in to the first forestry shelter, and we'll see you there tomorrow night. We'll have a feast up here, just like the good old days. Then we can all pack out together . . ."

Nabu was flushed and frazzled when he hung up, his hair frizzed up out of its braids, traces of beard on his face like charcoal rubbings.

"They're going to pack in and meet us tomorrow night," he said, panting slightly, brow furrowed with the effort of overcoming his lack of conviction.

We were all so sick of wild game and dehydrated pork we could hardly swallow it. Deer meat had started to make me retch, at which times I ate nothing but plain rice or noodles. Culinary fantasy was a form of escape, but there was no way in hell our driver would come up a day early and pack in fifty pounds of food and drink just to relieve our gastronomic monotony. Nabu's fibs about the direness of our situation were utterly transparent.

"Anyway, I've been meaning to drop a few pounds," I said to Nabu, a grim attempt at humor as we hefted our packs like corpses onto our backs.

"Hunh, me too," he said with a laugh that sounded like he'd been punched in the gut. He appeared disgusted both with his attempted phone deceit and with its obvious ineffectiveness.

Up ahead, Biung stumbled, his legs buckling beneath him, but he straightened and began whistling between his teeth, step step step on down the trail.

• • •

By the last day of the trek, my brain was a clot of clay and lime, a single neuron fluttering somewhere within, making my legs step forward bereft of thought. No aspirations on the downward leg of the journey, just empty-headed return to whatever you left behind. Nabu walked like he was asleep on his feet, his goatee matted with dust. Ishigaki had descended to some preverbal state of animal survival, his face slack and blank, *eat walk sleep, eat walk sleep* . . . Li-an was fresh and spry, taking everything in. Biung stopped to light a cigarette and lowered his pack for a brief rest. This time he remained silent, as if there were nothing left to say. Hushong and Nabu lifted Biung's pack to his back, he bit down on his cigarette, and we continued the final hour down the trail.

Back at the A-frame, our harelip driver was waiting with the dented van. We dropped our packs and exhaled the fatigue of the past twelve days. A shiny four-by-four SUV was parked next to it, belonging to the boss of the backhoe crew, a tall, hunched man, lean and stringy, his teeth black from betel nut, arms flapping at his side like wingbones. "Waa, where you been?" he said with a heavy Taiwanese accent, offering cigarettes all around.

Biung was illuminated. Bottles of *mijiu* and fresh packets of betel nut appeared from the van. Our driver threw a few sticks on a fire smoldering within a ring of stones. Biung had Deqing unpack a bag of meat and lay it out to display for the flatlanders. "Who shot that?" the boss asked, and Biung thumped himself in the chest with the flat of his hand. He grinned and began to recount the highlights of the hunt. This was the first of many recountings, as if the telling of the story was necessary to complete the journey, an element without which one has not arrived back home.

We sat in a circle around the fire. Meat was roasted and offered to everyone, a tactile illustration of the journey, as well as a ritual of gift giving. Having received the game as a gift from the spirits, the hunters now passed it on in turn. This was similar to the gift culture of other hunting peoples. For the Guayaki of Panama, it was taboo for a hunter to eat an animal he

HUNTING WITH THE BUNUN

had killed, the meat had to be given to others outside his own family. Among the !Kung in the Kalahari in 1961, Lorna Marshall recorded that an eland tracked by hunters for three days was divided into more than sixty gifts and distributed to the community. Rather than feeling lessened by dispersing one's bounty among others, the !Kung were "sustained by a web of mutual obligation . . . There are no haves and have-nots" (Marshall, quoted in Mintz, *Sweetness and Power*).

I was still on the wagon, but everyone else gulped down *mijiu* as a sacrament of return, blurring the edges of the worlds we were navigating between—and maybe numbing the friction of returning to issues of marginalization, dependency, and lack of recognized value for the skills and knowledge that had been primary during these two weeks in the mountains.

· · ·

We bounced down the dirt road in the dented van. I felt solemn and hollow, the silence and simplicity of the mountains like a glacier moving through me. But the van rocked with singing and shouting, everyone drunken and jubilant, with the exception of Nabu, who remained reserved, his smile either tranquil or preoccupied. Ishigaki sat next to me, his face glowing like a Christmas bulb, grinning like he could smell that tenure-track position on the horizon already. He clapped along with the singing, percussing the air inches from my ear, until I finally shouted at him to shut up. He apologized, forgot what he had apologized for, and continued clapping.

The valley opened out before us. Straight lines of cultivation slanted across a slope a thousand feet below. "That's where Hushong works," Nabu said, pointing to the fields. Hushong, stoic even when drunk, turned and nodded with a fuzzy smile.

"Down there in the fields? What does he do?"

"Yep, he works as a day laborer spraying pesticides," Nabu said. "He walks up and down those rows all day with the chemical tank strapped to his back. That's why he stayed up in the mountains so long. We give him and Biung a stipend to come with us as guides. They make about the same money trekking as they do at their jobs."

"That farm is straight up the hill from our village," Hushong said, speaking thickly through the wine. "We can't drink the water from our wells any more. They're too full of pesticides from the runoff. Now we have to buy water from the county. They bring it in tanker trucks."

Hushong recounted this with no hint of irony at the fact that the job he worked to sustain his family made their water undrinkable.

"What does Biung do?" I asked Nabu.

"He works for us, roasting peanuts for tourists in the Culture Village."

. . .

Down in the Bunun village, the old men emerged, arms opened wide to receive us. Biung returned the rifle to them and presented them with a bag of meat. We piled out and stood as a drunken herd in the dust and broken glass of the street. Standers-by and *mijiu* bottles aggregated around us. Strange hands put betel nuts and cigarettes in my hands. A plump woman on a motor scooter pulled up to the edge of the scene, her mouth painted like a rose, a chaw of betel nut swelling out her cheek. Two small children sat on the seat before her, another one clung to her from behind, and an infant was lashed to her breast with a sling. She called out into the tumult, smiling coquettishly, and with a toss of her head drove away. Everybody slapped Hushong on the back and cooed in falsetto, "See you soon, honey! Come home quick, sweetie!" Hushong blushed like a schoolboy.

"Whooboy, Hushong, hawww," Biung shouted. "You see how she did up her makeup real nice? And damn me if that wasn't a new dress. Look out!"

We scrummed back into the van, a jumble of reeking breath and feet, and drove to the Bunong Culture Village. We arrived into a fevered reception. Old and young jostled to touch and embrace us. One of Su-zhen's coworkers screamed and hugged her, they both burst into sobs. Blurry-eyed men shook my hand and small children climbed my legs. Biung was nearly senseless. Two men hefted him to their shoulders and carried him off to be feted a night before coming back to work to turn the crank on the peanut roaster. Nabu's secretaries and assistants appealed for instructions, and he did not disappoint, speaking firmly and pointing in various directions with his meaty fingers. Ishigaki spoke to three old Bunun women, his face shining with sweat. They answered in Japanese, speaking all at once. Li-an's parents lifted him in their arms and held him between their bodies, sandwiching him in an embrace, and spoke to him in Bunun. He didn't say anything, just watched the moil of rejoicing swirl around him, one final piece of information to ingest.

"Come on," Nabu shouted to me above the fray. "We're having a banquet at a restaurant, everybody is coming."

But one of his assistants pushed through the crowd and handed me a message. My record company had called a week before, trying to track me down. They'd set up a TV interview for me. They had faxed a long list of questions I'd be asked on the show, and I was supposed to do a live performance on camera. I looked down at my hands and laughed. My fingers looked like filthy grubs that would need a million years of evolution to arrive at musical articulation.

"Nabu, thank you, but I want to go home."

"Okay, I understand. Hong-mei, help Scott get the things he left here, and anything else he needs. Scott, we'll talk more soon . . ."

I stepped aside, and Nabu was borne away on the tide of celebration. I washed my hands and face and looked in the mirror, not quite recognizing myself in my two-week beard. Out on the cut lawns of the Culture Village every step felt like a reinitiation into a world I'd recently forgotten, the world of taxes and traffic signs, orders and decrees.

A handful of tourists sat in the rows of chairs around the

stage, where a Japanese drum ensemble was set up to perform as part of a cultural exchange. Their largest instruments stood six feet tall. The performers held thick wooden clubs and wore only loincloths and headbands. The group leader spoke into a microphone, and his words were translated into Mandarin.

"We are honored to be here from Osaka to perform today. We feel very moved because we see the roots of your culture, but in Japan, our roots are lost—only the forms remain. We lack this deep connection to our past."

The leader gave a martial shriek, and they threw themselves at their drums, beating them with wild violence, thighs quivering. They paused in perfect synchronicity, raised their heads and screamed at heaven, then flailed back into their rhythmic pugilism, human muscle thrust against animal skin stretched across the wooden frames, secured with round brass nails.

· · ·

My car was filmed with dirt, but it was the same, still rusted and crappy, with the blue-green Jackson Pollock designs I'd painted across the hood. I opened the door to a musty vinyl smell, white splotches of mold spread across the seats. I climbed in and turned the key, the engine started up and idled quietly.

I drove south along the valley, over the Beinan River, and turned north up the coast toward Dulan. The ocean was slate-gray as evening spread across the sky from the horizon to the central range.

I parked by the betel nut stand across the street from the *tangchang* and opened the plastic bag that held my portion of meat. It had already begun to putrefy and stink. White maggots squirmed in the crevices of the dead flesh. There was nothing I could pass to friends, no bounty to share with the Dulan elders and the Chief. The vestige of all those flashing wild beings was rotted and decayed, as if it could not exist beyond the domain of the mountains. I threw it in a dumpster and drove away, leaving behind everything from Takivahlas except that which flowed already in my veins.

FOURTEEN

Live Music

I began playing music once a week at the *tangchang* café as I worked on recording *Ocean Hieroglyphics* in my studio. I foresaw subdued folk recitals, and the night of the first gig I was crooning away like Leonard Cohen. The audience sat politely on chairs set up in rows, but after a couple of songs, Dou-dou called out, "Can't you play something we can dance to?" I hadn't planned any such thing, but sure I could. So I banged away at my guitar and opened up my throat to sing an old two-chord wonder of a song, "Something to believe in, you've got to have something to believe in . . ." Yiming and the others quickly pushed the chairs out of the way, the crowd swelled to its feet, and everyone began to shake, step, strut, skank, swivel, and stomp. The sugar factory gig became a folk-groove party, a vibe that remained as the performances continued week after week.

Down on Jinzun my ambient guitar music had been part of the plasma of life and the sea we all moved within, part of a larger whole in which everyone was engaged. But here, no one wanted to be relegated to nonparticipation, to sit still and observe a performance as a static audience, to passively receive.

Xiao Ma and Xiao Zhu, the benevolent café managers who topped up vodka tonics so high you had to bend down to them like a hummingbird coming in for nectar, bought a crackly second-hand PA system and a couple of mics. The gig gained momentum, and soon a variety of Taiwanese, aboriginal, and Western musicians came from all up and down the coast to play, and from as far away as Taipei. This was the only original music venue within a hundred miles, despite the fact that many of the best and most popular new musicians in Taiwan were from this stretch of coast, and that the Amis and other "tribal" songs were more gorgeous and alive than anything released by the record labels in Taipei. Live music in Taidong was usually a girl singer who looked like she'd just stepped out of a shampoo commercial, on a stage with a strobe light and a disco ball, warbling pop songs over a prerecorded sound bed—essentially a performance of karaoke. Most young people, whether aboriginal or Han, were so infatuated with real or imagined progress, development, and modernization that anything electrified and mechanized, lit up and amplified, was considered superior to cultural expressions from a previous era. Pop music was simply another commercial industry, purveying a saccharine mythology of eternal love and eternal heartbreak. Karaoke itself was a form of social engagement with modern technology, in which friends gathered in a room to sing to lyrics scrolling down a TV screen, combining an inherent love for singing and technology with a dose of self-aggrandizement, the personal authority of holding the microphone, the appendage of the machinery, everyone else frozen as an audience listening to the amplified sound, the echo effect set to infinity.

I thought of my own music as "organic folk"—musical seeds emerged inside me naturally and spontaneously, and I simply gave them space and attention to allow them to grow into songs. We called the weekly sugar factory performances the "Dulan Organic Folk Music Series," and the Taidong County Culture Bureau held a press conference to publicize it. They were thrilled to be able to attach their name to this event without having to spend a dime, and used it to promote the southeast coast as a tourist destination. The Dulan elders did an opening ritual at the press conference and arrived formally dressed in turquoise tunics and brightly patterned leggings, and wearing their usual truck-tire sandals. The Chief raised a cup of *mijiu* and said in Amis, with Siki translating, "We are here to mark the beginning of this performance series. We wish the best for all involved and hope this music will be blessed and free from trouble." He drained the cup and Kala-OK rubbed his throat thirstily, but the Chief launched them into a song. The journalists flashed their cameras, and the government officials smiled their official smiles.

· · ·

When folk or aboriginal music is moved from the living room, stage, or street to a recording studio, it is usually ruined, because the result when you try to fix something already whole and living is to break it. The only musicians who escape this are those so far out of the loop that the machinery doesn't pick them up on its radar. Long-ge, the Amis singer whose music Jie-ren had been working on in Taipei, was one such artist. His album had finally been released, augmenting his abiding local fame from winning a singing contest thirty years before. He had a soulful, funky guitar style, a combination of slapping and picking. Half of the album had been recorded by Tero through the lo-fi PAs of Taidong's backwater pubs, full of karaoke reverb and hisses and pops. The other half was recorded by Jie-ren in the TCM studio and at various remote locations. Long-ge came off like a Far Eastern, tribal Tom Waits, world-weary and world-wise, with a gravelly baritone delivery that swerved in and out of a sweet falsetto. The medium and the music combined into a rough, raw jewel that would have been ruined if it were cut and polished.

Long-ge rode his three-wheeled motor scooter up to the *tangchang* to play one night. He had been crippled by polio in his youth, and his legs hung lifeless beneath his waist— but this had perhaps given him greater freedom to disregard ambition and advancement, to step aside and let the machinery rumble past, to sing his songs of melancholy and wine in his own way and time.

I helped Long-ge do a sound-check, then we sat at the bar waiting for the audience to gather as he drank *mijiu* and chain-smoked Long Life cigarettes. He was mild and quiet, with a stringy mane of gray hair hanging tangled from the edge of his bald pate. As old friends came up to say hello and congratulate him on his album, he smiled and nodded and said, "Mmmmmmmmm . . ."

Long-ge levered himself up to the stage with his aluminum crutches and sat behind the microphone like a bashful, middle-aged prince. He thwacked out chords on his $20 guitar, extemporized, half-missed notes, forgot whole verses of songs, and spun stories like he didn't have a care in the world, working the gig for all the *mijiu* he could get. He was an infinitely charming performer, simply because he didn't do anything except be himself, which is harder and harder in our catapulting world, and nearly impossible in the music industry. The Open Circle women called out for him to sing "Rainbow" ("There's a rainbow that doesn't appear in the sky, but it's always in my heart"), and when he complied they sang in a chorus, "Long-ge, we love you!" He looked away, blushed all the way up to the top of his dome, with its few strands of gray hair, and asked for another cup of *mijiu*, which Xiao Zhu scurried to provide and pour, looking out to the audience with a goofy, squirrelish grin in her few seconds in the shared spotlight. Long-ge took a sip of wine, smacked his lips, and looked down at his guitar as he began to sing "My Drunken Self," a rambling, talking-blues song in which he bemoaned his lack of prospects within Taiwan's dollar democracy: "Drunken, who's never been? It's been a long time since I had work, a long time since I had a tomorrow, a long time since I had a future . . . I look at the calendar, already thirty years have gone by, but I'm still me, I'm still me."

Before the next song Long-ge said, "When I was young, I

went to Taipei to look for work . . . couldn't find anything, couldn't stay. From Taipei I headed to Taizhong, couldn't get a job there either. Continued all the way south to Gaoxiong, finally found myself a way to survive. But before long I just came back home."

Nomadic wandering was a common theme among aboriginal folksingers and echoed the experience of my friends, such as Yiming, migrating between jobs and cities before finally returning to Taidong. One of Panai's songs begins, "My mom and dad told me to go out wandering, I left, crying as I went. Where did I wander to? I wandered to Taipei . . ." This was the experience of many aboriginals, though most of them never made it home, but rather stayed in cities where they'd found work. Another of Panai's songs is addressed to city aboriginals and says, "Maybe one day you'll long to leave, the city will've tired you out. Maybe one day you'll long to see the 'place like Heaven' Mama told you all about."

The last two tracks on Long-ge's album are traditional Amis songs, recorded by Jie-ren in a field somewhere up on Dulan-shan, accompanied by a single strummed guitar and gorgeous harmonies sung by a childhood friend of his, with bird songs and crickets in the background. Long-ge ended his set with one of these songs, and it connected seamlessly with his own music, as if he had internalized his musical heritage even while evolving an individual style. When he finished, we helped him to a seat. The women in the audience came over and kissed him on the cheek, which made him blush all over again and call for another cup of *mijiu*.

Siki slapped Long-ge on the back and said to me, "Look at those hands. Know why he plays so good? It's from flattening out those *binlang* leaves day after day. You lay them out on the counter, then *whack* with your palm. Ha, you hear how that comes out from the guitar? Scott, if you want to play like an Amis, we've got plenty of leaves for you to practice on."

Unable to work because of his disability, Long-ge's only

vocation was to help out in his family's betel nut shop, pressing flat the leaves that would be daubed with lime paste and folded around the nuts. His hands were indeed broad as skillets, and his arms looked strong as a foundry worker's in comparison with his skinny, crooked legs. Long-ge's distance from the grid, and the beautiful form of self-expression that resulted from it, reminded me of folksinger Utah Phillips's warning that if you give your mind to someone else for eight hours a day, there's no guarantee you'll get it back in an undamaged condition. In response to Siki's comment, Long-ge closed his eyes and laughed.

· · ·

In the liner notes and promotional materials for his album, the label presented Long-ge as a sort of noble drunkard. This had come about partly in jest, because of his inability to record his songs sober. Without drinking, he couldn't inhabit the spirit of his songs amid the sterile terms of the recording studio. (This was at least part of the reason Jie-ren had taken Long-ge up to Dulanshan to record the traditional Amis songs.) But it was also a way to identify and market him through stereotypes, according to which aboriginals were great singers, drinkers, and hunters. These stereotypes were mutually created, in that many aboriginal individuals embraced them as a way of affirming an identity distinct from mainstream Chinese society. Yiming, for example, proclaimed and exhibited his love for all three at every opportunity.

But there was something hollow in the commercialized romanticization of drunkenness, just as there's something hollow in pop songs about eternal love, and the destruction I've seen come out of a bottle also makes me cringe. One night, riding back to Taidong from the sugar factory, Long-ge crashed his motor scooter, but with an innocent's or a drunkard's luck was not badly injured. He spent only three days in the hospital. But much later Ha-na's boyfriend rode away from the *tangchang* blind drunk on a motor scooter. He swerved into the path of an oncoming cement truck in front of Vadsuku's ghost house and was killed instantly.

. . .

Guo Ying-nan (Difang Duana in Amis), an elder of the Chief's generation from a village south of Taidong City, was even further than Long-ge from music as a commercial industry, but he came into unlikely and controversial fame. Difang was simply an elder Amis who had the best singing voice in his village and was brought to France in 1988 with thirty other Taiwanese aboriginals of various tribes for a performance tour. Unbeknownst to them, the performances were recorded by the French government, and Difang singing an Amis drinking song was included in an "anonymous" compilation of Taiwanese aboriginal songs produced for "educational" purposes. Enigma later sampled Difang's voice as the central motif in "Return to Innocence," the theme song for the 1996 Olympics, which sold eight million copies. Neither the singer nor the tribe was credited or paid by Enigma, or the record label, or the Olympic Committee. No one in Taiwan even knew this had happened until Amis kids watching TV heard the song and said, "Hey, that's Grandpa!"

A movement was initiated to get recognition and compensation for Difang. But Taiwan's Association of Copyright Owners claimed that aboriginal music was in the public domain, and singers who performed or arranged it could not claim any copyright. Therefore, this administrative body for the protection of intellectual property rights stood up for global corporate interests against the native cultures of its own country—a contemporary, intellectual rights version of internal colonialism. Eventually the record company paid Difang an undisclosed amount to settle the suit brought against them. Still, it's ironic that a song based on the appropriation of indigenous culture has the word "innocence" in its title.

. . .

Long-ge was famously incapable of singing a song more than once in a recording session, a Dylanesque don't-look-back approach typical of his inability to conform to industry agendas. This was not an act of petty subversion—it was as if the whole ethos of commercialization was an animal he couldn't comprehend. The usual recording protocol involves doing take after to take to get a song "right" (which is not the same as "good"), and then splicing many versions into one. In much commercial music a song is not produced as a whole but is made up of dozens or hundreds of fragments, small pieces from multiple takes, digitally edited together.

I was no one-take wonder in the recording process. I never formally studied music and aside from a few basic folk chords had learned to play guitar by trying to find ways to express the sounds I heard in my head. When I started to learn harmonica, I bought a rack to wear around my neck and simply played all the time, whether I was riding my motorcycle around Taipei or washing dishes. My ambient guitar music was something like landscapes paintings made with sound, which evolved through the resonances of unusual modalities I tuned the guitar to, defamiliarizing myself to the intervals of the strings and allowing my subconscious to come to the fore. In the same spirit of exploration, I had begun adding to my music acoustic bass, percussion, flutes, mbira, banjo, Jew's harps, and whatever else I could think of or get my hands on, including a *tonkori*, a stringed instrument from the Ainu of Hokkaido, in northern Japan, which I borrowed from Chen Jian-nian.

My anachronistic insistence on analog gear was a way to impose an organic shape on the recording process. The analogic need to record songs start to finish, without splicing different takes together or "fixing" them in the mix, forced me to sink more deeply into them and gain a greater fluency and absorption with the music I had composed—as if after writ-

ing a piece of music I had to reconsume it, redigest it, reme-
tabolize it, so that it would reemerge from within me whole,
through my guitar or banjo, a physical entity born into the
material world as sound vibrations, waves emerging from my
body, captured by spools of magnetic tape.

I loved the mechanical bulk of my old tape machines, the
reels turning like synchronized wheels across the tape transport, the motors that ran smoothly as a Swiss watch—in fact,
one of my tape decks was a beautiful Studer, a Swiss two-track
that an engineer from Taipei and I used to mix down the eight-
track recordings. I had a prejudice for the sound quality of
analog recordings, but in truth it was not the sound quality
but the more deliberate, unfragmented process that brought
qualitative improvement to the music.

With salvaged gear, the selection of mics I'd been collecting for years, and the driftwood aesthetic of the Open Circle
Tribe, I had the only analog studio in Taiwan, and the best
studio of any kind in my opinion, especially because it was on
a mountain above the Pacific, rather than locked in a sound-
proofed vault.

Inside the recording room the concrete floors reflected certain
frequencies that gave recordings a dull, boxy sound. I needed a
covering for the floor, to absorb and diffuse the sound waves,
and one day mentioned this to Diva, the Tao surfer girl from
Orchid Island, after she had begun working part-time in the
tangchang café.

"Well, I can weave a set of thatch mats for you," she said,
in the spirit of spontaneous giving so common here. "I learned
how to make them when I was growing up. It's the right time
to gather *yuetao* . . . but is that what you want for your studio, something handmade?"

"Of course it's what I want, everything in my studio is handmade!" I said.

Diva laughed at me, and in the coming days began collecting long, broad *yuetao* leaves, a yucca-like bush that grew

across the mountain, and laid them out in her courtyard. As they dried they took on striated shades of butterscotch, tan, and blonde, which she wove into cross-hatched patterns she'd learned from her grandmother. When she finished the mats, we drove them up in my car and laid them out in the studio, and they filled the room with the smell of sun and dried grasses. Before long the *yuetao* blossomed across Dulanshan. Long cascades of buttery white flowers trailed down like strings of moons outside the back window of the studio, so that these leaves and flowers blossomed both within and without the space where I played and recorded music, the two hemispheres connected by a gift from Diva, the dark and laughing surfer girl from across the sea.

FIFTEEN

Shelter from the Sun

In the spring the mountains rose lush green above the sea, the air became fragrant with new growth and the smell of plum blossoms. It was the beginning of my second year in Dulan. The sky was a blue poultice of heat, the sun rose orange and yellow straight out on the horizon, crashing in over everything like a train wreck. We hit a dry spell. There was no rain for weeks, and my water pipe and cistern were empty. I carried water bucket by bucket from the spring at the edge of the *shi-jia* orchard and bathed in the ocean. Out the back window of the studio the first wild raspberry ripened at the center of a white flower, ruby red among the thorns and buzzing bees. I picked it and popped it in my mouth when the petals fell away, the juice spread tartly across my tongue. A troupe of a dozen monkeys swung through the trees behind the house, marauding the persimmons that were still green and horribly astringent, but the monkeys liked them that way. Mull ran barking in their wake, inviting them to play, and then returned with a swagger, proud of chasing them away. I saw a bamboo snake on the side of the road, a squiggle of lambent, scintillant green that slid across the rough concrete. In the living room a tiny butterfly fluttered like a soft pink flame against the alternating light and dark of the ceiling beams. A gecko stole up and caught it in its reptile mouth, the wings still trembled as the gecko chomped it down. Everything flowed gold and blue and green, time running over my body in place of rain. The ocean molted a thousand shades of blue, and the sky became a white-hot void we all fell through, landing back on these radiant roads between the jungle and the sea in burnt skin and stained clothes, sand beneath our toenails, our hair all tangled and stiff with salt.

. . .

I rode down the mountain on a motorbike I had on loan for a few days from a friend in Hualian. At the *tangchang* Zhiming and Yiming were carving a piece of camphor wood to make a table, and a small mound of shavings was smoldering on the asphalt, releasing thick sweet smoke. Yiming swept a pile of shavings into a plastic bag for me and said, "Take these, you can burn them to keep mosquitoes away. And camphor smoke smells better than any incense you can buy."

"See any snakes up at your place recently?" Zhiming asked.

"Only some bamboo snakes."

"That's all right, their venom's nothing serious," Yiming said. "If one bites you, just slit your skin there with a knife. Let the blood flow out, and it'll carry the poison away. Might make your hand swell up a little, that's all."

"One time I was gathering bamboo up on the mountain," Zhiming said, pausing to trim his thumbnail with a knife. "I grabbed a stalk, sliced it off low to the ground, then looked down and saw two baby bamboo snakes writhing in my hand where I held the pole."

"Then what happened, Baba?" asked Zhiming's son, a thin pale boy with glasses who was visiting from his mother's place in Hualian.

Zhiming looked at him as if just remembering his existence and said, "That was the night your mother got pregnant with you."

I kick-started the borrowed motorbike and rode down to the beach. I parked by the tetrapods piled along the sea below the village and walked down the path to where the tide was coming in. The tetrapods were monstrous, otherworldly, like four-pronged concrete jacks several yards across and several tons each, stacked into a barricade against the ocean. Ostensibly they lined the coast to protect it from erosion or typhoon damage, but it was well documented that they increased environmental degradation, rather than preventing it. They had proliferated for no reason other than the political influence of the mob-dominated cement industry. Waves roared in rough and wild from where they broke a hundred yards out, ribbons of spray streaming silver in the sun. They hissed across the sand, swirled and pulled at my feet and calves, splashing up high before subsiding.

Out of nowhere a rogue wave surged in and rose up to my waist. I was suddenly surrounded by the sea, the ocean all around and trying to drag me away. But I stood rooted in the sand, the wave crashed against the tetrapods and dispersed, and the elemental strength of the ocean receded, like a sleeping god turning over and changing dreams. I remained on earth, still here, here again, still grinning and breathing in the sun, my skin shining with seawater and sweat.

I walked on to the far end of the beach, and on the rocky point found an almost circular curl of driftwood, a thick wreath of wood, perhaps once a root wrapped around a stone. It was dark purple or puce, almost the same color as the raw *shan-qiang* liver I'd eaten on the Bunun trek, and so heavy I could barely lift it. But I put it over my shoulders like a yoke, carried it back to the motorbike, and held it on the seat behind me with my left hand while I drove back to the *tangchang*. Zhiming and Yiming were gone, but E-ki's brother was sitting and smoking alone in the mouth of a bay door. "*Ge-ge*," I said, "brother, I need some rope. Is there any around I can use?"

"Sure, I have some right here," he said. He stood up and untied a piece of rope from around his waist, and handed it to me.

"What are you doing?" I said. "That's your belt—without

it your pants will fall down. All the girls will start chasing you, they won't give you any peace."

"Ha ha, don't worry. I don't have far to go to get home. They won't catch me. I'll be in the truck anyway. They won't see."

"How's E-ki these days? Is he back from China?"

"Yeah, he's been back a while. Why haven't you stopped by? Come see us this afternoon, I'm heading back right now."

"Okay, I'll stop by a little later."

. . .

I lashed the log to the back seat with B-*shifu*'s erstwhile belt, loading the motorbike like a truck, with the bag of camphor shavings hanging from the handlebars, and rode through town. The betel nut girls waved to me from their neon booths as I drove by, silver teeth glinting in their smiles, beckoning me to buy their wares, though these were family-run stands, not as libidinous as those on the lonely stretches of the coast highway up north. I pulled up to the cash machine by the post office to check whether the latest installment of my record advance had come through, but my account was still empty. Oh well, still plenty of wild *kugua* up on the mountain.

I sat down in the lunch shop next to the post office and ordered pork and rice, the only thing on the menu, if there had been a menu. The Hakkanese matron had plump, wrin- kled hands, pink and swollen from stirring a steaming pot of meat all day every day, and wore a scarf tied over her hair. She always picked out gelatinous globs of fat for me, fishing them out from among leaner chunks of meat, in honor of how far I was from home. Her husband sat at a corner table with the day's newspapers. He was lean and stringy as a range chicken, all tendon and bone, his face scab-red from accompanying whichever customers needed a drinking partner to help finish off a pint of deer antler liquor, a Taiwanese specialty. A dog sniffed at a severed pig's ear in an aluminum bucket by the door. I chewed and swallowed my fat-slathered rice as trucks slammed by and blew grit into my teeth and eyes.

I stepped next door at Chen's sundry shop to buy a bottle of *mijiu* to take to E-ki. Chen's daughter was holding down the fort, watching music videos on the TV suspended almost directly above her head, with stock prices rolling across the bottom of the screen. She waved one hand dreamily to help her nail polish dry, as a swirl of flies buzzed above a slab of pork atop the butcher's block. "How's your water pipe these days?" she asked me. Because of the rainless spell, everyone asked everyone about their water supply.

"It's all dry. How about yours?"

"Oh, we've got plenty. Our pipe is connected high up. It never runs out. How come you're not buying beer today? You like *mijiu*, huh?"

"Sure, sometimes. But this is for a friend."

The whole village was submerged in the siesta hour, a mummification of heat, except for the trucks hauling sand up the highway, which never stopped, and which didn't slow where the highway became the commercial strip of the village. I got on the motorbike and returned to the *tangchang* to have a cup of coffee in the café.

Within the dilapidation of abandoned administration, every wall and ceiling rafter seemed to list one direction or another, in a state of bohemian languor that inhered along with the Open Circle Tribe aesthetic of driftwood benches, seaweed lamp covers, and glasses made from beer bottles. Diva was working the counter, a shift of her part-time job here. She was alone in the café, and smiled at me from where she sat on a stool in cut-off shorts and a T-shirt reading a magazine. Her shorts were so tight and brief they had almost the cut of a bikini bottom, her thighs emerging smooth and dark among the white cotton threads along the edge.

My record company had agreed to include a set of poems along with the *Ocean Hieroglyphics* CD. Driving up and down the coast, cutting chips from driftwood logs, swimming in the salt and blue of the sea, I jotted notes on scraps of paper, which I piled on my driftwood desk, and which accumulated and distilled into a twenty-part poem, the ocean strung out the best I could string it, painted in words in green and blue.

I ordered a cup of coffee and took out my notebook, but words skidded bluntly across my skull, balky and abstruse. I felt steamrolled by the heat as I tried to slit open the reptile belly of the afternoon and spill it onto the page in color and blood.

"What are you doing?" Diva said, setting my coffee down in front of me and lighting a cigarette.

"Trying to juggle some words into poems, but not making much progress. Doesn't smoking make you even hotter on a day like this?"

"Yeah, but . . . ah, I can't help it. You know, it's just my addiction. Want one?"

"What the hell, why not." She lit and handed one to me, I inhaled her smoke into my lungs.

"You have any of those poems in Chinese?"

"Yeah, a few have already been translated. Do you want to see them?"

"Sure, let me have a look."

Diva sat down next to me, her legs splayed out in lazy, half-conscious eroticism, and read the translations, while currents of magnetism curled between us, swirling with smoke and steam. I gulped my coffee and looked out onto the street. There was no sign of life, except for the gravel trucks with their flumes of dust, and three schoolgirls who stood laughing together in blue skirts and pressed white shirts in the blunt sunlight across the road.

"Hmm, not bad," Diva said. "I don't know what the English is like, but in Chinese the language is strong. Did you do the translation?"

"No, an old friend did. A Taiwanese poet I know from America."

"Yeah, I like them . . . I'm not an expert on poetry, you know. My family forced me to study engineering in college.

But I come from Orchid Island. We're an ocean tribe, always touching the sea. Some of the people there, some of the elders, they know, they really know the ocean. And those who really know the ocean, well, maybe they don't have to write a poem about it." She shrugged and grinned. "That's just what I think."

"Yeah, probably you're right. But I'm stuck with writing, it's what I am. And anyway, language is just another kind of ocean I like swimming around in." I stubbed out my cigarette and said, "I'll have another Americano. Better make it a double in fact."

"Sure thing," Diva said as she got up and walked back to the counter. "But you're going to crash if you drink any more caffeine."

"I don't care."

"You won't be able to sleep tonight."

"Doesn't matter."

"O yeah? What else you going to do all alone up on your mountain all night long?"

The espresso machine hissed and shuddered. I picked up my pen and stared at the page hard enough to burn it. The words conveyed no evocation of the ocean or any other meaning to me. Diva brought my coffee. When she set down the cup I turned and her face was inches from mine, her eyes crinkled with mischief. I reached out and seized her waist, our sweating bodies mashed together.

"I could devour you in three bites and one swallow," I said.

"Yes, please."

I pressed my lips against her silken neck, drunk on her soft dark flesh, my blood surging like electricity in a dynamo, my heart jumping like a horse. I stood up, the chair fell over, coffee spilled across the table and stained my notebook. I lifted her in my arms and walked toward the door.

"Where are you taking me?"

"Home."

"*Fuck*," she said in English, "I have to work till closing!"

"It doesn't matter. There are no customers. Everybody in the world is asleep."

"Wait, I can't leave now. I'll meet you after work."

"Ah . . ."

I set her down. My hands were a swarm of bees, her body a sculpture of honey and blood. A dark sea power radiated from her, ten thousand pearls compressed in her belly, her hips a kelp forest, a shimmer of sun slanting through her salt and leaves.

We panted and sweated. I couldn't unstick my hands from her skin. She smiled impishly and said, "Don't let anybody see!"

· · ·

My hands on the handlebars were jittery as wild birds in a cage. I rode the motorbike south toward E-ki's workshop through heat gelatinous and greasy as the pork fat I'd had for lunch. E-ki's brother was weed-whacking waist-high grass at the side of the road, a bandana over his face like a bandit, his shirt sweated through and plastered to his skin. I pulled up the concrete ramp, and he shut off the engine of the grass cutter. "Scott, I'm cutting the weeds, but the pigs won't eat this stuff."

"Why not?"

"I don't know, maybe too many thorns. I got them a whole truckload of wild vines and leaves yesterday."

"You need a goat to eat this stuff. They eat everything."

"Yeah, but we don't like goat meat. Hey, stay with us for dinner tonight."

"I can't tonight. Next time."

"Are you looking for E-ki? He's across the road."

"Where?"

"Go on over, you'll see him." He started the weed cutter and raised his bandana back up over his nose and mouth.

I walked across the highway. A narrow trail wound into thick brush, then opened onto a small clearing fronting the ocean. E-ki sat on a low platform with a pair of pliers in his hand. He had cleared the bushes and bunch grasses and built a deck from the skinny, knotted shore trees he'd cut, two-inch wide stumps of which now stuck up from the dirt. He'd set four poles into the earth, attached cross pieces two feet above the ground by looping thick steel wire around the joints, then levered and twisted the wire tight with the handle of the pliers. He laid more unhewn poles across these to form a platform, and strung wire between the tops of the vertical poles to lay palm fronds for shade.

"Ho. It's about time you showed up. You have a cigarette?" E-ki asked me.

"Not on me."

"Good, and don't give me one if I ask for it."

"What's going on here?"

"My sun deck. For naps. Fuck the middle of the afternoon. Too hot to do anything. The light driving straight down in columns from the sky. Everything white and blinded, your eyes, your guts. Better to sleep through it. Listen—you don't even hear the cars here, just the waves."

We looked out to the ocean, and it was true. The light was flat and hard, the colors washed-out with glare, and there was no sign of the highway, only the murmur of the sea. The ocean looked like a mirage of itself, glossy and receding. Small waves rippled over everything. A stone jetty extended half-heartedly into the surf just to the north. A fisherman sat at the end of it where the stones sloped into the water, his head slumped forward beneath a bamboo-leaf hat, his fishing pole held loose between his legs.

"He won't catch much out there," I said.

"Depends what he's after," E-ki said. "He might have it on the line already."

The sea and sky whitened and blurred in the metallic light, like grinding a lens, glass dust in your eyes.

"You know that lung problem I told you about?" E-ki said. "What I've been going to the hospital in Hualian for?"

"Yeah."

"Well, turns out it's—you know—*cancer*."

E-ki said "cancer" in English. He looked down at the dirt and then back out to sea.

"How's the treatment going?"

"I don't know. They don't know. They're trying something new. This is step two."

"Is your hair falling out?"

"No, not yet. This is chemo. In the end it will, I guess. That's stage three, if things go that far. I told them, I don't care about my hair, but let me keep my dick. Who cares about hair anyway? You lose your hair or your hair loses you, damn stuff growing on after you're dead and underground."

"I lost my knife."

"Hmm, that's no good. What happened?"

"I was cutting weeds in the rain a few weeks ago, and it slipped and flew out of my hand. By the time I looked up it was already gone. The undergrowth is so thick I couldn't find it."

"No good to lose a knife. You did your handle all wrong. You've got to bring it down in the middle and leave an edge to grip."

"I know, I'll make another one."

"You got a carving knife?"

"Yeah, Yiming gave me one."

"Any pretty girls around these days?"

"A couple. Around, but too far away. Or too near."

"Get yourself a wife."

"Too much trouble."

"Ho, less trouble than not having one. Less trouble than being on the chase all the time."

"How many times you been married?"

"Enough. Numbers don't matter. Do the right thing at the right time—that's what counts. But it's not easy."

Out on the jetty the fisherman reeled in his empty hook, strands of sea grass hanging from the line.

SHELTER FROM THE SUN

"Look, about my—*cancer*—don't tell anyone. No one knows."

"Okay."

"Nothing anyone can do."

"I know."

"We may have to leave here. The owner's talking about selling."

"He's got a buyer?"

"Maybe. Everything's maybe."

"What'll you do?"

"Wait and see. When something happens, then we'll do something. The court case for our land is getting started. My mother . . . we may have to send her to the city, to Gaoxiong, to live with my sister. My brother and I can live anywhere. We can live in the back of the truck."

"You can stay at my place."

"What, way up there with the monkeys? Ha. We'll stay down at the *tangchang* if we have to. How you going to make your music with chainsaws going in the yard? We need to make noise to work, you need quiet. Plus, we like to be closer to the shops, and to our friends. Can't spend all day driving up and down the mountain."

"Let me know if you need a hand with anything."

"No, we've got everything we need."

. . .

B-*shifu* sat wiping grit and grass stems from his face, wiping his stubble clean, his hair lank with sweat. The weed cutter lay on its side, a dragonfly stripped of wings, the cutting blades plastered with cuddish green. "How's E-ki?" he asked as I walked to the motorbike.

"He's okay."

"Stay with us for dinner. I'll kill a chicken."

"I can't, but I brought you some *mijiu*."

"No, you keep it. E-ki doesn't drink now. He quit smoking too. He says smoking's no good, but I still smoke."

"I'll leave the *mijiu* here for you."

"Is E-ki really okay?"

"I think so."

He reached out and clasped my hand, his grip rough and hard. I gave him the bottle and drove up the mountain to wait for Diva.

SIXTEEN

Coupled Orbits

Diva drove her beat champagne-green motorscooter up the
mountain after work. She sat out on the porch sipping ice coffee from a plastic cup and smoking roll-your-own cigarettes,
reminding me of Jack Kerouac's words in *The Dharma Bums*,
"there's nothing better in the world than a roll-your-own deeply
enjoyed without hurry."

"Won't drinking coffee at night keep you awake?" I asked
her, but she just laughed.

"I'm so used to this stuff, it doesn't affect me at all." Her
smile was a dazzling radiance, an added coruscation to the
night that was alive with trilling and chirping insects and
other creatures. Diva was so at home in her own skin that she
seemed perfectly at ease in every situation, as if perfectly content with the rotation of the earth and stars, perfectly happy to
spin along with them. And now she stepped from the mirage-
like mythology in which I'd first seen her, a dark pearl rising above waves of silver-blue, into my physical space, her
skin warm and soft, her breath sweet and stale with tobacco
smoke, her eyes so bright and flashing I almost ducked when
she turned her gaze to me.

"Where'd you get the name Diva anyway?" I asked her.

"Oh, I don't even remember. I just heard it somewhere and
decided to keep it . . . why, is it a stupid name?"

"Not at all, it means a great singer."

"Ha ha, well then it doesn't suit me at all . . ."

But when I asked her to sing a song from Orchid Island, she only briefly demurred, and then sang out a melody so full of freshness and yearning it made my heart ache. I thought I'd never sing again, so far did I feel from that vivid evocation of life on earth.

Diva had gone to college in Tainan, and by virtue of her entrance exam scores was placed in an engineering program. She hated the flat, industrialized western plains, where there were no waves, just a flat brownish sea, which was so fraught with fishing nets and military patrols (because it was the coast facing China) that you could barely find a place to enter the water, and surfing was a bald impossibility. She had wanted to quit and return to the east coast many times, but her family coerced her into finishing her degree, and she became the first college graduate of her family.

Like many natives of Orchid Island who had worked or studied on "mainland" Taiwan, Diva had little desire to return there to live, even had there been waves to surf. She'd become used to the freedom of anonymity that she could never have on an island a dozen miles in circumference, in the small community where she had grown up.

The Japanese had preserved Orchid Island as an ethnographic study site, keeping the Tao people "pure" in order to study them, as in a human zoo. Because modernization began late in their communities, Tao culture remained the least eroded of indigenous Taiwan. Orchid Island was an eddy in the current of modern progress, but it was also insular, impoverished, full of superstitions and taboos. The Tao's lack of contact with the modern world seemed to have made them more vulnerable to damage when it finally arrived, as if they hadn't had a chance to build up resistance. On the first day of the month, old men would collect their welfare checks from the post office, spend all their money on liquor, lie drunk in the village street for three days, then white-knuckle it twenty-seven hungry days till the next check.

The Tao are the only indigenous Taiwanese whose language does not belong to the Formosan language family. Centuries ago the Tao migrated from the Batanes Islands north of Luzon, in the Philippines, and their language belongs to the Batanic dialect cluster of the Austronesian language family. The Tao are considered the most egalitarian and nonhierarchal of Taiwan's indigenous tribes, and are the only ones whose traditional culture did not include alcohol. Perhaps this latter fact is the reason they have been susceptible to such abject alcoholism—or, maybe there was just nothing else to do on Orchid Island, with the traditional economy dismantled but few jobs available, and no place to travel without taking a boat or plane. For many young Tao, like Diva or Feiyu, moving away was like escaping from a bucket of crabs, slapping away the claws of personal and cultural obligation that had once been sustaining, but had less and less relevance in contemporary society and might now be burdensome rather than mutually supporting.

After the KMT takeover of Taiwan in 1945, Orchid Island remained off-limits to the public. In 1967 Chiang Kai-shek and his wife visited and were horrified that citizens of the Republic of China were living "underground," which they considered dirty and uncivilized. Tao houses, adapted to local conditions and materials, were built into the sloping hillsides of the island, inlaid with stones and hand-hewn planks, so that the earth protected them from the violence of typhoons and the bludgeoning heat of summer. Isolated in the sea, the island was exposed to the full force of both. After the Chiangs' visit, the traditional homes were bulldozed, and the government began to build new concrete structures to replace them. But the funds for "civilized" dwellings ran short, which left the island scattered with half-built concrete shells, with rusted rebar sticking up from unfinished walls. The new houses absorbed so much heat that they were miserable to live in anyway. When I visited Orchid Island, the villages were rows of crumbling, dystopian houses, where sows rooted through roadside garbage piles, trailed by strings of black and hairy piglets.

The Chinese name *Orchid Island* was derived from a profusion of phalaenopsis orchids, but these had been harvested to oblivion. Today orchids no longer exist on Orchid Island. Its indigenous name is *Ponso no Tao*, or "island of the people."

The island's current and future generations were saddled with another curse of civilization, which Feiyu had raged against in his protest diorama on Jinzun. In 1970 the government told the Tao people it was planning to build a fish cannery, which would bring jobs and income to the community. But when the project was completed in the 1980s, it turned out to be a nuclear waste storage facility instead. Orchid Island did not even have electricity at the time. The Tao elders, removed from the realities of contemporary life, had no idea what nuclear energy and its waste were. When younger Tao returned from studying in Taiwanese cities, they explained radiation in terms of *anito*, evil spirits in Tao cosmology, to help the elders understand what had been manifested in their community. Ironically, an international campaign to remove the waste has brought more attention to the undermining of Tao agency than would ever have come otherwise. Maybe this malevolent spirit, if it does not irradiate the island into a wasteland, will help preserve Tao culture longer than it would have survived on its own within the tide of industrial progress.

After realizing what had happened in their midst, the Tao began protesting the facility and demanding its removal. These protests have now been going on for more than twenty years, and despite government promises to remove the waste, it is still there. Meanwhile, mobilized into political activism, the Tao managed to defeat, or at least forestall, a second nuclear waste dump that was planned for Orchid Island, which was to be covered over by a national park. A national park built on top of a nuclear waste dump seems a cruelly appropriate metaphor for our world in which facades of sustainability are rolled out like wallpaper over terms of absolute destruction.

Perhaps Orchid Island has become the ethnographic display the Japanese authorities had hoped to make it. But rather than an unpolluted bubble enclosing a "pure" culture and ecosystem, it is now an exhibit showing the effect that exotic social and political forces can have on an indigenous system of culture and sustenance. Orchid Island is now a diorama of itself, a real-life illustration of a people subjected to internal colonialism, in which the conflicts and contradictions of contemporary society are not glossed over and sanitized, but are right there on the surface for anyone to see.

. . .

In the morning Diva came with me to fix the water pipe. I carried a machete and wore rubber boots, a blue bandana tied around my head. From the bridge where the road crossed the stream, we picked our way down the steep path to the streambed. Diva kicked off her flip-flops, and we headed up the stream bank, hopping stone to stone.

"Are you all right going up barefoot?" I asked her.

"Don't worry about me, I'm an aboriginal," she said merrily.

She knotted her T-shirt up high beneath her breasts and took a cigarette from a pack outlined sharply against her thighs. Insect songs pulsed all around us, the air was humid and damp. High up the ravine, where jungled slopes converged, a ten-foot waterfall fanned down from a cleft between two boulders and poured into a broad, deep pool. Diva waded into the pool, then turned around and slung a spray of water at me. I pulled off my boots and waded in after her. Tiny fish swam around my feet. She jumped into my arms and wrapped her legs around me as the waterfall roared beside us. Soon nothing separated us, we were skin to skin within the gushing current. She threw back her head and laughed, "Now we're really savages, aren't we?" My legs trembled and we fell over with a splash.

Diva lived in a listing concrete shack a few villages up the coast from Dulan. It had nearly been knocked down by an earthquake some years back, and she rented it for almost nothing. When not out surfing, she would sit there for hours weaving grass mats or making strings of shells to hang from the cracked support posts, occupying a contentment of being with no need for stimulation or agenda. Sometimes on my way up or down the coast I drove through the dirt alleys of her village to see her. The house faced east toward the sea, so in the afternoon the sun hit the back wall and heated it like a kiln. Hot bronze light burned in through the single window to the dimness of her room, where we lay across the *yuetao* mats and cotton quilts of her bed, listening to Nora Jones on a cheap CD player.

My relationship with Diva was surreptitious, partly because my relationship with Ming-sho was never fully resolved. There was a heightened element of play in covert meetings with Diva, which were more delicious simply for being secret. Flashed glances between us could be signals in an unsuspecting crowd. If we talked or danced together, electric currents flowed between us, invisible to anyone else.

I had wanted to grasp and hold Ming-sho, to integrate her into my life moment by moment, and it hollowed me that I was incapable of doing so, that I could not make a place for her in my days, my house, my life. I loved Diva but protected that love with distance. I was sure that a formalized relationship between us would be polluted with expectations, at least from my own expectation-polluted self. Diva and I expressed love not by grasping but by letting go. We were autonomous and self-determining within our secret love affair. One time an ex-boyfriend of hers came down from the north and stayed with her for a few days. When she brought him to the sugar factory the sideways smile she gave me was more impish and sly than ever, a playful acknowledgment of the ever-proliferating game of sex and love.

I made no effort to grasp and hold Diva, enclose or engulf her, to emotionally colonize or restrict her. Because of this she said one day, "You've seen through all the bullshit," meaning I had let go of ego attachments. In fact, I was at least as full of shit as anyone, and my balance or detachment with respect to her was only due to the remoteness with which I insulated myself, unwilling or unable to share my emotional or physical space with another. Unable, in other words, to open my heart.

I loved both Diva and Ming-sho, each love refracted by different prisms of distance, different ambers of emotion. My relationship with Diva remained secret until much later, when she moved back to Orchid Island. There she and Ming-sho became best friends and shared everything.

• • •

Meanwhile Ming-sho continued her life on Orchid Island, the furthest corner of Taiwan. Orchid Island was full of tribal taboos, stigmas, poverty, insularity, but it was also wild and gorgeous, a place of simplicity, primitive and lazy, an emerald set amid a lapis sea, with a volcano at the center and a shore fringed with coral. Ming-sho found a traditional Tao house to live in, one of the last remaining, and made a new life for herself. She worked for a social service organization taking care of Tao elders who needed help getting food or medical attention. It was as far from Tainan as one could get and still remain in Taiwan, probably the perfect antipode to her home environment in helping stretch and reconceive her identity and trajectory.

Every few months Ming-sho had a holiday, or a work meeting back on the "mainland," and at such times she would come to stay with me for a day or three. Strands of our intimacy remained, as if we were unwilling or unable to let them go. We would reinhabit the closed circle of our relationship, returning to the shared patterns of cooking, swimming, sleeping, walking, and reading together with or without words.

Mull was even happier than I when she returned, I think, because she was the gentler arm of the oligarchy and allowed him to break all the rules set for him, such as not entering the house—a rule Yiming demanded I enforce, that a dog's place is outside. When we sat to eat dinner on the tatami mats in the living room, Mull nosed his head through the door, and slunk around to Ming-sho's side, arcing as far from me as possible, as if hoping I wouldn't notice him, and then plopped down with a sigh, resting his bewhiskered head upon her lap. Mull had grown up with only A-dong and her kittens for animal companions, and he thought he had learned to stalk from them. He would creep through the grass in the yard as if on a sly mission to pounce, not realizing his ass and wagging tail were sticking way up in the air behind him. He would try to steal thus into the illicit territory of the living room, but with Ming-sho there I couldn't say no to anything. I just laughed instead, which Mull took to be consent, and his right to enter became *fait accompli.*

And then I would drive Ming-sho down the mountain, to the Taidong train station if she was going home to visit her family in Tainan, or to the ferry pier if she was heading back to Orchid Island. We were even more wordless than usual on such drives, because nothing remained to talk about except her departure, our impending separation, the question of whether and when we would meet again, and we were so saturated with these things already that I could only frown and grip the wheel and ask too many times what time her boat or train left. After dropping her off and watching her recede, I would drive up the coast and flop into the sea, to let the waves wash over me. But eventually I would have nothing left to do except drive back up the mountain, home.

Every time Ming-sho left, I wandered in a daze for three days, from the studio to the living room to the kitchen, as if trying to locate myself within an emotional geography with which I was no longer familiar, the rooms and painted walls all resonating with both her presence and her absence. Mull looked at me despondently, as if wondering where Ming-sho had gone and why we couldn't go there, or at least go to the beach.

One day, returning home after driving her to the ferry dock, I became infuriated with the betel nut trees that grew behind the lower house and diminished my view. The whole fucking twenty acres had been left to go wild and would never be harvested again. What the hell did anyone need those trees for? Without a moment's thought, I took my Japanese hand saw, a curved blade about eighteen inches long with a round wooden handle, marched down through the overgrown elephant grass, and cut down a dozen of the trees. Pulpy and fibrous, the saw made short work of them despite their age. I sawed off the crowns and lopped off the fronds in order to remove the "hearts," which are like the palm hearts eaten in many tropical countries, but with a kick to them. They gave you heart palpitations as if you'd just chewed half a bag of the nut itself.

Later a friend of my landlady raised hell over this, and I had to pay compensation for the trees—but really the friend was just sore that she'd rented the place to me instead of letting him have it for free. Yiming said it was a travesty to have to pay her since the trees were completely valueless. But I had acted spontaneously, without permission. I knew all along I'd have to pay one way or another, and I didn't care. With the view opened up, a constraint on my residence was removed. Now, waking in the morning, drinking coffee and sitting on one of the broken chairs I'd picked up somewhere, I looked out to a greater vision of the sea, and to the alternating presence and absence of Orchid Island on the horizon.

SEVENTEEN

The Chief Is Dead

The Chief lay on a cane divan with a blanket up to his chin, his arms outside the covers and seeming to dangle, though they were laid flat next to his body. His wife sat next to him on a low stool. The Chief had been hale and strong a few months before, despite being seventy-two. Now, wasted by stomach cancer, his flesh was flayed away, his skeleton almost visible beneath the skin and rising fast. His arms, which had been like the mooring ropes of tanker ships, were thin as string, blotched with bruises and needle sores, the veins all jerky and broken.

His wife's body was enormous still, amorphous with bulk, but with an almost equal sense of wreckage. She was a sloughing mountain, decaying back to component parts, her face blurred with dissolution as if some essence were being erased from inside out.

"Fifty-five years, Rekal," she said. "In a few months we'd have been married fifty-five years."

The Chief lay unseeing, unhearing, his eyes fluttering upward in his head, his face so eroded that it was an act of faith to say, "Yes, this is the Chief." There'd been a bait-and-switch, this harrowed skull put in place of the man we knew. He was reduced to a rasp of pain, heaving with the strain to breathe. He shuddered and spasmed as bile drained into a plastic sack on the floor. The Chief and his wife were probably married before they ever heard a word of Mandarin Chinese, but in the corner of the living room a TV was tuned to a Taipei news show, the picture cut with diagonal bands of interference over a pert, pretty news anchor speaking perfect Mandarin.

I sat silently with the Chief and his wife for half an hour, then stepped outside. Rain pooled in the street from the night before. The sea was a swirl of grays, with low clouds blowing over. I drove home, put a beer in the freezer to cool, and sat out on the porch with my guitar. I could see already that my friends here—virile, bear-chested and half-wild, lifting whole logs to their shoulders, pouring wine past their teeth straight to their guts—would soon be frail, gray-haired, mystified to have grown so old. What dies with a village elder? The moon waxed and waned across the sky and raised up waves that splashed ten feet high against the stones of earth. Nothing sounded right on the guitar, as if my fingers and the wood and the steel strings were all disjunct. Through a break in the clouds the sky was vanilla blue, I wished I could reach my tongue up and taste it. The plum blossoms had fallen from the trees in the orchards that quilted the flank of Dulanshan, but new fruit had set on the branches, and flowers were growing up through the petals strewn across the ground, deep green stems and leaves preparing to bloom into gold and blue.

I remembered the beer and took it out of the freezer just in time. It had nearly frozen and exploded. I popped it open and drank half in a gulp. I put a recording of Ali Farka Touré guitar music on the stereo, but I wondered, *Where is Africa? Where am I?* There was no problem with drinking a beer at ten in the morning. The problem was where to go from there.

· · ·

I drove down to the Chief's house the next morning. Old women milled around the doorway in the early light. One crooked her index finger to me in a "come here" signal. But in Chinese this gesture indicates death. The Chief was dead.

"When?" I asked.

THE CHIEF IS DEAD

"Just now," she said. "Within half an hour."

The Chief's middle-aged sons and daughters, back from their homes in Taipei and Gaoxiong, were weeping loudly. The living room quickly filled with mourning bodies and sounds. But the Chief's grandchildren, in their late teens, were cool and composed, dressed up neat in city fashions, and spoke to me in English, asking my name and where I was from.

The Chief's wife had not apparently moved. She still sat by his bed, with red betel nut juice spittled on her lips as she rocked back and forth. I sat down next to her. The Chief's dead eyes were half-open to the ceiling or whatever lies beyond that. He didn't look to be at peace, but his face was no longer chewed with pain.

"Fifty-five years," she said. She took my hand and guided it to the top of the Chief's skull. She placed my hand on the crown of his dead hair and skin and rested her meaty hand atop mine. She released and leaned back, and I touched the Chief's hands where they were folded together on his chest, still almost warm, hard and smooth with calluses.

Tears welled from her eyes, shrunken and blurred with cataracts. "Fifty-five years next January," she said. "We'd already planned a celebration. Siki was going to kill a pig, but now he's gone . . . *Ayah*, Rekal, he couldn't wait. He was holding on for his brother to return, trying to see him one more time, but he couldn't wait, he couldn't stay long enough to say good-bye. It was the last thing in this world he tried to do . . . but he had to go."

Someone poured her a slug of Wisbih, the bubblegum-tasting truck driver hooch. She knocked it back, swayed slightly as if about to topple, but straightened and handed back the plastic cup.

"Give one to Rekal," she said.

"The same cup. Give me the same one," I said, as one of the Chief's daughters went to find a clean glass. "The same," I said, half-rising in the space where bereavement swirled in the void of the Chief's absence. No one had yet adjusted to the world as it had just become.

"They're embarrassed to give you a used cup," someone said. "It's because you're a guest."

A new plastic cup came and filled my hand. I dripped out three drops of Wisbih to the Chief. We were of different worlds. I had no words to offer, even if he could have heard. What could I say of this land, this time, of his life, and of the emptiness left by his passing? I wished to inhabit my life as solidly and completely as the Chief lived his, to quietly love a people and a place as integral aspects of my being, but I didn't know how to say that then. "I like your songs, Chief," I said. "I like your voice." I lifted the clean glass and drank down the dirty wine. Everything was inadequate, my words and bones all hollow.

The Chief's wife closed his eyelids one at a time. She pulled the quilt up over his face. People stood around in the asphalt courtyard and hunched near the doorway, looking past each other, smoking and talking in scattered voices. The Chief is dead. The bottle came back, but I stood up to go.

"One more, Rekal," the Chief's wife said. "Don't go so soon, have one more." I took the cup she held out to me. I tossed the Wisbih down in a swallow and stepped through the dim doorway, staggering slightly in the diffusion of light swelling gray and pearly through the clouds, and from the alcohol diffusing through my brain. A few raindrops spattered the asphalt and the shallow puddles in the street. I got in my car and drove up the coast, the sea like wrinkled iron, whitecapped to the horizon.

Some drink and work, some just drink, some just work. The sun beats in across the ocean, rising bright and gold above the blue lips of the sea. We pound against the days, pound them into something graspable when we can. Drunk at 10 a.m. There's nowhere left to go. We drink the bile down. It fills us; we are empty. You can go to the city to work. You can stay home, and there's nothing, less every day. This culture, language, way of being evolved for centuries across these cliffs and bluffs above the sea. Now a handful of threads where there once was tapestry. What dies with a tribal elder? Many things I will never know. The Chief is dead, long live the Chief, wherever he may be.

. . .

Squalls slid across the ocean. Rain slanted to the sea as a flock of pigeons cut through the air in tight turns, then dispersed. I stopped to buy a white envelope from Mrs. Chen to enclose my contribution to the funeral fund. In Taiwan each guest makes a cash donation at marriages and funerals. The envelopes are opened by a friend assigned to do the accounting, and the amount of each contribution is entered in a ledger. These donations comprise a floating slush fund that is funneled into the pocket of whoever is the victim of tragedy or celebration, to pay for expenses and provide a little extra. Everyone in a community pays into it and receives a lump sum when it's needed. This legiblized gift exchange had become part of the public ceremonies of the Amis, perhaps dovetailing with their traditional systems of community gift exchange.

"Who died?" Mrs. Chen asked. She had seen the funeral vehicle parked down the road, and a white envelope could only mean one thing (white is the color of death in Chinese symbology). But she was mystified—she hadn't heard of anybody passing away.

"The old Chief," I said, equally mystified. I couldn't imagine anyone in Dulan not knowing the Chief was dead.

"What are you doing? You don't have to give anything," she said. "You won't get married here, so you'll never get it back."

Systems of gift exchange are traditionally codified with an obligation to give, to receive, and to return. From Mrs. Chen's point of view, I was under no obligation to take the first step in this social and financial relationship, to *give*, because I would not necessarily be present to eventually *receive*. (I ignored this slight to my marriage prospects.) But from my perspective, I had already been given everything here. I had been welcomed, accepted as a resident of this place, invited to join feasts and dinners, allowed into song circles, and offered uncountable *mijiu* toasts. I could never repay these debts with any number of KMT-issued bills. My contribution to the Chief's funeral was not the inception of the gift exchange relationship, but rather the fulfillment of it. And by fulfilling it I was also reinitiating it, as this act of *giving* would be *received*, then answered by further *return*. The gift cycle perpetuates itself, each step in the process extending and deepening social relationships through material exchange.

I stuck a 1,000-NT bill in the envelope and headed over to the Chief's house. The wind blew in gusts, shuddering and snapping the tarps set up for the funeral service. A flatbed truck with a boxy trailer-like structure built on the back, covered with orange and yellow paper flowers, was parked out on the street. Despite the spitting rain, shards of blue sky shone far out to sea. I arrived five minutes early, but the service was already in full swing, an inversion of the usual relationship to punctuality here. A voice droned through a PA system as down the road in the village the metal clang of some machine rang out. I handed in my envelope and signed the register. The woman handling the donations offered me a betel nut from a basket set out for guests. I stood at the back of the crowd, the courtyard seats already filled with row after row of grease-parted hair and clearing throats. A one-armed chaplain stood by the casket, delivering a sermon on the pain and death of the valley of the shadow, the empty left cuff of his suit coat pinned to his heart. Cell phones went off in the crowd like stranded birds.

A heavy shower swept through without warning. Two men ran to string up another tarp and set out plastic stools for those of us at the back. I crowded in with all the other on-time latecomers. We squeezed in from the edges to avoid the runoff rain. We were far away, up an incline from the striped tarps covering the podium and the casket and the flowers. From

THE CHIEF IS DEAD

this distance, we were removed from the formal reckoning of grief, crammed into a small space with tension sweat and the hard seat of the plastic stools and our memories of the Chief. All we could do was bunch together away from the strings of rain running from the edges of the tarp and share cigarettes and wait for things to move along.

The rain passed, and someone started a roll call of the dignitaries present. When their names were called they stood up and bowed in all directions in their suits of undertaker gray. Suddenly my name was called—out of courtesy, I suppose. By the time I stood up they'd moved on to the next name on the list, though my neighbors gave me a polite round of applause.

The crowd struggled to its feet and began to shuffle past the casket, where the family lined up, ritually weeping, to receive and greet the guests. Even the Chief's great-grandchildren, four or five years old, were in the handshake line, genuinely sobbing, terrified by the tears and anguish around them, holding out their hands like flags of surrender, no comprehension of death except that because of it they had to shake too many strangers' hands. Their right arms became too tired to extend, so they propped them limply with their left hands as the line of mourners continued past them.

In his final resting bed the Chief looked like his face had been whittled out of bone, but cut down too far, like the carver had nothing to do after finishing so just kept going. "Where are our friends, Rekal? Everyone is gone," the Chief's wife wailed to me, though she was surrounded by her friends and family. She looked disheveled as a falling mountain, skin sagging from her bones. The chaplain stood at the head of the casket as the guests filed past, his empty sleeve hanging from his breast, looking somewhere beyond the crowd with a serene smile on his lips. Everybody shook hands with everyone. No one knew what was happening, but there was a sense of finality in the air that made individual striving and complaint seem small. Still, belt buckles were shined up bright, and hair that had not known a comb's attention in months was neatly parted. The single women had dressed up nice for everyone's benefit; it would have been almost disrespectful not to. Xiao Hua, a sexy Amis divorcée and friend of Ming-ling's, had cut her bangs and wore a new pair of calf-length leather boots. I walked around feeling volitionless as a beast of burden and found myself facing Siki. A few nights before, we had nearly come to blows over the unspoken question of whether Ming-ling was or was not single, but now we shook hands in grim reconciliation, didn't pump up and down, just grabbed hard and held, both of us looking elsewhere. The old men of the Chief's generation wandered through the crowd, dry-eyed and preoccupied.

· · ·

The casket bearers loaded the Chief into the paper-flowered funeral truck. A few raindrops fell. A six-piece brass band in baby blue sailor uniforms looked dubiously to the sky from beneath their battered captain's hats and launched into "Onward Christian Soldiers," a bass drum thumping out the beat. The engine idled as the mourners gathered in the rising smell of wet earth. Then the procession pulled forward, the hearse-truck in front, followed by the band, and then the rest of us, trailing a susurrus of plastic raincoats. We walked along the main road, through the village, then turned down a two-track lane toward the ocean, to a graveyard on a rise just north of Dulanbi, a few hundred yards from the shore.

A funeral director had been hired to conduct the burial. He puffed a cigarette and guided the truck to back in as the crowd circled the open grave. The band stood to one side and played on as Siki and the other pallbearers hefted the coffin to their shoulders and staggered toward the hole.

"Turn it around, goddammit," the funeral director yelled at them. "Get the goddamn head around this way. Okay, now back it in. Jesus Christ, what are you afraid of?"

They stumbled over the mound of loose wet earth, tripping and sliding and almost falling into the grave, and lowered the casket down with ropes, nobody knowing what to do except the director, who wasn't helping. "Swing the rope over this way," he said, as a murmur of grief from the crowd grew louder, the Chief about to return to the earth forever. "Come on, you want to bury the sonabitch rope? Give it a jerk, no, jerk it *hard*!"

The pallbearers were disoriented, even Siki was confused, but finally the box rested on the floor of the grave, and the ropes had been recovered. A styrofoam cross was laid atop the mound of earth at the head of the grave, and the chaplain said a prayer that was like a damp wreath to drape over the occasion. As he spoke the director scrambled down and bored a hole in the foot of the coffin with an auger, and another in the head of it. Everyone tried to look away from this too-visceral reminder of the decomposition the Chief's body was about to undergo.

Family and friends stood on the overgrown grass of neighboring graves and strew flowers on the casket where it rested in the earth, and a steady rain began to fall. A man in a worn T-shirt with a cap pulled low over his eyes jumped forward and grabbed a spade and heaved a shovelful of earth down onto the casket and the flowers, *thump*. Others took up the two or three remaining shovels and worked furiously at filling the hole. All these men who had spent their lives in manual labor now channeled their strength into burying the Chief, seeming to work with anger, as if avenging a personal affront. Perhaps their work and strength were the last gift they had to offer to the Chief. Each man worked a few minutes then stepped back to let another take his place. A bottle of *mijiu* made its way through the crowd. The Chief's old man friends swigged from it and rubbed the whiskers on their chins. Kala-OK elbowed me and offered me the bottle with a wink, I took a drink and passed it on.

I wanted to step in and take a shovel. I wanted to touch the earth that would entomb the Chief, but I felt like an outsider, as if to intermix would break the contiguity of tribe. I stood at the front of the crowd and stared at the movement of the tools in the men's hands. A middle-aged man I'd met at the first dinner at the Chief's house saw my face and asked, "You want to help?" I nodded "Yes." He spoke to one of the men and took his shovel, gave it to me, and I stepped into the mound of soil with the smooth, cracked handle in my hands. The effort ran up my arms and shoulders and back, the burial of the Chief now in my muscles and blood and bones.

The earth mounded up above the lips of the grave, and that was the end. The chaplain said a few more words, which were lost in the shuffled dispersion of the crowd, and the band kicked in again. Their horns were bent and dented, patinaed with oxidation, but the baritone sax swung like he was in a Mardi Gras parade. The song sounded familiar, but they were into the third chorus before I recognized "I Ain't Got No Home in This World" from an old Woody Guthrie recording. Originally a Gospel song about having no true home on earth, but only in Heaven, Woody rewrote the lyrics to talk about the dispossession of dust bowl farmers who had no home in this world because a bank had taken it away. The band led the procession back up the road to the Chief's house, playing that song all the way, and I sang Woody Guthrie's words to myself:

> I ain't got no home, I'm just a-roamin' round,
> just a wandrin' worker, I go from town to town,
> the police make it hard wherever I may go,
> and I ain't got no home in this world anymore.

Tables were laid with slabs of cold pork under the tarps outside the Chief's house. The old men sat in circles wearing their stained shirts, polyester trousers, and truck tire sandals. They hollered me over to sit down and eat, but I waved and hollered back and continued walking south through Dulan. In an empty lot a vine of pink flowers twisted and bloomed through a pile of dead branches. A line of tour buses high-balled through the village without slowing, driving up the coast. Faces pressed to the bus windows to take in the mountains and ocean through rain-streaked glass. I turned off the main street. Betel nut trees swayed in the wind where they grew in dooryards. The back streets of Dulan were empty except for a few motorbikes navigating through the rain, the drivers steering with one hand and holding umbrellas with the other. Opposite the *tangchang* I crossed back over the highway and continued walking down the dirt road to Dulanbi, the rocky elbow of earth that extends into the sea.

Waves rolled in gray and green along the shore. Sheets of rain like falling sails slid in along the coast. But further out the sun shone through a breach in the clouds, and the sea was turquoise and ultramarine, cobalt and indigo, like a field of violets and irises churning. The heart of the sea was rippled and azure, the blue of sky reflected in the undulations of the sea.

EIGHTEEN

An Apartment in Town

I drove south along the coast from Dulan, past the gravel-crushing plant painted backhoe yellow, then crossed the long, four-lane bridge over the Beinan River, which thrashed and roiled ash-gray, with rounded marble stones along its bank. Across the river Taidong City rose against the sky, with billboard advertisements for wedding services covering the facades of ten-floor apartment buildings. White-veiled brides reclined with bare limbs splayed in all directions, and a tuxedoed groom drove a black Mercedes through a rain of confetti and streamers. In town, cars moved like herded beasts through chutes of concrete and metal. I navigated through the grid to the address B-*shifu* had given me. I parked in an alley, stepped out into a smell of fruit rinds and wet paint, and walked up a stairwell to the fourth floor.

E-ki lay on a couch beneath a flowered quilt. It had been half a year since he'd told me he had cancer, when we sat on the platform of his half-built shelter looking out into the sea. Plastic tubes stuck out his nose, connected to a steel cylinder. His mouth was half-open, like a fish trying to breathe air, except that it was backward, his lungs were filled with liquid that sloshed as he tried to inhale.

"Scott, come in, welcome, sit down . . ." E-ki half-rose, indicating a chair. His elbows were knobby, loose skin hung from his arms and neck.

"I brought some juice," I said. "Do you want some?"

"No, I have plenty here, keep it for yourself. See there, on the table, there's plenty of fruit. In the old days everyone brought me whiskey. What the hell's gone wrong?"

A TV stood against one wall, and a wooden crucifix hung on another, a bearded Jesus, varnished and factory-sculpted, strung up mournful as ever with his hands and feet bound to his cross. Bright prints of landscape paintings were hung amid expanses of bare white wall. Sunlight sifted through lace curtains and the metal mesh of a sliding door. Chinese books lined the shelves of a maple laminate bookcase, plates and bowls were stacked behind the glass of a china cabinet. Concrete apartment, concrete box, slack skin and obtrusion of bone. E-ki wore a red bandana on his head like a member of a motorcycle gang, tufts of gray hair stuck out like wings. Beard stubble speckled his chin and jaw. A night light glowed in a socket, pastel orange like the night sky above Taipei. The refrigerator hummed from the kitchen. Greenish fluid drained through a plastic tube that emerged from beneath E-ki's quilt, air bubbles pushing through recalcitrantly.

"How are you?" I asked E-ki.

"Fine, I'm fine, fine. I have to piss into this plastic bucket. I watch TV. My wife is here at night, after she closes her restaurant. She has a dumpling stand out at the edge of town, you know, and stays open late. For truckers and kids."

"I brought my guitar. Want me to empty that bucket for you?"

"No, it's okay . . . Yeah, I see, that's the one with the cedar top. I remember it. That's a beauty. I wish I could play it. How is everyone anyway? I haven't seen anyone for a while."

"They're all busy, working up north on a county project. Still collecting logs that washed up from the last typhoon. How's your treatment going? Hurt?"

"No, no, doesn't hurt. Doesn't hurt. I stopped going—too hard—to get to the hospital in Hualian. And the one here is no good. They can't do anything for me. Now I stay home. My workshop—we lost it, did you hear? The owner wants to sell the place . . . he tore down all the buildings, we slaughtered the pigs. My brother couldn't . . . take care of things on his own."

"I know, I saw. The lot's empty. Trucks carted away the rubble. Where is your sculpture now?"

"Siki . . . Siki helped me move it. He put it in his warehouse. He took care of it. The government wants to do a big exhibit of my work . . . after all these years . . . Siki will organize it."

E-ki's breath became short and quick.

"What's wrong?"

"Nothing, just can't talk too much."

"Want me to play something for you?"

"Ho, yes, yes . . . that'll be good. What you going to play?"

"Maybe I'll try 'Purification,' an instrumental song. It's about trying to strip off old skin, strip down to the bone. I wrote it when I was moving here from Taipei. You remember, when we met down on the beach at Jinzun. You'll hear a little Amis melody in there too."

I put my fingers to the strings, steel vibrations were amplified through the thin-planed wood braced and epoxied into a body. The song is based on harmonics, a technique in which instead of pressing a string down onto the fret board, you touch it lightly at specific nodes. This creates a standing wave, a double- or triple-resonance that sustains between the nut and saddle, the slivers of bone carved to suspend the strings.

"Ho," said E-ki when I finished. "Well, that's good. I like that. You got everything in there, the sea, the mountains, our songs. I could hear it all. Let me see your fingers—"

He took my hand, touching the calluses on my fingertips. His hands were cool, veins stood out blue on the backs of them, the skin pale, as if diluted with milk, but his palms were like sandpaper still. E-ki closed his eyes, seeming to slip into a dream. "Purification . . . crawl up on the shore . . . crawl back to the sea," he said, then opened his eyes and looked at me. "Can you help me? Can you empty this?"

"Of course."

"I like that bit of Amis melody in that song."

"Yeah, that's in there . . . you know, all those hours around the fire."

"Good . . . that's good . . . there are so many wounds . . . in what we were . . . as a people."

He let go of my hand, and I picked up the beige pissbucket. The bathroom smelled of perfumed soap. Dried flowers stood in a glass vase on the toilet tank. I emptied the bucket and looked in the mirror. Gray had infiltrated my three-day beard, seeping into me day by day. Sediment of years, a stain of age. I took the empty bucket back to the living room.

"Thank you."

"Them're fighting words," I said.

"Huh, now you sound like Dou-dou . . . but it hurts too much, don't make me laugh. Did you finish recording your album?"

"Yeah, it's done. They even paid me."

"It's going to be a big seller, I bet. You got a copy with you?"

"They haven't sent my copies to me yet, but I'll bring you one next time I come."

"Yes, as soon as you can. How's it going up at your place these days?"

"I made a new knife, but the blade is all nicked and dented. When I cut through the brush I always hit rocks."

"You can grind that out."

"Yeah, but I need a harder blade. These iron ones dent too easily."

"No, it's not the blade. You don't know how to use it. It's not a gun. You're not in a movie. You can't shoot your way through. I've been in these mountains all my life, and I never dented a blade. Well, maybe once or twice, but not like you.

You're hell on a blade. How come I can hunt wild boars with the same knife for twenty years but after a couple of months of cutting grass you've ruined yours? When I'm better I'll show you, you have to learn. You can't use your American brain in these Amis hills. You think you're going to teach the mountain something with your knife? How old is the land? You have to listen to it, learn from it. You know, it's the same way with women. If you try to force them to do anything, you're kidding yourself. Torturing yourself, in the case of women."

Blurred spots of sun slanted across the floor. The room sagged with heat and stillness. E-ki turned his face away and coughed. The air punched through him like a barbed fist. He seemed to have aged in the half hour I'd been sitting at his side. He spat into a handkerchief and said, "It's a gift, your mind, your body . . . it's all a gift. You have to give it all back in the end . . ."

E-ki glanced past me to the paintings and the crucifix on the wall, then turned his head to the screen door and the light that filtered in. "I have to rest now. I have to sleep. But before you go, give me a hand. Help me turn toward the door there, toward the sun. Put that bucket down here next to me. Come again when you can, and bring your guitar. Next time I'll play one for you . . ."

• • •

I walked down the stairs and drove away. At the edge of town a thin rain began to fall across a teal sea. As I crossed the river I saw an undulating V of migrating birds wedging north along the coast. I turned off the highway before Dulan and drove the back roads through plum and mango orchards, past large boulders that had risen from the ocean floor and tumbled down from Dulanshan, now surrounded by meadows luminous with rain. I cut the engine next to a mound of raw earth heaped into a trapezoid, with a massive backhoe parked atop it. The machine listed seaward on its muddy treads, the long shovel arm stretched out and resting in the soil. Rain beaded on its yellow hull and ran off like pearls, the rod of its hydraulic arm was mercury-bright. Three gravel trucks sat in an empty lot fringed with sprays of golden grasses. A freshwater crab scuttled across the road as rain tap-danced on the roof of the car.

Back home, I pulled on my rubber boots and grabbed a bamboo flute from my studio and walked down the road to where a bridge formed a square concrete tunnel over a stream. I walked down the embankment, stood in the middle of the current, and wove long notes into the hush of the rain, the water swirling and gurgling around my feet. The fragile, hollow-sounding flute notes sustained and piled upon each other, layers of resonance accumulating in the long echo of the tunnel. The stream was full of green stones with bands of white quartz running through. I chose three of these to take to E-ki next time I visited. I put the wet stones in my pocket, tucked the flute under my arm, then walked back up the road as the sea fell across the mountain as rain.

· · ·

A week later I pulled into the sugar factory at dusk and parked next to the café. Mull jumped out the car window and was intercepted by his best dog-friend, Monk. They crashed into each other and sprinted across the lot in a jumble of jaws and limbs. The air was thick with moisture, salty sea air rolling in and mixing with cool jungle air flowing down the mountain.

When I stepped inside, Xiao Zhu set a beer out for me before I could even say hello. Bottles and ashtrays crowded the chainsawed-log bar. My Open Circle friends were huddled together in conversation, words rose like bubbles from the bottom of a glass. Mosquito coils trailed smoke up to where seaweed lamp covers encircled bulbs hung from the ceiling. The evening was heavy and sweet, as if the sunset sky were an overturned flower, sifting pollen down upon our words, our glasses, our senescence, all the desires and aspirations in our hearts.

"What's going on here?" I asked.

"They're going forward with the beach resort on Dulanbi," Ai-qin said.

"Sure, they want to pave the whole coast. That's nothing new."

"But it'll destroy the ecosystem along the coast here," Zhiming said. "Plus Dulanbi is sacred to the Dulan Amis. It's where the ancestors are buried."

"Good for tourism, man."

"They're breaking ground for the hotel development up on the mountain too."

"It's like this," Ha-na said. "They develop the mountains, develop the coast, develop till there's nothing left but a road between developments. Where are we supposed to live? My place on the way out of the village is nothing but dust and noise anymore, with the trucks driving up and down all night long."

"You know, they don't even let us hunt the land, our own land. Who gave it to the Han tribe to tell us what to do?"

"It was like this, our ancestors had to choose, and they choose to live, so that we could live. They had to quit the fight for the land. The tribes that didn't, well, we got no brothers and sisters from those tribes no more."

"They say we can't hunt 'cause we need to protect the environment. Fuck man, it's only aboriginals who understand 'ecology.' How do they think we lived here thousands of years? For civilization it's just another word, just another law to enforce. The 'Republic of China' has only been here fifty years and look what they've done already. There's hardly anything left to fuck up."

"I can't see what civilization has done except wreck the earth. Hell, the Han tribe can't even sing and dance."

"We must be stupid. Everyone counts money better than us."

"I'll stay stupid. Once you learn to count money you're not good for anything else."

"Yeah, but then they calculate your land right out from

under you. You know, I can't even keep dogs any more. Where I live on the side of the highway, I've got no space for them," said Ha-na, who loved Dalmatians. "I had three run over last year and finally gave up."

"The developers want to pave us over, the anthropologists want to bury us in a museum."

"Either way it's good for someone's dime, just not ours."

"What can we do to stop that beach resort?"

"We'd have to fight the mob, plus the developers in Taipei who don't know or care whose home is being ruined, plus the government officials who don't want to give up their kickbacks."

"Scott, what's it like in America?" Zhiming asked me.

"Different postage stamps, different TV."

"Yeah, but in America you have an environmental movement, social ideals, and there's not so much government corruption, right? What do you do in these situations?"

"Well, I used to tree-sit in the old-growth redwood groves, the virgin forest. We climbed up and lived at the top of the ancient trees so they couldn't cut them down. One girl lived at the top of a thousand-year-old redwood for two years without coming down."

"That's what I'm talking about! So you saved the forest?"

"No, in the end they cut them down anyway. Except for a few the government paid a fortune to the lumber companies to preserve."

A-sun came in, followed by Ming-ling and her daughters, four and five years old. Ming-ling was sobbing. Xiao Zhu mixed her a vodka tonic and topped it up with liquor till it was convex above the rim.

"Ming-ling, what happened?" Ai-qin asked.

"We've just come from E-ki's," A-sun said. "We went to see him at his wife's apartment in town."

"What's wrong, is he bad?"

"See him while you can. He'll soon be gone. Soon he'll be no more," A-sun said. He tore the plastic seal off a pack of slim menthol cigarettes and lit one up. "Not bad," he said, looking at the cigarette, "not bad at all."

"A-sun, those are women's cigarettes."

"Who can say for sure?"

"How can you say that about E-ki?"

"What I say or don't say won't change the facts. He's dying."

Ming-ling had not stopped weeping. She sat at the bar with one hand on her drink, the other covering her face. Dou-dou and Ai-qin leaned in and put their arms around her.

"God, how could this happen to E-ki? He's still young," Dou-dou said.

"He worked too many years in his shop, enclosed in spaces filled with dust and fumes and wood smoke," Ai-qin said.

"Is it cancer?"

"No, it couldn't be cancer."

"What can we do?"

"Just see him while you can," A-sun said. "He's alone all day in his wife's place in town. Go see him while you can."

Ming-ling took a sip of her drink. By the doorway her daughters played with a puppy and sang a song.

"Who wants another round?"

Light drained from the sky. Bubbles rested in the last half-inch of liquid in a glass. Lipstick the color of sunset stained the filter of a cigarette. Tobacco smoke swirled with smoke from the mosquito coil and rose to the ceiling, illuminated by the seaweed lamps. Ashtrays overflowed and spilled onto the floor.

NINETEEN

Homecomings

Biung, the Bunun folksinger I had known in Taipei, was headlining a government-sponsored fish festival in Taidong. I hadn't seen him in the year and a half since I'd moved here, so I drove down to a cement-tiled plaza at the center of town, where a crowd was gathered before a stage. Electronic music blared and neon lights lit up a sashimi-eating contest, where skinny men with fat ties wolfed down raw fish, embarrassing their wives and delighting their children.

There was no sign of Biung, but I saw a member of his band sitting on a concrete retaining wall drinking a beer. He wore a rugby shirt and was about as wide as a steer. When I walked over and said hello, he offered me a betel nut and spat some red juice into the soil of a potted palm.

"Hey, what's going on?" I asked him.

"Just playing the bongos with Biung. What about you?"

"I just came to say hi to Biung. I haven't seen him since I left Taipei."

"Hold on a sec, I'll call him and see when he's coming."

He dialed Biung up on his phone, then held it out to me. Biung sounded harried and distracted, as if he were in the middle of a frenzied auction for his soul. "My friend, my friend," he said, "yes yes yes."

Biung is from Hong-ye, a village half an hour north of Tai-dong City in the rift valley, near the Bunun Culture Village, and his albums were ubiquitous in Taidong County. Dance groups from all the tribes practiced and performed to his songs, despite the fact that a hundred years ago Bunun and Amis had headhunted each other. All the adolescent aboriginal boys could play his songs on the guitar, and when they talked about him they would shake their heads and grin and say words like *idol* and *star*.

Biung had showed up in Taipei a few years before as a skinny kid trying to get attention with a new CD, and started playing in underground pubs. He and I played consecutively at a music festival in 2000, and he did the longest sound-check I've ever seen, testing and retesting the levels of his guitar and four back-up vocalists, the whole group decked out in brightly embroidered Bunun tunics and headbands. Biung had a jittery enthusiasm that turned some people off in conversation, but on stage that keyed-up energy came across as passion and made him seem to reach out to bring the audience into his songs. His first, self-released album did respectably well, his shows grew more popular, and by the time his second album came out he had a following, though his band still called around to borrow guitars every time they had a gig. The second album was produced with studio players and some computer-programmed music but listed only halfway into mainstream pop. When it won a Golden Melody Award, his career trajectory was sealed. Biung was now signed with a major label, had a new album about to be released, and had even parlayed his popularity into a job hosting a TV show.

. . .

I sat down on a plastic stool at the back of the crowd. The local entertainment arranged for the festival was a broken-down variety show. A troupe of old matrons in bumblebee corsets danced the fandango. Little girls with microphone headsets recited government-sanctioned speeches. A faded Liberace in a checkered beret and fuzzy pink stole crooned Spanish madrigals and pranced around the stage. Someone played a song on a kazoo. The MC made tired jokes about farting and his own corpulence. The jokes tried to limp away unnoticed, but the crowd ran them down and beat them to a bloody pulp with their distracted laughter.

I was almost ready to give up and head home when the MC announced the "Song King" was ready to play. The crowd erupted, and Biung walked out with his guitar. He was followed by the percussionist and the lead guitarist from his band in Taipei. Biung walked slowly, hunched over a little, like his spine was tired, but he still managed a bit of a strut, wearing a knit cap and plain t-shirt, the fashion disregard that only stars and bums can afford. "You're too far away," he cooed to the crowd, his hips quivering. All the girls ran to press themselves against the stage.

I once asked E-ki if it was hard to come home again after he'd worked in Taipei. "What's hard about it," he said, looking to the sea. "This will always be home. That can never change. I was born here and I know I'll die here. Who cares where you wander in between."

Biung hunch-strutted to the center of the stage and plugged in his guitar. "Here's a new song from my next album," he said. "What's the matter, you all didn't bring your hands? Put 'em together for me so I feel like I've come home, will you?"

The crowd didn't clap, but screamed. A scratchy beat started up from some canned music Biung had brought, a music bed without the vocals—karaoke, essentially. Biung strummed his acoustic guitar over the beat, and his guitarist came slashing in with an electric guitar. I remembered this sidekick as a shy, bashful kid, but now he had a mop of pink hair and grinned with the cultivated aloofness of a guitar hero. The percussionist banged away, an oasis of physicality amid the prerecorded and electrified sounds. He was like a walrus thwacking at the hull of a ship with wooden flippers. The sound system was terrible, a churning mud from which Biung's voice struggled to emerge. But Biung shook and cooed like his body was a love letter, personally delivering it to the crowd. He raised his arms above his head to lead the crowd in clapping to the beat. He played a couple of songs from his second album and invited members of the audience up on the stage to sing. They knew all the words, and the crowd began to dance. "I got a new TV show and a new album coming out," he said. "Come on, babies, give it up a little for a neighbor. You all know it's not easy for a local boy to make good up in ol' Taipei town. Give it up a little, where are your hands?"

The songs he played from the upcoming album sounded like hip-hop, with acoustic guitar as an afterthought, a long way from the earnest innocence of his first CD with its heavy tribal chants. The new songs with their prerecorded beats were pop music—music of a marketing plan, not music derived from place or tribe, as I heard Biung describe his first album on a radio interview.

But he twitched and shivered, and stood tall at the center of the stage, though he still seemed to stoop a bit. He sang to the people, as if he didn't have anything better to do with his heart than give it to them, and the sound mix got better as the show went on, the voice emerging surer and clearer song by song.

Someone in the audience shouted for an old song, one from his first album, and then everyone else joined in the request. Biung stepped back and looked lost for a moment, looking down at his feet. He scratched his head and said, "I don't know . . . I haven't played that song in a long, long time. I don't know if I can remember it. You may have to help me."

He stepped back from the mic a moment, then began to slowly strum his guitar. He sang the song with no karaoke bed and no electric guitar. It was a delicate ballad that hung like gauze in the night air above us, and the crowd helped, singing along, buoying, and then at the front of the stage they began the traditional Amis dance, hands linked, dancing in a line that spirals into a circle. They danced right up onto the stage, slowly stepping to the rhythm of the song, wreathing Biung in bodies until he was lost among the revolving ring of fans, barely visible with his guitar, cut off from his pink-haired guitarist, only the percussion player ensconced and grinning there next to him. Despite all the marketing and city slickness appended to him, Biung was alone within the swirl of bodies, a Bunun singer wreathed in Amis dance, tribal distinctions dissolved into a deeper indigenousness, in which he belonged only to this place and community. As with all my aboriginal friends here, it didn't matter where Biung wandered. Like E-ki or Yiming and many others, he had had to leave but he would always return, he was always coming home.

· · ·

In Amis legend the people of the world were originally one but were dispersed into the sea by a flood. When they washed back ashore, they were separated into different tribes, some settling in mountains, some on the coast, resulting in different languages, customs, and faces, all arising from a common origin.

A few days after Biung's fish festival gig, I drove into town again to see a theater performance organized and directed by A-dao. The group, called Mo'k'da'ai, spoke in Amis, sang traditional songs, and enacted tribal myths. The performance was called "The Great Flood" and included an angry sea god, marriage between a god and a mortal woman, the burial and reexhumation of a daughter, and of course the inundation of the earth.

When I first met A-dao I took him to be a gregarious and useless drunkard, a perception he did nothing to dispel. He looked like an abo-hippie, with tangled ropes of gray hair and an old discolored cloth tied around his head like a turban. His face was pocked and creased, and a shaggy Pancho Villa moustache hung from his lip like a gut-shot apology. Everything about him had the look of sea wrack, washed ashore, salvaged, accepted and assumed without circumspection—his clothes, hair, skin, and smile all salted and wrinkled and worn.

A-dao shared whatever he had with whoever was around him, and usually this was a bottle. I thought he spoke in platitudes, but as time went on I realized his words contained emotion that was original and real. Which is more platitudinous, gut emotion expressed with clichés, or shallow emotion with ingenious phrasing? A-dao assumed the best of everyone and spoke to children, friends, dogs, and government officials with equal humility and respect. He would have offered a cigarette and a shot of *mijiu* to anyone who showed up at his doorstep, whether it was the Queen of England or a betel nut girl.

I began to realize I'd misjudged A-dao one day when he was preparing for a three-day theater workshop he'd organized on the beach at Jinzun. "Our Amis culture has all forms of artistic expression," he told me. "We have songs, stories, dance, even painting and sculpture. But we have no drama. This is what I am trying to do—bring theater to the tribe, to tell the stories to the young people in a different way. They're the ones we have to reach."

It was midsummer then. The sun swung down from the sky like a cudgel, and on the beach it was even hotter as the heat radiated up from the sand. It was so hot that any moment you were in the sun you could only think of how to get out of it, get into the shade. But A-dao was building the stage for his workshop, digging post holes in the sand three feet deep and a foot wide, wearing his usual stained sweatpants and long-sleeved shirt. His skin was awash with sweat, but he worked with the same beatific smile with which he drank and sang. He paused and lit a cigarette, first offering one to me. But I couldn't stand that skillet heat and couldn't imagine breathing hot smoke into my lungs. He laid his cigarette down carefully on the sand and continued digging.

One evening when I stopped by his house to say hello, A-dao sat cross-legged on the floor writing at a low table, rectangular reading glasses balanced on the tip of his nose, looking like a cross between a professor and a guru. "Ah, come in, come in, sit down," he said, continuing to write. "I'm working on a grant proposal."

"I don't want to interrupt."

"No, you're not interrupting, you're always welcome. I'm trying to get government funding for a youth theater festival. You know, we still need to pay the rent while we work on our art."

He continued writing, making me feel both welcomed and ignored. I think the whole village could have crowded into A-dao's room, and he would have continued pensively working while reverie thronged around him.

When I left that night I said, "A-dao, I have to go. Do you want a beer?"

He looked up and squinted at me like a drink of alcohol was the novelist idea he'd ever heard. He took the can I pulled out of my shoulder bag, set it on the corner of the table and went back to writing as a smile cracked through his face, and he whispered, "You know my hearrrt . . ."

• • •

The theater group was made up of Siki, Xiao Hua, and a few other Dulan Amis. They had only begun rehearsing two days before and didn't have any other scheduled dates. Still, they succeeded in expressing a resonance between the movements and cycles of daily life (weaving, carrying water, harvesting millet) and archetypal stories that recur across the globe.

At the time I assumed this flood narrative was derived from the Bible, but I later learned that Austronesian-speaking peoples, whose migrations predate the Bible by millennia, have the greatest incidence of flood myths of any language group in the world. Many stories I had always thought of as "Western" in fact belong to a global mythological consciousness. A version of the "Icarus" myth, so iconically Greek, was recorded by Pierre Clastres among Guayaki Indians in the Panama jungle in the early 1960s. In *A Pattern of Islands*, Arthur Grimble writes of hearing a local legend "astonishingly like the tale of man's fall in Eden" from "unchristianized" Gilbert Islanders in Micronesia in the early twentieth century.

The Chinese translation of the Amis dialogue was projected to the right of the stage, and my seat was on the far left. Fearing a neck injury, I ignored the words and just watched. Free tickets had been distributed to the Dulan elders, and a soft echo of the songs rose up around me as they sang along, but quietly, as if not wanting to disturb the performance but unable to refrain from joining in.

I laughed out loud at one point, realizing I was watching my friends do on stage the same things they did in real life. A-dao had fallen down drunk, and Xiao Hua was smiling with a look of emptiness or bliss on her face. Siki, crawling along the floor, raised his eyes to the audience, and said, "If you got no wine, you got no friends," Kala-OK's famous dictum. A hen-like chuckle fluttered through the crowd.

A-dao had a hemp rag as big as a beach towel wrapped around his head. Siki strode the stage shirtless, as the sea god, his enormous muscles swelling and glistening beneath the lights, his face square and slanted, framed beneath a bandana. A disco tune suddenly blasted over the PA, and Xiao Hua, as the sea god's stolen bride, stripped down to a strapless top and a flimsy skirt and began to bump and grind to the beat. I guess this was the part that was meant to engage the Amis youth.

The last act was a postdiaspora gathering, a reunification of tribes. The performers knelt and sang a song around a fire; then they stood up, linked arms, and danced in a spiral, a high-stepping, swaying dance with a rhythm like ocean waves. They turned and asked the audience to join them. A-dao invited the new Chief up onto the stage—he was bespeckled, shorter and slighter than the old Chief but with dignity befitting his position—then the rest of the elders, the old men with stubbly chins, wearing collared shirts buttoned over their work

T-shirts, the women in embroidered tunics. Children wandered around amid the adults, half mimicking the songs, half making up their own. Xiao Hua walked to the edge of the stage and called out, "Anyone who wants to dance with us, come on up!" She smiled and reached out to me. I took her hand, as we all stood up to join the circle.

TWENTY

A Long Swim

I walked down to the lower house, where A-cai's wife Xiao Hua was burning the last of A-cai's things. (She was ethnic Taiwanese, from the west of Taiwan, not Ming-ling's Dulan Amis friend with the same name.) Farmer Huang putted up the hill on his old motorcycle, swung off, kicked out the kickstand, and stood next to me chewing a stem of grass.

"Bound to happen," he said. "Everyone who ever lived in this house either died or went crazy. Hard to say which the lucky ones are. Those sarcophagi buried beneath the foundation, what did I tell you? The place is cursed. Years ago, before Tang and his wife moved down from the north, they let a nephew of theirs come stay here. He had a test to study for. His family wanted him to be a dentist or lawyer, something like that. About six months he stayed here, all alone. Reading his books, I guess. Nothing else for him to do. Then one night, no warning, he took off down the hill. You know that place below mine a ways, there's a sort of greenhouse reinforced with metal bars, right? It's empty now, but that's where old Zhang grew his orchids. Fifteen years ago, you know, there was an orchid craze in Japan . . . they were selling those things for tens of thousands of NT, sometimes hundreds of thousands. Zhang had a fortune there in that metal cage. Back then, lots of farmers became rich overnight. You wouldn't believe it, one day riding a crappy motorbike like this one, next day driving the biggest Benz they had in the showroom and dressed in a silk shirt from Hong Kong. Still wearing plastic sandals and with dirt in their toenails, of course. Some things never change. So the kid walked down the hill and somehow got into the cage with Zhang's orchids, the dogs barking like mad, but Zhang was out that night, and by the time he got back, dogs still howling like all the souls in hell, the kid had destroyed every last one of those orchids, chopped 'em up with a machete, and he was just sitting there in the middle of the mayhem talking to himself. They took him away, kept him in the nuthouse for years. Poor boy never did take that test of his."

Huang shook his head and gave a sad grin, revealing his silver teeth, ruing either the boy's insanity or the lost fortune, then remounted his bike and coasted down the hill. Xiao Hua looked up at me, shrugged, and tapped a cigarette from a pack. She prodded at the fire with a stick. The air filled with an acrid reek of burning polyester and mold. A-cai's old clothes and wigs, coconuts carved into heads, papier-mâché masks, water-stained magazines, and other items of a lifetime's accumulation were all going up in smoke.

. . .

A-cai was a cult movie star among his friends, though maybe we all can claim such fame. He had lived down in Dulan village for a few years and had recently worked out a deal with my landlady to rent the lower house, with the provision that she could stay there when she came down from Taipei. Down in the *tangchang*, A-cai used to tell me about experimental performances he'd conceived with horses, elephants, jugglers, fire dancers, trapeze artists, electric guitars, and Taiwanese opera. A-cai was afraid of the ocean, but his last swim was straight out to the horizon.

During the few months he lived in the lower house, A-cai occasionally wandered up the drive and stood in my yard looking bewildered and adrift, shirtless in the sledgehammer sun, wearing a pair of shorts six sizes too big that hung below his knees, his glasses resting bulkily on his face because of electrician's tape wrapped around the joints to hold them together.

"How's it going?" I'd say, when I emerged from my studio to greet him.

"Fine. Yeah, fine. How's it going with you?"

"Fine, fine. Want some coffee? I got some good stuff here. Real beans. Italian roast."

"No thanks."

"A beer?"

"Nah."

We'd regard each other for a minute, our minds clearly in separate orbits, then he'd turn and shuffle back down to the square house, scuffing his plastic sandals on the drive, his shorts pulled up above his navel but the hems still hanging halfway down his calves.

I was engrossed with recording the ocean music and simply didn't know how to talk about myself or what I was doing, or how to relate to others at all. My focus was fiercely inward during this period, and I could only grunt and nod in conversations and hope my friends realized I was just preoccupied, not generally misanthropic. A-cai seemed to be on about the same level of communication, similarly engaged with something he couldn't articulate.

As I drew toward the end of the recording process, I was working madly, recording guitars, banjo, acoustic bass, percussion, flutes, harmonicas, mbira, Jew's harps, straining to achieve some overarching expression of the color and texture of the ocean. I worked late every night, then woke early and started rolling the tape on the machines, thinking about what to add or what mic to use, or practicing parts over and over to get them right.

When everything was down on tape, I hired Chen Guan-yu, a Hakka recording engineer, to come down from Taipei with a high-end analog-digital converter and some other fine outboard gear. We mixed the music through the Studer two-track machine, adjusting fader channels on the fly, controlling the levels almost like a symphony conductor, though the "orchestra" was the different instruments recorded on my eight-track tape machine. Guan-yu returned to Taipei and gave a mastered disk to the record company. *Ocean Hieroglyphics* was done.

Then one day I got a call saying that my friends were searching the sea for A-cai's body. At dawn a fisherman had found a farewell note, A-cai's shorts and sandals, and a half-empty bottle of liquor on the rocks of Dulanbi. Everyone swam out into the sea with face masks, looking for traces of A-cai, sick at heart and hoping not to find any. Helicopters and boats combed the pellucid sea, the water so clear it seemed impossible not to detect anything that lay beneath the surface. But nothing turned up for two days, and then a typhoon hit, battering the shore with wind and waves. If there had been anything to discover it was surely gone now.

"Fish food," Siki said with a frown.

A surveillance camera had captured grainy video footage of A-cai buying a bottle of liquor and a loaf of bread in the Dulan convenience store at 4:30 a.m. on the morning he disappeared. There was enough evidence to know he was gone, but not enough to dispel a sense of mystery—or maybe just enough to engender a sense of mystery. Had he simply swum straight out to sea from Dulanbi? If so, why was his body not found in the transparent water? Had the currents carried him away so quickly? Had he used an inner tube or other flotation device to get far enough out to disappear in deep water? If so, where had it gone? Were all the clues at Dulanbi a red herring he'd laid before drowning himself in another part of the sea? But how could he have gotten there, since his car was parked at the *tangchang* with the keys in the ignition? Was he incognito in some mahjong parlor in Taipei? Had he procured a fake passport and begun a new life in the Argentine Pampas?

Everyone had a different theory. Some said A-cai had sacrificed himself in an act of protest against the corporate resort slated to be built on Dulanbi. Farmer Huang claimed a friend had seen A-cai on the street in Taidong the day after the alleged suicide. A rumor circulated that this was a tragedy of lost love, with a love letter to prove it, though no one ever saw the letter. Others said he was the ultimate thespian, and this was his greatest performance. At the *tangchang* the night the search was abandoned, someone said A-cai had just discovered masturbation, at forty-four, and killed himself out of despair at having lived his life without it.

We don't know the reasons for anything, but usually we don't pay this any mind. I don't know why the plum and persimmon trees flower and fruit, but I seldom gave this any thought. Why do the waves roll in endlessly across the shore? I know they are pulled from the sea by the moon, but why is there a moon? What is the reason for the sea?

One of the behemoth Malaysian logs processed by the Taidong sawmill washed ashore in the typhoon that followed A-cai's disappearance. The Open Circle Tribe built a memorial for A-cai on Dulanbi, on the cliffs above the sea where his note had been found. They asked a friend with a crane to erect the enormous log in the center of a circle of boulders—an amusing monument to a man barely five feet tall.

Friends, acquaintances, bit-part actors, Taiwanese opera singers, and street musicians from all over Taiwan converged on the *tangchang*, drinking in ragged groups at all hours of the day and night. They formed an amoebic wake, which self-propagated spasmically, reproducing and dividing in an agar of spilled beer, bare arms sticking to the tables. We talked and talked in circles with nowhere to go. Everyone wanted to know, to understand, to comprehend motives, means, ramifications, consequences, and to have a sense of resolution and conclusion, but we would never know why A-cai took that last long swim.

Aside from my shock and confusion, and the sense in which one man's desperation is every man's defeat, I absorbed the loss and returned to my studio. Maybe I was isolationist to a fault, but the reasons for what had happened didn't matter to me. There are so many tragedies in the world, repeating day after day, and I just wanted to keep living, breathing, embracing the world the best I could, while trying to touch and know the tiny corner within my reach. A-cai had apparently chosen to die. I chose to live, to the best of my ability, within the terms of my own limitations and shortcomings. There is always a way to love better and give more, and that's probably the only way to make sense of tragedy, or make the world a better place. My personal failure was that my isolationism and inward focus kept me separated from others, and I could not even let beautiful women I loved, like Ming-sho and Diva, become more integral to my life and days. At the time the only way I knew how to open my heart was with music and poems, in solitude and introversion, so it was to these that I returned.

• • •

At the lower house smoke rose from Xiao Hua's fire as the sky turned toward dusk, the last rays of afternoon slanting in from behind the ridges and peaks of Dulanshan.

"Come on in, see if there's anything here you can use," Xiao Hua said.

I agreed to take a few ragged tatami mats and an old *guzhen* (Chinese zither) with most of its sixteen strings missing, more to help her clear out the place than because I wanted them. The fridge was unplugged, sitting on a damp spot on the concrete floor.

"Here's some soy sauce," she said, walking to the kitchen. "How about some garlic?"

I took the bottle of soy sauce but left the garlic to sprout in the darkness of an empty shelf.

"Want this fan? It still works."

The truth was no, I didn't want anything from a dead friend, but there was too much obfuscation. All these possessions were suddenly repulsive, but I hauled them up to my place and dumped them in the yard. I leaned the tatamis against a wall, and A-dong's three kittens immediately began clawing and scratching them, climbing up as high as they could and then leaping down to ambush each other, frolicking and playing with crazy joy. I stuck the ugly red fan behind the house where no one would see it, that is, where I wouldn't have to see it, goddamn red plastic swirling bullshit. What foul wind, what miasma would it blow?

The phone on my desk rang. I answered sullenly, sick of the impositions of death and smoke from the outside world. But it was the postmaster calling to say a package had arrived for me, and that I had fifteen minutes to get to the post office to pick it up if I wanted it today. *Fuck the tatamis*, I thought. *Let the cats scratch and piss all over them.*

I backed the car down the incline without starting the engine and stopped at the lower house.

"I'm heading down the mountain," I called out to Xiao Hua. "Want me to bring you anything?"

"No, I'm almost out of here myself," she said. "But there's a stack of records here, do you mind dropping them at the *tangchang*?"

I stuck them in the car and fired up the engine and continued down, past the place where my landlady's husband had crashed into the ravine and died three years before, past the wild boar in its cage at Water Running Up, through the village, and got to the post office just as the doors were closing.

"I know you've been waiting for this," the postmaster said. "That's why I called you as soon as it arrived."

"Thank you, it's kind of you. I'm sorry to have troubled you," I said. For the past week I had stopped in every day to ask whether it had arrived.

"Not in the slightest," he said, with Buddhistic forgiveness or disregard.

The package held my copies of the *Ocean Hieroglyphics* CD, just released by my record label in Taipei. It was a miracle to hold them in my hands, the impossible dream of moving from the city to a mountain above the sea now manifest within this box. The songs that had emerged from my fingers through a guitar, and from all those driftwood hours around the fire, as an expression of this landscape and time, were now carved into these disks as 1s and 0s. They were complete, independent. They had become discrete things of the world, and for well or ill would make their own way to sink or swim beyond me.

I took A-cai's records to the *tangchang*. Most of the gypsy thespians had dispersed to wherever they'd come from, but all my friends were there, still lingering in each other's presence, holding together as a collective body. Watching A-cai's things rise into the sky as smoke had made me feel heavy, weighted, as if the earth were tugging at me a little harder than usual. Receiving the box of albums made me feel I was outside my own body, half euphoric and half insane. I was intoxicated by the convergence of these two imbalances of consciousness. I asked Xiao Ma for a glass of whiskey, drank it in a gulp, and asked for another, trying to catch my body and brain up to the abstract drunkenness of soul I felt rushing in on me. I became lost in heat and alcohol, and in the entirety of my life stretching before me without the lifejacket or anchor of *Ocean Hieroglyphics* to buoy or locate me.

"I'm going to buy some tobacco," I said to no one in particular, and stepped out the side door into the parking lot. I took off all my clothes, then walked naked across the street to the betel nut stand.

"A pack of triple-5s, please," I said.

The boss jumped up from his chair and shouted, "What do you think you're doing! We're not going to sell you anything when you come up to us like that!"

But his wife scurried up behind him and said, "Don't worry, honey, what is it you want?"

I paid for the cigarettes and walked back over to the *tangchang*. My friend Brian, an American who'd moved to a village a few miles north with his Taiwanese wife Rita a while before, was waiting for me and shoved my pants at my chest, saying, "Goddammit, man, my wife told me to come out and get your clothes on you. Put your pants on, will you?" But we both wore cheesy grins. How angry can you be at someone for doing something as stupid as that? It's got to be forgiven on grounds of temporary insanity. Something in me had required a gesture of abandonment, self-abasement, release, to strip off and strip away, to crumple up and discard my sense of self and agenda, throw it like chaff out into the world, and then return. But now this was over, it was enough, done.

I stepped back inside. Yiming held out his hand to me with his little finger extended. We interlocked our right pinkies, a gesture of sealing a promise—but he didn't say anything, just looked steadily into my eyes, as though silently eliciting an oath to stay alive, to stay here, to keep being and doing what we most truly were. Whatever the wordless promise was, I ratified it by holding on and returning his gaze. I said Yes.

Xiao Ma was A-cai's best friend. He flipped through the records I'd brought and said, "How could that idiot kill himself when he owned music like this?" He took one out of its sleeve, put it on the turntable, and lowered the needle. It scratched and skipped, then Marvin Gaye began to sing, "When I get that feeling, I want sexual healing."

A drink appeared in my hand. I looked up, and Diva smiled at me, her eyes crinkled with affection and sadness. She was working at the bar, but I drew her to me anyway, and we danced close and slow, our hearts beating against each other in the twilight. I closed my eyes and pressed my face to her hair. It smelled like plum blossoms on the mountain after rain. I touched my lips to her neck, her skin tasted of the sea. The sun turned to stone and tumbled from the sky. Nobody knew anything and none of us desired to wonder. We were adrift, swimming deep into the night.

TWENTY-ONE

Betel Nut Brothers

The Betel Nut Brothers came down from Hualian to play at the *tangchang*. It was the most exalted sugar factory gig so far, in the half year the series had been running. The Betel Nut Brothers were one of the first aboriginal bands to release their music through a label in Taiwan, and were legends up and down the coast. Zhiming had been in a state of rapture from the moment he heard they were booked to play. Like the Brothers, Zhiming was a Hualian Amis, or Pangcah, as Amis are known in the northern half of their range. They were his musical idols, and for Zhiming their arrival was a convergence of worlds, of reality and myth.

The album *Betel Nuts* was released by an independent record label in Taipei in 1996. The first half of the album was recorded in the Trobriand Islands, Papua New Guinea, a whole village and three generations of harmonies singing along with a strummed guitar. Trobriand Islanders speak Kilivila, an Austronesian language descended from the sea migrations that probably began in Taiwan five thousand years ago. The second half of *Betel Nuts* consists of Huegu and Abi, Amis/Pangcah twin brothers, singing traditional songs on their porch in Hualian. The album traces linguistic connections between Amis and Kilivila, and between a shared anapest, "three stomps," at the end of the lines in the songs—and between the culture of betel nuts in indigenous Taiwan and the Trobriands, which presumably traveled along with the Austronesians in their out-rigger canoes. According to the liner notes of the album, when Trobriand singers sailed between nearby islands to perform, they were paid in betel nuts. (This reminded me of playing for a lump of hash and as much beer as I could drink the night of the gig in anarchy bars in Barcelona.)

Betel Nuts launched the career of Huegu and Abi, who have recorded and performed as the Betel Nut Brothers ever since. *Betel Nuts* was an underground classic in Taiwan and made the brothers famous, but they were never anywhere near being able to quit their day jobs as construction workers in Taipei. The band had morphed and expanded, taking on several cous-ins and an uncle. At the *tangchang* Huegu and Abi showed up with a third guitarist and a percussion player. They had just released their fourth album, *Hunters Who Lost Their Land*, and their record company had set up a series of gigs to pro-mote it. The music had changed, however. The first album consisted of traditional songs and spare harmonies sung over a single guitar, but now they had added elements of blues and rock and sang some songs in Chinese. When I wrote up the album for an independent weekly in Taipei, I interviewed Huegu and asked him how they saw their music, and about the shift in musical style.

"We're trying to dig the ancient songs out from the past so they won't be forgotten," he told me. "We're singing these songs for our aboriginal brothers working in cities, to remind them of home. And we sing so that our aboriginal culture will be recognized by the Chinese. We also feel a connection with the music of Black America, and we hope that by add-ing blues and rock to our songs, they will have more appeal to young people."

The Betel Nut Brothers' music had become less "pure" than it had been in their first recording. There was something naked and innocent in both halves of *Betel Nuts*, something shining and mysterious that resonated with the connection between community and place. Singing and strumming among friends on their porch, the Betel Nut Brothers seemed to be simply playing music, with no agenda or self-consciousness. In the following, studio-produced albums, they were playing music to be recorded and released as a product, with the dual goal of retaining a sense of physical and spiritual home and connecting with a broader audience.

The Betel Nut Brothers represented a pan-aboriginal cultural identity that Amis and other aboriginal peoples embraced. Their recent albums were similar to Biung's music, in being a form of creative expression that offered an alternative to mainstream-purveyed identities. At the same time, they illustrated the position of contemporary indigenous peoples who may be wholly integrated neither with their traditional cultures nor with the prevailing values and structures of industrial society, and are therefore in a constant process of navigating between the two.

. . .

The Betel Nut Brothers pulled up in a van and unloaded their guitars. Three of the four members of the group who'd come to play were middle-aged and slightly graying. Huegu and Abi were angular and strong from the physical labor of their livelihoods, though their extra guitar player, an elder cousin, was tending toward rotundity. The percussion player was their nephew and in his early twenties. They stepped inside and looked around in awe at the driftwood aesthetic of the place, the abo-bohemian consciousness manifested here in the old sugar factory, with Japanese calligraphy still hanging on the wall, a recolonization of the colony, or a re-indigenization of it.

There was instant affinity between the Open Circle Tribe and the Betel Nut Brothers, as if this were a long-overdue reunion. They were welcomed as if they were returning home. Xiao Zhu had lit candles all around the space, and we had rigged up a couple of small spotlights to cast blue and green light across the stage area. The band sat down and accepted a drink and an offer of betel nuts before commencing with their sound check, and the space began to fill with bodies in the warm and humid evening.

The café buzzed and tingled with excitement. From the first time I came down and crooned my songs in the sugar factory café, these gigs had become an event where the Open Circle Tribe congregated every Saturday night. They formed the core of the audience and led the evening from musical performance into a freestyle, freeball dance party. Locals and out-of-town visitors alike were seduced by the swirl of music, rhythm, bodies, and dance, and by the community togetherness and spontaneous generosity that was manifest here.

The performance series helped resolve the strange paradox in which many of the best musicians in Taiwan came from Taidong, but there had been no local venue for original music. Established aboriginal singers such as Long-ge, Panai, Jie-xing, Hu Defu (known as Kimbo in English), and even Chen Jiannian, the undisputed king of aboriginal folk music in Taiwan, had taken the stage at the sugar factory. Between the music series and the Open Circle Tribe, Dulan was entering national prominence as a cultural center.

Today, ten years later, ten years after these events I'm narrating, the music series at the *tangchang* is still going. A number of young Amis singers who played their first gigs at the sugar factory have gone on to national fame as recording artists. In addition to providing a link between generations of aboriginal musicians, the Dulan Organic Music Series has served as a bridge between local singers and a larger audience.

• • •

The Betel Nut Brothers adjusted the mic stands and tuned up their guitars. The place was packed, everyone sweating and high with anticipation, buzzing with wine in the burnished candlelight. With the first note, Zhiming threw his head back and whooped, and from that moment led the spiral dance all around the crowded room, managing to simultaneously dispense *mijiu*, sing along, pass out betel nuts, and pull everyone out of their chairs as he went, smiling beatifically all the while. Zhiming was radiant, his face luminous with the interface between times, places, lives, these Dulan days juxtaposed with his Hualian past, a slopping over of myth and history into skin and breath, into wine and songs, into sound waves transmitted directly from hearts and tongues into the air.

It was the wildest, most illuminated night I'd seen at the sugar factory, the candles on the tables reflected back on us by fogged-up window glass, everyone dancing along in the winding spiral behind Zhiming, or simply following the rhythm where they stood. There was no differentiation between Amis, Puyuma, Chinese, Taiwanese, Americano—these distinctions of headhunting and dominion all dissolved away. We were swirling currents of bodies conjoining and diverging from each other. Everything was a gelatinous mix of culture and skin and song, a petri dish of music and bones all mixed up with a swizzle stick to dance.

I held my arms out to Ha-na as we passed close to each other. She stepped over and embraced me, and we danced body to body, the implicit eroticism of rhythm and music flickering between us, but she giggled and pulled away. Ai-qin's laughter resounded from somewhere—it was such a primordial force it would not be out-competed even by the amplification system. Dou-dou and Dafeng moved past me in a chain of dance. Dou-dou let out a shout of happiness. Dafeng sang along calmly but with a euphoric smile, he too was a Hualian Amis. Siki had always been too busy to be much engaged with the *tangchang* gigs, but when I met him in the convergence of waves of dance he grinned an unfettered grin and nodded, "Not bad, not bad." Yiming appeared and enveloped me in a bear hug, then handed me a betel nut, which I popped in my mouth and chewed.

I made my way through the crowd to adjust the sound on the mixer, then stepped up to the bar to get a beer. Xiao Ma was standing there, shirtless as usual, and offered me a hit from a bottle of *gaoliang*, 116-proof sorghum liquor. He was the titular manager of the café, along with his wife Xiao Zhu, yet he sometimes seemed removed from what was happening even as it surged around him. "To A-cai," he shouted to me above the music. "I miss him so much."

I took the bottle and tilted it into my mouth, the burning liquor washed down the betel nut juice I'd planned to spit out somewhere. Xiao Ma took a hit himself and seemed to stall with a sense of loss there in the midst of gyring movement.

"I'm sorry," I said, putting my arm around his shoulder.

He stared down at the ground a moment, then looked up at me with a wistful grin and said in English, "Life is such."

He flourished the bottle and took another swig, then said, "I'll save the last drop for you."

This caught my heart, as if he were offering me his last drop of blood, of his soul. I also stilled for a breath or two, as if a slow root connected me in this moment to the center of the earth. I couldn't imagine another place I would ever hear such words.

The gig was acephalous and anarchic, as with all things connected to the Open Circle Tribe, the Consciousness Tribe. The audience sang along with the Amis songs and those they knew from the Betel Nut Brothers' albums, but did not protest when the band broke into a refrain from John Lennon's "Give Peace a Chance." You could clap or dance or sing along or howl to the moon, as you liked and as you loved so you were free to do. I sat down next to the stage and picked up a hand drum and played along. Huegu and Abi shook their heads and smiled with the same beatitude as Zhiming. Everyone seemed to feel they were coming home to something they hadn't even known they'd missed.

The Betel Nut Brothers finished their last song, but the audience shouted "Encore!" so loudly and insistently that they were barely three steps off the stage when they turned back and picked up their guitars again. But now they unplugged the guitars and stepped out from behind the mics and into the crowd. They started an Amis song and joined the movement of the dance, moving from performance and purveyance into undifferentiated participation, strumming as hard as they could to make the guitars heard in the chorus of sixty or eighty voices rising together. The guitar cables lay on the floor, and the PA buzzed. There was no stage to step down from, no difference in elevation, only an area demarcated by mics and wires that separated performers from audience, and they crossed over this imaginary line with one step. Nothing remained of music as an industry now. This was music as the Amis had grown up with it, not as a performance or product. Unplugging the guitars and forsaking the microphones was one more step away from the hegemon, one more step of return. For sure no one thought of it in those terms at that moment, but there was a surge of energy when the crowd saw the band had disconnected from electric amplification, from the Taiwan Power Grid, and were singing and playing directly from their guitars and bodies to the ears and hearts around them. Whoops and harmonies rose up above the melody as sweat ran down faces and arms and wetted our clothes.

The last paragraph of the first chapter of *Ulysses* is a single word: "Usurper." Glum and melancholy Stephen Dedalus flings this at the English race from his role of gloomy servitude. Ireland usurped by the English. But who did the Irish usurp? It goes on and on. Evolution is usurpation. Hunting and gathering usurped by agriculture. Usurped by fossil fuels, usurped by corporations and machines, usurped by television. Usurped by governments and banks taxing land out from under you. The Austronesians walked overland from China to Taiwan when sea levels were low, but Taiwan was not empty when they arrived. Who did they usurp? A thousand years later they spread across the sea, inhabiting islands already inhabited. Usurping. Usurped by the way things are, by the inertia of the previous five billion years. Life pulsing on anyway. Usurpation in every process of becoming. The past usurped by the present, the present usurped by the future. Yesterday usurped by tomorrow. Life usurped by death, death usurped by the new life it nourishes. The land no longer belonged to the Amis, but the Amis still belonged to the land. Usurped and still making room at the dinner table, usurped and still passing the wine bottle to strangers and friends. Usurped and still standing up to dance. Usurped and still belonging to the mountains and the sea. My life in Dulan usurped by my departure from Dulan. Usurped and still alive a little longer. Usurped and still in love.

The sugar factory café shook and grooved in a collective mass, a rhythmic innocence of love for this place and these people and for life on earth, a sound wave transcendence of bones and time. Everybody twined together in a soulful ululation except for two crew-cutted men standing at the bar. They looked around as if they had beeswax in their ears, sealed tighter than Odysseus's crew when he sailed past the sirens. Tie me to the mast, boys, I can't live without hearing, but you'll have to pass by deaf to that seduction. The two men stood staid and solemn with untouched mugs of beer before them, tiny bubbles streaming upward to the surface in the amber liquid. Their glasses sweated and wetted the wood of the bar as one of the men pointed a video camera around the room, and the other clicked a camera, flash flash flash.

TWENTY-TWO

E-ki on the Boulevard

I was sitting at my driftwood desk with a mass of papers when the phone rang. "Scah-ott, this is Aii-qiiinn," Ai-qin said, drawing out the syllables with foghorn deliberation. "Have you heard?"

"No, heard what?" I said. I was alone and hadn't seen anyone for two days. It was autumn, the wild grasses all russet and tan across the mountain. The betel nuts hung large and orange as apricots from trees with fronds that were browning, drooping, and falling to the underbrush.

"*E-shifu zou le*," Ai-qin said. "E-ki has gone."

"Ah."

Silence filled the space between us and spilled over.

This wasn't like A-cai's death, grotesque and sudden, a freak act of man and nature against which you could curse and rail. We had known E-ki was dying. No violence or surprise was involved. This was simple mortality asserting itself, the fact that we're all going to die stepping into the place where our friend had been. This whole life is a devil's bargain. You buy your time on earth with the fact that you have to leave it, but at some point everyone feels cheated. There was no shock or anger, only absence, now absolute, and the remorse of those left behind. I felt I'd done nothing for E-ki when he was an invalid, alone in a concrete box with a respirator and a plastic sack draining bile from his lungs. I hadn't even made it back to give him a copy of the ocean songs.

"Ai-qin," I said, "are you alright?"

"I'm in Xinzhu in the north," she said. "I can't return to the coast for two more days. The wake is tomorrow at his wife's apartment, but you don't have to go to that."

"I'll go."

"The wake's not for his close friends. It's not for us, it's for his wife and her church friends. It's a formal thing. No one expects you to sit through that."

"I'm going."

"The day after that is when you can see E-ki in the funeral home, and that night is his farewell banquet. We're putting everything together for that."

"Where's the funeral home?"

"Next door to the morgue, on the boulevard where they have the night market."

"Is there anything I can do?"

"We're holding the banquet in a park in town. We'll be working there the day after tomorrow. Just come when you can. I'll be coming south by train."

"Okay."

Silence pooled along the wires between us. I placed the receiver back in its plastic cradle. I sat down at my hinoki desk and stared at the mess of papers, the whorl and grain of the wood.

· · ·

I walked up the stairwell to a sea of shoes. Black shoes, brown shoes, solemn shoes. Dou-dou stepped out as I arrived, and we bumped into each other on the dim landing outside E-ki's wife's apartment.

"Scott, Jesus you scared me. I thought you were a ghost. What are you doing here?" She wore a frilled purple shawl and a matching headband, along with her camo pants and work boots.

"I'm here for the wake."

"Ah, you didn't have to come for this. It's the church service. But it's good of you. Everybody's asleep in there."

"Where are you going?"

"Home to take a nap. Church always does this to me. Later Shen-hui and I are going out to gather reeds and wildflowers for the park banquet. Siki and those guys are bringing some of E-ki's work. The banquet in the park tomorrow evening, that's our goodbye to him. You'll be there, right?"

"Yeah, I'll be there."

"Come early to help us set up. We're going to turn the whole park into a memorial. The next morning we'll drive him north to the burial ground."

"Why bury him? I thought you were all cannibals."

"We eat people, but only our enemies. And white meat. So be nice. If you die we won't bury you, don't worry. What a waste that would be. Even though your liver'll be no good."

· · ·

Gray heads were lined up in rows above folding metal chairs. A wreath of flowers was placed around an old photo of E-ki. Though he was Amis, E-ki had acquiesced to the Chinese tradition of taking a somber black and white funeral picture at about age forty. It made the death of a friend seem even more improbable and surreal to see him looking down at you stern and hale, nailed to the wall but looking better than he had in years.

It was a solemn gathering. I handed my white envelope with 1,000 NT to someone taking contributions at the door. The gray heads slanted forward, some snoring inaudibly. Solemn silence prevailed. A mountain of fruit was piled on the table. Amid the silence one of the old men would humbly stand, head still bent forward, hands clasped in front, and speak a few words. They spoke about E-ki, but not the real E-ki, rather E-ki-no-more. Really, they were speaking words out of a ledger, inserting E-ki's name into a blank. Still, this was a form of endearment—a way of touching and handling something that no longer existed, a box of absence you could hold in your hands. It was a closed box, but you could imagine what was inside, especially with E-ki looking down from the wall solemner than he'd ever been in life, looking at the camera like he was not posing for a portrait but waiting in line for a colonoscopy.

And it was a form of pain. A way to palpate loss, the irrevocability of change, the blank where a name was filled in but where it had not been written two days before because then there'd been a living man, breath, muscle, bone, sweat and obscenity, movement, the slow thresh of years into language written across his body, language you could read to read the man. This was the paradox the old men held in their mouths and in their folded hands—the closer you come to self-knowledge and self-exposition, the less time remains to BE what you most truly are. It takes a lifetime to become.

I sat in a chair at the edge of the assembly but didn't stay long. No one looked up when I entered; no one noticed when I left. This was a private gathering, each of the church elders saying farewell to E-ki as he had known him, and hello to E-ki as a memory, and as an entity toward whom they all drew near. The greater collectivity of the ceremony bound them into a body, but it also defined a space in which they each could be alone.

· · ·

Yiming called me on the phone the next morning. "*Shi-kao-te*, Scott, we're going in . . . we're going in to town." He spoke high and fast, and sounded like a sergeant in a foxhole, calling for reinforcements.

"Okay," I said, "I'm with you. What are we doing?"

"We got to get E-ki from the—morgue, where they put him in his coffin. Then we got to drive him to the—we got to put him in the freezer." At every pause I heard Yiming swallow, and in my mind's eye I could see him grimace as at a splinter in his toe, a pain he tried to push to the edge of perception, but insistent, sharp and throbbing, unable to be ignored.

"When do we go?"

"Now . . . right now—we're at the *tangchang*. Hurry, we're waiting for you."

I rushed to lock up the house, my hands stuttering with the keys. When Mull saw me getting ready to leave, he ran and jumped up through the window of my car and looked at me from the passenger seat, *Hell yes, going for a ride.* "God*damn* it Mull," I hollered, "get out!" He jumped back out the window and trotted to the front door, where he sat with exaggerated erectness, the particular dignity dogs manage when they're certain they've been wronged. I thumped him fraternally on the ribs, then started the engine and backed down the drive. Mull didn't move a muscle, his posture of injured pride seeming to call out, *Okay, I'll guard the house then . . .*

. . .

Yiming, Siki, Dafeng, Zhiming, and Siki's apprentices sat in a circle in the asphalt lot of the sugar factory. Yiming moved over to make room for me on the half-carved log he sat on. They were discussing what to do with E-ki's work, and everyone nodded to me without breaking the conversation. Siki didn't look up when I sat down, but Yiming poured out a shot of *mijiu* and signaled me to knock it back.

My mind rambled off on its own. No one asked for my opinion, and I didn't have one. E-ki was not my blood, this soil was not mine to bury him in, I hadn't known him for decades as the others had. I helped myself to another shot of wine and looked beyond the intermittent cars driving north and south on the coast highway. The sky slanted like gray-white marble across the sea toward the horizon. *Toward home*, I thought, *America. But is that home? When I'm away from this village, even just a day's drive to Taipei, I can't wait to get back to my farmhouse, to my friends, my recording studio and guitars. My house here is the only space in the world shaped around what I am. I feel like a stranger when I visit America. But is Dulan really my home? Would I stand and fight if the Chinese invaded? Do I want to live here forever? Do I want to die here?* And here at least I reached a certain extremity of my residence on this cusp of earth where mountains sloped up from the sea—I couldn't imagine being buried here. At some level I didn't belong to this soil. This was the conundrum of my expatriatism. I lived in a home where I did not wish to die, but I had chosen not to live in the home where I was born.

Everyone stood and moved toward Siki's van. The apprentices ran to gather tools. Tools traveled everywhere in this crowd, even to the morgue.

"Let's go," Yiming said to me. "We'll ride together."

I climbed in the van. We crowded into the metal space, it filled with smoke and sweat. Siki revved the engine and jammed it into gear but just then received a phone call. We sat pressed against each other's skin and opened the tinted windows. The engine idled as Siki spoke on the phone, leaning on the wheel. Yiming pressed a bill into A-zai's hands. Yiming threw the sliding door open, and the apprentices ran off as if tethered by string. We flicked the ends of our cigarettes out the door onto the asphalt, where they continued to burn. Siki finished his call and raced the engine again. The sharp hardness returned to his face, a wedge of bone cutting into the onus of what lay ahead. He popped the clutch and wrenched the wheel. The bald tires crunched wood shavings and gravel as we turned. I held on to Yiming, who held the opposite window frame, my body halfway out the door.

Beyond the *tangchang* gate Siki pulled right onto the highway, the two lanes of narrow speed that led to town. We passed the spot where Mull later took to sitting like a sentinel for hours at a time. Siki kept to the shoulder of the road, driving slowly till the apprentices caught up and tumbled into the van in a tangle of limbs and grins. A-zai, with his brass-colored hair and silver earring, handed Yiming a plastic bag with condensation beaded and rolling down the outside. Yiming reached in and handed cans of Taiwan Beer all around, delicious aluminum cold sweating in our hands. We broke them open and poured them down, replacing the sweat we were losing. A-zai held a beer to Siki's lips. Siki twisted his head to drink while taking another call, one hand on the phone and one hand on the wheel.

"Where we going?" I asked.

Yiming slugged down half his beer and said, "To the fucking meat locker."

Siki hit the gas and A-wei, the other apprentice, let out a whoop. "Who the hell you think you are?" Siki growled, and grabbed his beer from A-zai. He looked at his apprentices like he was looking at shit on the sole of his shoe, like they'd gone and crapped in the exact spot where they knew he would step. The wind blasted in, and the ocean blurred by on one side, Dulanshan on the other. Beer cans blew out the door. A-wei leaned into the handle and slammed it shut with a metal crash.

We sped south toward town, jammed together in the van like knuckles in a metal fist, swaying through the curves of the highway. We were slowed briefly by the tourist traffic at Water Running Up, with its optical illusion of reversed gravity, vendors of steamed corn and sausages, and its imprisoned wild boar. We broke free from the traffic and jammed on along the flank of the coast range till the mountains subsided and the rift valley opened outward to the sea. We crossed the Beinan River, whitecaps flashing in the slate-gray current. Dump trucks rattled across the bridge and drove down an access road to the riverbed, where bucket loaders filled them with sand to haul away. At the highway bypass we continued straight downtown, where on the first corner a shop sold tropical songbirds, living bits of vibrant color enclosed in bamboo cages.

Siki was on the phone again. We drove in circles through the congestion of town, a holding pattern, waiting for something to happen, what I didn't know, I don't think anyone did. We didn't speak, sweating against each other with our sticky skin, just stared ahead or out the side windows, each of us stuck in a holding pattern of memory. Smoke and steam boiled up from food stalls along the road. Yiming passed around a plastic sack of betel nuts. I took one and bit off the cap, chewed the nut wrapped in leaf and lime paste, and spat out the window, but the red juice ran down the door panel. I moved the fibrous wad between my cheek and gum, and Yiming handed me another beer.

We broke out of our puttering circles and accelerated back toward the edge of town. The morgue was on the broad boulevard that ran from the center of town to the highway bypass. Political rallies were sometimes held here, and the weekly night market, which stained the asphalt with grease and left trash scattered in the gutters.

We jumped out of the van and trotted toward the entrance of the complex like commandos, passing through a sliding iron gate. Electric jelly flared in my legs, as if at any moment we would break into a full sprint for our lives, mortars would crash down upon us, shrapnel rip through our guts. But the compound was empty. We went around knocking on doors, till finally someone told us we'd come too early. We had to wait.

We sauntered back out to the van, past the Buddhist, Taoist, and Christian chapels annexed to the morgue, trying to hit a cool stride after our nervy run. The street was empty except for a couple of old men sitting and snoozing on the median island beneath trees with crinkled yellow leaves. We sat down on half-broken plastic chairs someone had abandoned here. A-zai went and got the beer from the van. Sun beat through the frail leaves above us. "What are we waiting for?" Yiming asked. Siki frowned and shook his head. We drank beer and chewed betel nuts and smoked. One of the old men started up from a dream, looked around at us, then dropped his head back on his chest and began to snore.

Across the street a silver car pulled up and parked, and Ming-ling stepped out in a tight shiny dress and faux-designer shades. She came over and sat down, lit a cigarette, and pointed to the beer. Siki opened one for her. She looked around at us in our stained clothes and confusion and managed to wordlessly convey disdain.

"What are you all doing?" she asked.

"Waiting," Siki said.

"For what?"

He just smiled. "What are you doing off work at this time?"

She took a drag from her cigarette. "I get off when I want to. Everybody's coming to see E-ki." Her eyes flicked over us once again. I stared hard at her, but her gaze didn't even pause. "It's too hot here," she said. "I'm going to wait in my car."

But just then A-zai said, "Look!" Down the street Vadsuku was walking toward us, bare-chested in his army pants with cigarette holes in the crotch.

"Fuck," Siki said, "hide the beer." He bunched the bag beneath his seat but he was laughing. Vadsuku walked up and stood before us, snot crusted on his moustache, and looked intently at each of us in turn.

"E-ki's gone," he said. He squatted down, put a hand on Siki's shoulder and reached into the bag for a beer. "What are you doing here?" he said, squinting his eyes at me. But then, catching the tone of accusation in his question, he said, "No, what I mean is, what are *we* doing here? Who here is a better man than E-ki? Not me."

"We're here to carry the box," A-zai said.

"Yes," said Vadsuku, opening his eyes wide, "but whose box? Who is it for? Never mind, I don't want to scare you." He drained his beer, then held a filthy, crumpled bill out to A-zai. "We need some Wisbih. Do me the favor, boy."

A-zai took the money and headed off to the nearest betel nut stand. We watched him shuffle down the street and talk with the girl behind the counter.

Ming-ling had forgotten to wait in her car. We all sat slumped like marionettes cut loose from their strings. Then someone shouted from the morgue and waved us over. We jumped up and ran toward the gate. A-zai sprinted up the street to catch up with the action, Wisbih bottle in hand. Vadsuku followed with his usual saunter-strut, and Ming-ling returned to her car.

· · ·

E-ki's body lay on a gurney in a room like an airplane hangar, with high ceilings and bare concrete walls. The corpse was thin and pale, but also somehow bloated, as if E-ki had been drained of all tendon, muscle, fluid, bone, and then half-filled with air. We stood staring in disbelief. Close enough to touch but far too far to fathom. "What the fuck is this?" said Yiming, looking around as if for a perpetrator.

After a few minutes an attendant appeared and said, "We're ready to put him in the casket." He pushed the gurney through a door, and we were left in the cavernous space.

"I need to take a leak," Yiming said, and I said, "Yeah, me too." At the urinal we looked at each other for an instant—then shook our heads and spit into the piss splash in the stainless steel trough. Yiming went back inside to wait, and I sat down against a wall to let the sun beat down against my skull.

They wheeled out the casket. A yellow plastic cover was fitted over the open half of the coffin. E-ki's head rested on a purple cushion. Somehow it looked more like E-ki than it had before, as if the cover acted as a lens, magnifying some residue of E-ki into a facsimile, but he also looked artificial, like a waxed apple, shined up for display. Not E-ki, but what someone thought his memory should be. I looked away, and through a doorway saw thousands of candles guttering in the Buddhist chapel.

E-ki's friends began arriving, milling around the casket and bumping into each other. E-ki's wife came in, practically carried by several church friends, her legs dragging dead behind. A woman in a red dress wept loudly. Small groups stood around the periphery looking sour.

A nucleus of empty space surrounded E-ki. People peered

into the coffin from a step or two away but always kept a distance from it. The room filled up, with murmured conversations echoing off the empty walls. Right when the crowd was at its densest, Vadsuku stepped through, nodding and salutating politely, then suddenly commandeered the center space, bare-chested and wild-eyed, like a horse breaking loose from a barn fire. He put his hand on the plastic cover, right above E-ki's dead eyes and face—the room stopped, all breathing caught. Vadsuku held the death space in silence for a long moment, then bellowed, "E-ki!"

A woman wailed and fainted. Vadsuku went down on one knee, keeping his hand on the casket. The crowd buzzed and crackled like static electricity and arced into shouts and moans.

"E-ki!" Vadsuku bellowed again. "E-ki, where are you! E-ki, why did you go? E-ki, my brother, how could you leave me so alone!"

The crowd broke down and quietly wept, sorrow flowing like pus from a wound. Vadsuku stood up and blinked at the faces around him, as if emerging from a trance, then moved away saying, "'Scuse me, 'scuse me, pardon me . . ."

Siki and Yiming pushed through the crowd. Yiming called out, "We're loading him on the truck!" The crowd wailed, Aaaahh! and began to bustle and agitate like herd animals. E-ki's brother appeared, looking astonished and betrayed in a clean white shirt buttoned to the throat. Yiming held his shoulder and guided his hand to one of the brass handles on the casket. Zhiming and Vadsuku took positions. I stood in the space between the casket and the crowd, the crowd now spooked and stinking of sweat. There were five bearers, one handle still unmanned. They started to lift it.

My body sucked in all the nerves and death energy of the room. My muscles twitched and quivered like snakes of hate, hating their mortality, hating the task of lifting E-ki's body's box, hating being left out of it, hating my own hatred. Siki was facing me but wouldn't look up. Yiming shouted, "Scott, help us lift it!" Sweat and tears streamed down his face. I grabbed the brass handle next to Siki. We lifted and strained, grunted and cried like galley slaves, my arm pressed against Siki's, our muscles tensed against each other. We lifted the coffin to our shoulders and staggered toward the exit, the crowd stumbling before us. We carried it outside to where the sun cracked down on us like a whip and rose back up at us from the pavement. We moved through the compound gate and slid the coffin into E-ki's truck, now E-ki's brother's truck, along with beer cans and frayed rope and sawdust in the bed, *great amis* spray-painted on the side, to drive E-ki to an ancillary storage space where he'd be kept till tomorrow's procession north. The engine was running. E-ki's brother stared at the open door as if he couldn't conceive its use or meaning. "I'll drive," Yiming said. He helped B-*shifu* into the passenger seat and took the wheel. Across the street Ming-ling's car pulled away, a sleek silver ghost. The apprentices waited at the van, and Siki talked on his phone.

I walked aimlessly up the boulevard beneath the yellowed trees, kicking a styrofoam cup through crackly brown weeds. Rusted cars sat in a dirt lot on flat tires. A phalanx of refrigerators stood like a palace guard in front of a used appliance shop, but nothing moved except a black dog that scratched an open sore on its ear and turned its head to watch me pass.

· · ·

There was a betel nut stand on each corner of the junction with the highway bypass. I picked the sexiest betel nut girl and bought a pack of *binlang* from her, then crossed the highway and walked aimlessly north. I stuck my thumb out and the third car stopped for me. It was a family of four in a small maroon hatchback. They made room for me in back, and I folded myself in. "Where are you going?" I asked.

"We're driving back to Taipei," the father said. "Eight hours to go. You can come along with us if you like." The mother turned and gave me a look of alarm.

"Me, thanks but no, just up to Dulan, that's where I live."
They offered me an ear of steamed corn from a plastic bag, and
a juice drink in a box. "No, no thank you, I'm fine," I said.

Aside from my having no appetite, the car was filled with
a foul, fetid reek of decay and rot, like fermented shit. *How
the hell do these people live like this*, I wondered to myself as
we made polite conversation about the weather and where I
was from and where they were going. I tried to roll down my
window but the electric switch didn't work. I didn't want to
shame the mother by asking them to turn up the fan. I wondered if I would be able to make it the whole twelve miles to
Dulan—the man seemed intent on driving slowly to take in
the view, and I cursed him silently for not flooring the gas.

"You sure you don't want some corn?" the father asked.

"No, thank you, but I'm not hungry. In fact, here's the sugar
factory, this is my stop." The father pulled over, I stepped out
and thanked them, and the mother looked back at me with
dread and relief. *Poor lady's embarrassed*, I thought.

"Say goodbye to uncle," the father said.

"Goodbye, uncle," the children said.

I slammed the door, and they drove off. I stood in the sun
soaking in the salty afternoon air. I caught a whiff of that
foul stench, and for a moment thought it must have adhered
to me in the fifteen minutes in the car—but I looked down at
my clothes, faded and torn, stained with sweat and beer, and
realized it was me that stank, it was the acrid reek of rot and
sorrow, and the death in my meat and bones, all mashed up
and sweated through my skin. "My god, those poor people,"
I said aloud. But by then they must've had the windows open,
with a cross breeze blowing through, with their corn and soft
drinks and a view of the open sea.

TWENTY-THREE

E-ki across the Ocean

A banyan tree grew at the center of the park, in the box of soil contained within a low retaining wall. Thin, brittle tendrils descended like whiskers from the tree's limbs. Some of these would have grasped the soil and grown into roots, forming a sinuous lattice beneath the canopy, between the branches and the earth—but here all the hanging roots and leaves broke and scattered as detritus on a flat shell of concrete. Concrete extended to the edges of the small, enclosed park like ice-nine, Kurt Vonnegut's fictional polymorph of water that consumed and converted everything it touched. Flowers grew from squares of earth left in the pavement.

A-dao sat on the wall beneath the tree, dappled by afternoon sunlight filtered through the leaves, drunk and happy next to a virtually limitless supply of *mijiu*. He stood up and sloshed over to Dou-dou and offered her a bottle.

"Ahh, no, A-dao, I don't feel like drinking anything," she said.

"For E-ki," A-Dao said. "E-ki can't drink now, we have to drink for him."

"Ahh, okay then. Poor E-ki."

She tilted the bottle and dipped in her right index finger, dripped out three drops as an offering to E-ki, and took a sip. Dou-dou set the bottle down and continued weaving a braid of reeds. A-dao returned to his seat, where he remained, drinking and smiling, singing softly to himself amid the work going on around him.

· · ·

Yiming and Zhiming built a twisting fence from long, femur-shaped lengths of driftwood, to display poster-sized photos of E-ki that Dou-dou had printed. Siki and his apprentices set up a projector and screen to show a video. Pieces of E-ki's work were set all around the park, and wreathes of grass and flowers decorated chairs and tables brought in for the banquet. Vadsuku built a fire in a steel barrel sawed in half the long way, and unloaded a large pile of wood to feed it through the night. In a few hours the Open Circle Tribe transformed the park from a blank concrete topography into a ritual space.

Ai-qin arrived from the north and came straight from the train station, wrinkled and pale after her overnight journey. She didn't speak to anyone, just set her travel bag on the ground and sat on the wall on the opposite side of the banyan tree from A-dao. She raised her hands to her face and silently cried. Tears rolled down from behind her sunglasses, dropped to the concrete, and evaporated.

The work continued on around her. More plastic tables and chairs were set up around the tree, and pictures of E-ki were leaned up around its trunk. There was shouting and commotion as Dafeng and Siki and several other men carried in a massive cross-section of a tree trunk, six inches thick, three feet wide, and twelve feet long. It was a piece of E-ki's work, with abstract and archetypal designs carved into it in relief—bird-men and totemic fish, triangular eyes, women with double sets of breasts, animals with human faces and protuberant phalluses. This was the banquet table, where food and drinks would be laid out for guests.

As they set up the table on a couple of sawhorses, A-dao came around and sat down next to Ai-qin. He put his arm around her, and she turned to embrace him. Then the rest of us came and hugged Ai-qin in turn to welcome her home. Yiming was last. He encircled his wife in his bearish arms and chest with fierce passion and grief.

"Shhh," Yiming said, "what are you crying for? Crying doesn't help anything." She laughed with relief while continuing to cry.

. . .

The sun reclined behind the high, far ridges of the central range, and guests began to arrive. The Amis elders came dressed in their turquoise tunics with bright colors embroidered along the seams, leggings wrapped tight around their calves.

"Scott, why don't you go pour them some *mijiu*?" Yiming said.

I twisted open a bottle and moved around their table clockwise. Several of the men said they wouldn't have a drink till I had one first. One of the old women said sternly that she wouldn't accept anything from me unless I got down on my knees to serve her. I did so, she smiled coquettishly, and the whole table roared with laughter. Food was brought and set out on the banquet table—bamboo shoots, raw oysters, roasted pork, freshwater snails that had to be picked from their shells with toothpicks, slimy and delicious, and a big plate of sashimi Siki had carved from a fish caught that morning. I stood staring at the carved table, the feast spread upon it as if it were laid upon E-ki's body and his work. I had become a bit drunk and ate some sashimi, the fresh raw fish flesh so delicate it seemed to melt in my mouth, swirling with the taste of soy sauce and wasabi. Yiming put his arm across my shoulders and grinned.

"That sashimi's good, huh?"

"O yeah, I love this stuff," I said, taking another piece with my fingers and dropping it in my mouth.

"We all do, but we always serve the elders first. We'll eat what they leave later."

"O fuck!" I said, and took a platter over to where the elders were drumming their fingers on the plastic table.

"Okay!" they shouted when I put the sashimi down before them.

E-ki's wife's church friends arrived in gray trousers and white shirts. The tables filled up, and guests milled around looking at the photos: E-ki with his carving knives and chainsaws, E-ki playing a guitar, photos of laughter, his hands strapped across his belly. Most of the guests were dressed in work clothes, but some of the women wore dresses, make-up, and lipstick, and a few bouffant hairdos were debuted. Platters of roast pork were served along with pots of soup and bowls of rice. At sundown everyone slapped at mosquitoes, and the night sound of crickets rose up in the dusk.

Siki set up the video to play in a loop at the edge of the gathering. It was a documentary about E-ki and his sculpture produced by Taiwanese public television some years before. We saw E-ki driving his truck along the shore of the Pacific, loaded with driftwood stumps and logs, and E-ki carving a block of wood with a chisel and mallet. Then a scene of E-ki talking about his work, his face strangely grave and solemn, his hair looking almost combed. He gestured with his hands as if grappling to express himself with words, but the sound was turned off, he spoke silently to us.

I sat down on the retaining wall next to Dou-dou and Shen-hui as images of E-ki shuffled past. Dou-dou sighed and said, "Ah, E-ki . . . he was so good-natured. He never lost his temper with anyone, no matter what happened."

I nodded in agreement. I once saw a passing stranger verbally abuse E-ki for no reason, ranting and flailing his arms, flinging insulting accusations. Rather than flare up, defend himself, or retaliate, E-ki turned to me and lifted his eyebrows with a look of mild surprise, and said, "That person seems a bit bad-mannered."

E-ki's nonjudgmentalism came from an acknowledgment of cycles and factors beyond himself, beyond his control, beyond his ability or need to understand. Not to be angry is not to wish another person, or the world, to be any different than they are, and that's a form of enlightenment all the more luminous for being ordinary.

Dou-dou and Shen-hui stood up and moved off to greet a new arrival. Yiming came over to grab a bottle of *mijiu*, then sat down when he saw me there. He opened the bottle and dripped out three drops, silent for the two or three seconds this required. He took a shot and passed it to me. Zhiming passed by, and Yiming caught him by the arm and pulled him down to sit next to us. I dripped out my three-drop offering to E-ki and took a swig and gave the bottle to Zhiming.

"Hey," Yiming said, "you guys remember that time E-ki came down to Jinzun? He had a girl with him and told her to wait in his truck while he came down to get something from the campsite. But once he came down, we were all there, someone gave him a shot of *mijiu*. He sat down at the fire and started to tell a story. The bottle went around again, he was feeling high, man, he didn't want to leave! The girl started calling him, but he wouldn't answer his phone. It kept ringing, so he turned it off. This was back when he was healthy, you know, when he was strong. Well, he finally went back up the stairs to the parking lot, and I went with him. The girl was gone. She just took off or called someone else to come pick her up. And she'd written on his windshield in lipstick, 'E-ki I hate you!' In lipstick! And the lipstick broke! It was broken right in half, lying there on the asphalt of the parking lot. She was so mad she broke her lipstick in half writing 'I hate you!' on his truck."

Yiming repeated the detail of the broken lipstick over and over till we were all laughing unrestrainedly at this memory of E-ki. Yiming laughed so hard tears spilled from his eyes and ran down his face.

As the feast wound down, the elders began to sing. A-dao came to their table and asked the new Chief to stand up and lead the dance. The elders stood up from their plastic chairs and joined hands in a line. The Chief, lean and bespectacled, with a spray of eagle feathers in his hair, sang out a line and stepped forward into the ebb-and-flow movement of the dance. We ran forward and moved the tables and chairs out of the center space, as the elders answered the Chief in a chorus and fell in with the rhythm. All the guests stood up to join the spiraling line as it wound around the banyan tree, around the pictures of E-ki and the banquet table, the turns widening outward to the edges of the small square park.

Vadsuku's fire burned on, though he had disappeared as soon as the guests began to arrive. The flames cast flickering light on the photos of E-ki as they became gray outlines in the dark. The video ran on silently, its glow illuminating the dancers when they passed near: E-ki in his newest plaid shirt and his half-tamed hair, speaking stiffly, like he was suddenly trapped outside himself, bewildered, trying to talk himself back in through the camera lens. Round tan lines showed on his face from his oversize sunglasses. He blinked distractedly against the too-bright light of the sun shining down on him with the ocean in the background, rubbing his belly for reassurance.

The elders continued to dance and sing as if they had nowhere to go and nothing to do for the rest of their lives, for the rest of all time, and everyone held on, opening our throats and bodies to join the songs, all the Amis friends and relatives, all the friends from other tribes, and all the Taiwanese and Mainlanders and Hakka, holding to each other arm to arm, reaching forward and back to grasp our neighbors, arms crossed across our bodies, foot stomps accentuating rhythms like the slap and break of waves, everything rising and receding in the half-light. Dancing for E-ki as a memory and as a presence, as part of all of us, part of this landscape and community, E-ki as a convergence of continuums, who had emerged from the waves in order to return to the sea again. And dancing not for E-ki at all, not for memory or loss, but for the same thing we always danced for, which people have always danced for, an embracing of life in the rhythm of bodies and songs and blood, which was both E-ki and not-E-ki, which is every individual and no individual, love and sorrow as they mutually engender, with no wish for anything to be different, for anything to change.

E-ki remained with us as we remained with him. He was gone just as we all would soon go. We would join him in the overlapping orbits and continuums in which we have never been separated from this earth or from each other. We would return, as E-ki had returned, to the place we all came from, and we continued on, a spiral braid of songs and memories in the night.

· · ·

The next day, when my friends drove E-ki's body north to bury him, I remained at home. Somehow the final interment of E-ki in the earth was not for me, but only for those who'd shared this land and its songs with him for decades. Maybe I felt I had interceded in the exequies too much already and needed to retreat back to my solitude, return to my desk and papers, my poems and guitars, to the point of stillness where the living flesh of the world pulsed and revolved around me.

Autumn sun sifted from the sky. Cicadas roared through the morning, swelling into funnels of sound. At noon, clouds appeared from nowhere, precipitating from air currents blown in from the sea. Shaded by the cloud cover, I walked around the back of the house, clearing away the weeds along the water pipe. I cut a stalk of sugarcane, skinned and chewed it, sucked out the sweetness, and spat the dry pulp. Mull followed along as I walked a game trail through the briars and elephant grass erupting between the rows of betel nut trees. The trail twisted around to a large boulder that had tumbled down from the face of the mountain decades or centuries ago. I climbed to its crest, which rose above the tops of the trees to an open view across the coast range north and south, and out to the open sea.

A fork of lightning flickered like a snake tongue, a platinum flash against the low lead sky, and a rumble of thunder bellied down the ridges and bluffs, enfolding me. The air thickened, and scattered raindrops fell but evaporated instantly from the accumulated heat in the boulder. Down below, unshielded by clouds, the coast was still gilded in heat and sun. The zinc roofs of Dulan gleamed silver, the road shimmered like a river, and rice fields swirled gold and green, stirred by the breeze. Slow undulations curled in along the shore, breaking over stones. Beyond them the autumn ocean churned green and blue, whitecapped to the horizon. Green Island rose clear and dark, a lumpy crocodile head in the belly of the sea. Far off to the south and east, a faint shadow rose on the horizon, at the extremity of vision, between presence and absence, at the seam of sea and sky—it was Orchid Island, pale and alone, like the sail of a ship disappearing from the edge of earth.

TWENTY-FOUR

Departure

The police with their dull blue uniforms, a medium, middling blue of so little pith, panache, or pride that it may as well have been any other color, like the beige of their computer monitors, or the metal gray of their air conditioners coughing dust. Their sting operation against me the night of the Betel Nut Brothers gig had been successful. It was a relief to find out the undercover cops were really cops. Who else would have a haircut that bad, who else would dress so square and point cameras like accusations when all we wanted to do was hang out our bellies and dance?

At the police station in Taidong City, the cops had a document typed out in skinny vertical lines of Chinese for me to sign, a statement to the effect that the statement I'd stated was my statement. The desks were crowded with teacups stained pee-yellow, the ancient air conditioners wheezed and groaned. The Taidong mayor had brokered the deal: Ezell will sign the statement that he's innocent, and then just leave him alone, or something to that effect. Everybody knew I was innocent—I'd been accused of playing my guitar in public, of which I was guilty, but no one believed it was a crime, not even P. Chin.

P. Chin was a police officer notorious for hounding Westerners in Taiwan. His family was said to have high government connections, which protected him even when his maverick operations caused embarrassment for the police department.

He had begun his career in Taipei, where he had made a series of bogus arrests of locally employed Western TV and radio personalities. Because they couldn't fire him, they transferred him to Gaoxiong, Taiwan's second largest city, but he caused the same problems there. Finally, they sent him to Taidong, the most remote backwater of Taiwan, where from his superiors' perspective he would be least able to cause trouble. But in Taidong the most high-profile Westerner was me.

Rather than come after me directly, P. Chin threatened my friends. He told Xiao Zhu and Xiao Ma that as the *tangchang* café managers, my involvement in the Dulan Organic Music Series could incur upon them a fine of 150,000 NT, roughly five thousand dollars.

"They say they have evidence," Xiao Zhu told me.

"But I didn't even play the night they filmed the gig," I said.

"They said they have footage of you playing the drum in the audience, and that's enough."

"Oh for Christ's sake."

According to an antiquated statute left over from Taiwan's martial law period, it was illegal for a foreigner in Taiwan to engage in any occupation not specifically indicated by one's visa. This law was so obscure and anachronistic that no one had bothered to strike it from the legal code, much less try to enforce it. Though I had a resident visa from a record company, it did not specifically include a permit to perform music in public. This was the technicality with which P. Chin was coming after me.

P. Chin must have known his ridiculous accusation would never hold up in court, but that I would have to act to protect my friends. The threat of the fine was too serious to take chances with. It was a pusillanimous move and caused outrage in the local government, which had only benefited from my residence here and the performance series. The Taidong mayor intervened on my behalf, and the local politicos lined up on our side to get the case dropped.

"Well, we've got the file open now," P. Chin replied to the

mayor. "We can't close it till we get an official statement from Ezell. As soon as he signs the document the case will be shelved forever."

So here I was. P. Chin squinted at me from a leather chair while a hench-cop went through the procedure. Yes, I'd started up the concert series in the *tangchang*. Yes, I'd played my guitar there. No, I didn't receive any payment. Yes, I'd helped schedule the other musicians who played. Just the facts, and we'll let it ride. Sign on the dotted line and nobody gets hurt.

"Thank you for your assistance," said P. Chin, with a bored professional smile. He held out his hand, and I shook it. It was like liverwurst taken out of the freezer and half-thawed, but it was too much of a relief to have the whole soap opera over to worry about details.

· · ·

At the Chief's funeral, I had yearned to step into the earth of his interment, to hold the handle of a shovel in my hands and feel his burial in my muscles and bones. But at E-ki's funeral, though he and the main participants were closer to me, I had refrained from attending his final burial. Perhaps I had become too involved with this community's questions of identity and realized the absence of answers for my own. When E-ki was laid out in the mortuary in a new plaid shirt, his face waxy and yellow beneath a plastic bubble, I asked myself into which soil I would wish to lay my bones, and had no answer. I began to wonder if after a dozen years in Asia, and two years in Dulan, it was time to return to America.

In the months after E-ki's death I continued with my life of books and music. But through the slow turn of the winter months I felt something was missing, that I had reached some plateau or limit of my life here and needed new borders or frontiers. And yet, it was impossible to consider leaving Dulan, even as I began to feel some emptiness that I did not know how to fill within the terms and orbits of my life. Dulan was the only place I was at home in the world, even though I had an itch in my heart that I would never wholly belong here.

During my grand inquisition by P. Chin, these issues of plateauing and belonging came to the fore. But after the resolution of the case they quickly subsided, and life returned to its usual rhythm.

. . .

However, rather than shelving the case, P. Chin took my signed statement, seemingly harmless as litmus paper, and hoofed it up to Taipei, probably in a squad car with the siren wailing like a Wagnerian soprano. He presented it to the Labor Bureau and claimed I had confessed to violating the terms of my work visa. Gullible or ignorant administrators took his official word at face value, and rescinded my residence permit.

Dou-dou called me one Friday afternoon in the spring. "Scott, there's some problem with the deal between the mayor's office and the police," she said.

"What kind of problem?"

"I don't know, but they just heard P. Chin was up in Taipei last week. And not on any official business."

"Well, they already closed the case. I guess it doesn't matter."

I was convinced everything was back to normal, and that my life in Dulan would continue to coast on ahead indefinitely.

But two minutes later my phone rang again. It was the postmaster, telling me I had received a registered letter. From the sugar factory, I drove through the village to the post office, midafternoon, all the shopkeepers snoozing out in front of their shops.

The postmaster smiled his benevolent smile and handed me an envelope, embossed with an official seal from the Ministry of Labor. He held out a receipt for me to sign.

"Just sign here," he said.

"Hold on one second. I have a call coming in," I lied.

I stepped out of the air-conditioned post office and called

Roger Wang, a Taiwanese lawyer friend in Taipei. He had advised me on my case and told me to call him if anything else happened.

"Roger, I just got a registered letter from the Ministry of Labor."

"Did you sign for it already?"

"No, not yet."

"O thank God! Where are you now?"

"I'm here at the Dulan post office. The postmaster just called me to pick up the letter."

"Scott, whatever you do, don't sign for that letter! As soon as you sign for it, the clock starts ticking. Get away from the post office. The longer you wait to receive the letter the more time we have. Meanwhile, I'll start making enquiries and see what we have to do to fight this."

"Fight what?"

"Whatever it is. Now leave the post office, and I'll call you later."

I stuck my head in and told the postmaster I was going to the beach, so would be back to pick up the letter later. Roger worked through the weekend trying to figure out what it was we had to fight. The next week I started getting phone calls from the postmaster, saying the Labor Bureau was pressuring him to deliver the letter. On Tuesday I finally went in and signed for it. It was the cancellation of my residence permit and notified me that I had to leave Taiwan within two weeks.

Roger began fighting the case. Bands all over Taiwan played protest songs on my behalf. My journo friends in Taipei mobilized the press, and I became more famous as a "dissident" than I'd ever been from my music career. A series of articles about the case came out in the English language press, though it was never reported in Chinese newspapers.

The mayor and other local politicos contacted the minister of labor on my behalf. The case, which exposed a schism between branches of the government, was supposedly being discussed in the president's office. Roger was able to win a stay on the cancellation of my residence permit for as long as the case was being heard. He told me that even if we lost the case, it could be appealed for years. And in fact over the next few years Roger filed appeals all the way up to the supreme court.

But I did not wish to live under the threat of being deported at a moment's notice, especially since I was no longer free to play music at the *tangchang* or anywhere else in public. The threat of expulsion from my life in this community and place catalyzed a process of departure I could not have undertaken otherwise, and I decided to leave.

. . .

Yiming drove all the way up to my place just to take back a pair of rubber work boots. He'd given them to me several months before, saying they were the biggest boots he'd ever seen, they would fit me for sure. But they were two sizes too small and sat out on my porch unused until he drove up and threw them in the back of his truck, cursing himself, saying they must've been bad luck, as if my departure were the result of an evil talisman, as if it were his fault.

Mull had taken to roaming around on his own and for some unknown reason would sit still for long periods on the side of the highway a half-mile south of Dulan. One night I couldn't find him when I was heading home from the *tangchang*. The next day when I went out looking for him a shop owner said he had seen Mull's body on the road when he drove into Taidong that morning, but when he returned an hour later the body was gone. I asked all around but never found a trace of him.

Ming-sho and Diva called me on consecutive days to say the same thing: our relationship isn't going anywhere, let's just let it go. At the time I thought it was a coincidence, a double-dissolution of heart strings I could never cut myself, either out of cowardice or love, but since they had become best friends and shared everything, maybe they had come to this consensus together.

And so, as I faced the prospect of departure, several emotional ties that would have held me to Dulan were severed already. I signed my lease over to a local journalist. He wrote an article about my departure and promised to feed A-dong.

. . .

I disassembled my recording machines, leaving square gaps in the counter Vadsuku had helped me build, in the slabs of driftwood Yiming had helped me haul up the mountain. Papers and books were strewn across the floor, my guitars lined up against a wall as if facing a firing squad, various cables and wires tangled in the corners. As I packed, every scrap of paper was saturated with memory and significance. The mass of remembrance grew exponentially in inverse proportion to the amount of what remained.

To clear my mind I hacked at the overgrown weeds in the yard. I had always imagined my life in Dulan would achieve overarching wholeness and resolution, but now I knew the door would never close cleanly—departure is fragmentation, not resolution, and whatever was incomplete would remain that way forever. At one point I felt if I remained any longer, the weight of nostalgia and regret would become insurmountable. There was nothing to do but stand up and walk out the door.

On the front wall some friends' children had painted pictures of flowers and mountains, and a little cartoon car, a depiction of their journey from Taipei. A-dong mewed at me from the empty kitchen window. I stood in the yard, the smell of cut grass and the falling summer sun rising all around me. I got in my car and drove down the mountain toward the sea.

. . .

I turned north on the coast highway, my car weighted down with crap I still had to sell or give away, including the car itself, boxes lashed to the roof so that it swayed back and forth as I drove. It was the end of July 2004, two and a half years after I had moved to Dulan and met the Open Circle Tribe. Yiming and a few others were having a work meeting at the Jinzun café. "Come say good-bye on your way north," Yiming said when I called him on the phone.

I pulled into the Jinzun parking lot. Yiming, Ai-qin, Dou-dou, and Yu-shi, a French-educated art curator with coiffed hair and a sparse moustache, were clustered around a table looking at blueprints in the open air café above the sea.

"How's the project going?" I asked.

"Fine, it's fine, fine," they said glumly, glancing at my car. "How's your packing?"

"Great, just great."

Yiming ordered me a coffee and handed me a *binlang*, then pressed the rest of the pack into my hand. "Better take these for the road, it's a long drive."

Dou-dou hadn't known I was leaving this day. Once I'd decided to go I'd avoided everyone—if I saw friends on the street in Dulan I turned away, almost hyperventilating, unable to speak, as if a single word would be a fissure through which departure would pour in and flood my heart. Now, Dou-dou finished a phone call and walked over from the railing above the cliffs. When she saw my loaded car, she punched my arm hard, then slapped me across the chest and said, "You can't go," and punched me again. I thought she was horsing around and laughed distractedly, but suddenly she heaved with sobs and threw her arms around me.

"Okay, okay," said Yiming and Ai-qin, gently pulling us apart, but Dou-dou didn't stop crying.

"Want to have a smoke?" Yiming asked me.

"Sure, why not."

We lit cigarettes, inhaling ash into our lungs.

"So where are you going?" Yiming asked, trying to kindle some flame of distraction while we sipped our coffee. He looked at me as if trying to fix me in his memory, and I realized I was looking at him with the same intensity.

"From Taipei I'm flying to Hong Kong, then traveling north through Tibet to the Silk Road, and west to the far edge of China, the border with Pakistan and Afghanistan. Then I have a job to do some music for a film in Beijing. From there I'll either take the train to Europe, or return to America . . . I haven't been back in five years."

"Ah, the whole world. You're lucky," Yiming said, grimacing.

I tried to feel lucky. I think my heart was cauterized at that moment and remained so for months or years.

"I guess I'm going," I said, and stood up.

"Call my sister if you go to Europe," Ai-qin said.

"I will."

"Let's take a picture," Yu-shi said.

"Yes, yes, of course."

We lined up together in front of my loaded car. Dou-dou hadn't stopped crying, and wiped her face with the purple shawl that matched her motorcycle.

"You're going to look terrible in this picture," Yiming said to her with a smile.

"I didn't know," Dou-dou said. "You shouldn't leave so soon."

We erected smiles like picket fences. The flash flashed silently, redundant in the sun. I imagine in this photo my face looks like silicon, a palimpsest of masks. Love and grief, the estrangement and elation of departure, of new vectors and migrations, all corralled within a rickety smile and written across one another over and over, hope and despair battling it out at the bottom somewhere. And across everything a mask of silicon confusion, plastic information with no sense, no promise, no heart. My heart remained in the place I was leaving, even as I tried to emigrate it to the road.

I got in the car and put Yiming's *binlang* next to the gearshift lever. I started the engine and released the brake to drive north along the two-lane highway, along the sea of three blues with waves curling in across the shore, the sky streaked with silver clouds above, green mountains rising like waves of stone between. Yiming grasped my hand through the window and said, "We'll be waiting here when you return."

Epilogue

Further Fields

In 2007 I met Yiming at an artist residency in New Caledonia, but otherwise I had no contact with the Open Circle Tribe for years. Our connection and communication was based on face-to-face interaction. I found no pleasure in keeping touch through the disembodied talk of phone calls, and most of my Dulan friends did not use computers or email. In 2010 I was in Jeju Island, Korea, playing music with a contemporary dance project, when I got the news that Vadsuku had died. From high rocky cliffs I looked out to the sea, my heart full of memories that felt cut into pieces by time and distance.

PhD dissertations were written about the Open Circle Tribe and the project at Jinzun as a turning point in contemporary Taiwanese art, with my name listed there with my friends', my "tribe" listed as "American." Roger told me that because I had not been deported or charged with any crime, I could reenter Taiwan at any time. In 2008, on my way to Hanoi, I booked a stopover in Taipei but was not allowed through immigration. The officials apologized and said there was a five-year ban on my entering Taiwan. My absence took on an inertia of its own after that, and even when the ban was up I did not return. I was always busy working and traveling, and then as I began writing and revising this narrative I told myself I would return to Dulan once the book was done.

· · ·

In the summer of 2013, nine years after I left Dulan, I was living in Yunnan, the southwest of China, where I had settled from an interest in border dynamics and ethnic minority peoples. I was working on the final revisions of this manuscript, when after years of chronic illness, my father went into a steep decline and passed away in California. The memorial service would not be held until the autumn, and my family encouraged me to stay where I was and finish my work before returning home.

In the meantime I had to do a visa run to extend my stay in China. I flew to Xiamen, Fujian Province, and took a ferry to Jinmen, an island five miles off the coast of China, which belongs to Taiwan. All I needed to do was exit Chinese immigration and get a stamp in my passport; then I would return to Xiamen the same day. But when I arrived in the Jinmen ferry port and entered Taiwan for the first time in almost a decade, I was seized with an uncontrollable desire to see my friends in Dulan. I simply couldn't turn around and get back on the boat. Instead, I caught the next flight to Gaoxiong and took a train to Taidong. That evening, just a few hours after landing at the ferry terminal in Jinmen, I was back in Dulan, with no plan and no change of clothes, no luggage except a shoulder bag with a notebook and a pen.

It was Saturday night. Vadsuku's son Jamulang, whom I hadn't even known existed, was performing in the sugar factory. Panai was there and introduced me to him, saying, "This is Scott. He was a good friend of your father." Jamulang looked at me with a friendly, open smile and shook my hand with a strong, firm grip.

Panai and Nabu had become a couple, and lived together in a town in the rift valley near the Bunong Culture Village.

"Do you remember the first time I came down here, with Xiao Lu?" I asked Panai.

"Yes," she said. "We drove to the bluff above the sea across from Feiyu's place. And you said you were going to move here."

I nearly fell to the floor right there. It was as if Panai had spoken words from the secret mythology of my own life. I couldn't believe that she remembered this sentence, spoken in a second then gone, from a dozen years before.

Jie-ren was there too. He had finally managed to leave Taipei and move to Taidong.

"What are you doing down here, keeping fighting cocks at Tero's?" I asked Jie-ren.

"No," he said, "I'm too busy . . . I'm running a performance series in Taidong City, and I'm even busier than I was before . . . nowadays when I want a vacation I go back to Taipei."

Standing at the bar of the sugar factory café, as Vadsuku's son played guitar and sang, Nabu told me that Biung the hunter, who had led us up to Takivahlas, had married Su-zhen, the woman who came with us on the Bunun trek. Ishigaki the anthropologist had married the younger sister of Biung the singer, and they now lived in Okinawa.

"How come that trek was full of romance for everyone except me, and I never even knew?" I said, laughing.

Nabu laughed along with me and told me the "cultural re-establishment" treks had continued, growing larger year by year, and that they'd recently built a house in Takivahlas.

"Is it legal for you to build a house up there?" I asked.

"Legal? Of course it's legal," Nabu said, as if affronted by the suggestion it wasn't. Then he shrugged and added, "Well, to us, it's legal . . . according to the laws of the Republic of China, it's illegal." We burst out laughing again, and Nabu said that the police were too lazy to go up into the mountains to stop the Bunun from returning to their old villages, but sometimes waited to arrest them at the trailhead when they came down.

The tourism boom that followed Dulan's reputation as an art center had gentrified and commercialized it a bit. Some of the Open Circle friends with whom I'd lived in bohemian abandon on the beach now ran shops or guesthouses. But the ocean was wild and gorgeous as always, and I felt complete release when I looked out at that plangent yawn of green and blue, flopped into it and let the waves wash over me.

The Open Circle Tribe was now at the center of a protest movement against a large resort on the coast halfway between Dulan and Taidong. It had been built illegally through collusion between local government and big business, but the protests had prevented the resort from opening for business. This protest had catalyzed similar grassroots movements all over Taiwan. Some weeks before I arrived, my friends had organized a protest march from Dulan to Taipei and walked fifteen days all the way up the coast to bring media attention to the issue. The harmony of these indigenous artists with a broad trajectory of life and time did not translate to political passivity. Rather they were fighting fiercely to bring agency to themselves and the larger local community, to bring a longer arc of perspective into the decision-making process, rather than ceding authority to the short-term gain of greased palms that usually paved the way for whatever development project the money gods wished to push through.

• • •

Sometimes I can't help thinking humanity made a wrong turn eight thousand years ago, from hunting and gathering to the beginning of agriculture, with its resultant hierarchies and states. Hunter-gatherers never created systems of regimentation and control. Sometimes the world seems like chaff, barely held together with a few strings of commerce, technology, music, a few echoes of poetry from the Alta Mira cave twenty thousand years ago, shards of myths and songs passed mouth to mouth along migration trails across continents, land bridges, and the sea. In the game of accumulation, maybe we're just like raccoons, who once they've reached into a cage to grasp a shiny object will never let it go, even though the closed fist of possession is the only thing enforcing their captivity.

In the contemporary world it's easy to feel suspended between poles of estrangement and belonging, half-integrated with the earth, half-invested in machines. Despite the sense sometimes that things should be better than they are, I think we love the endless flash and buzz and zip of progress, and the chance to look behind the curtain to see what's next, even if it opens to oblivion.

We are all destined to fade and pass away. But can anyone say the Chief's singing of Amis songs, or E-ki's acts of generosity and kindness, or the Open Circle Tribe's driftwood sculptures along the shore, will not exist eternally? Haven't these become part of the ever-changing fabric of the universe, as real and illuminating as the senescent and receding stars? Everything temporal may cease to be, may crumple and give in to the passing of time, but everything on earth is also ineradicable in the flow of life as a continuum.

. . .

The night I arrived back in Dulan, Ai-qin hit my shoulder hard, over and over, just as Dou-dou had done when I departed, saying "Where have you been, where have you been?"

Yiming lifted me up on his shoulders and spun around in circles. He put me down and began berating me, saying "What happened to you? You've grown so old, you've changed!" But it was Yiming who, in his late forties, had finally lost his boyishness, his face creased by cigarettes and laughter, by sun and wine.

Others, more polite or less critical, said I looked the same. My hair was still golden, bleached by the sun of the downslope of the Tibetan Plateau, though my sideburns and chin beard had gone white. I picked up a guitar and began singing all the songs I'd written in the past nine years, including "Departure," which I wrote to the Open Circle Tribe from New Caledonia. Yiming finally cried out, "*Shi-kao-te*, you haven't changed after all!" And then he opened up his throat and chest and sang a Puyuma song back to me, the sorrow of absence and the joy of reunion resonating in his voice as if they would sustain forever.

Zhiming grinned his famous grin, despite streaks of gray in his ponytail, and told me he'd begun making driftwood guitars. He introduced his son—the pale, bespeckled boy I'd known was now a tall, strong lad of seventeen.

Dou-dou was more matriarchal than ever, her long silken hair replaced by a short perm. She and Dafeng ran a gallery out of a *tangchang* warehouse bay. Dafeng looked exactly the same as a decade before, except for a slightly darker tint to the betel nut stain on his teeth, but he actually said hello and grinned at me rather than nodding a silent greeting. He admired my embroidered Hmong shoulder bag from Laos, and the third time I saw him looking at it I emptied my things from it and gave it to him.

Siki's crew-cut was speckled with silver, and the lines of his features cut deeper into his face. He was even busier than before with meetings and plans. His workshop had expanded to include another warehouse bay, and he had remarried, with two new children.

Shen-hui enclosed me in a powerful embrace, despite being a foot and a half shorter than me. Then she held my arms and took a half-step back. Looking into my eyes, she said, "I have to tell you something . . . have you heard about Vadsuku?" I nodded solemnly. She dripped three drops out of her glass, took a sip, and handed it to me to do the same.

Everyone knew I was only here for a few days, that I had spontaneously cut away on time stolen from other agendas and plans, that my father had died and I could not stay. I would have to leave again soon, but my friends still welcomed me like a long-paused cycle was finally complete, like a long-held breath could finally release, and we could inhale and breathe again. When Ha-na saw me she jumped into my arms and kissed me and began crying and said, "We've been waiting so long for you to come home."

ACKNOWLEDGMENTS

Thank you to the Amis elders of Dulan, who welcomed me
so warmly that their home became my own for as long as I
was there. No one even questioned what a two-meter American was doing in the midst of the songs and dance or at the
dinner table.

I was implicitly accepted by the Open Circle Tribe throughout my time in Dulan, and my greatest thanks go to Siki, Dou-
dou, Yiming, Ai-qin, Zhiming, A-dao, Feiyu, Dafeng, Ha-na,
Jian-wei, and Shen-hui.

E-ki and the old Chief were elders of their respective communities who died during my residence in Dulan. Chief Konuy
and E-ki, thanks always for your generosity and your songs.

Special thanks and three drops of *mijiu* to Vadsuku, who
died in an accident while loading driftwood logs onto a truck
at a beach south of Dulan in 2010.

Thanks to Nabu and the Bunong Culture Village for inviting me on the two-week hunting and cultural re-establishment
trek to Takivahlas, their "old village." Thanks to Biung and
Hushong for their guidance on the Bunun trek, and another
three drops of *mijiu* to Biung the hunter, who died in a traffic accident in 2012.

My connection to Taidong and the Open Circle Tribe began
with my musical community in Taiwan—thanks to Jie-ren,
Xiao Lu, Panai, Chen Jian-nian, Hao-en, Tero, Zhang 43,

Taiwan Colors Music, Wind Records, and others too numerous to name.

Thanks to Roger Wang for pro bono legal representation and indignation during my residence permit issues in Dulan, including several years of filing appeals after my departure, and for warm friendship before and after these issues existed.

One day in 2003, journalist David Frazier called to tell me he'd taken on the editorship of an independent English-language weekly in Taipei, and asked if I had anything to contribute. I began writing a column called "A Far Corner" about my life in Dulan, which became the seeds of this narrative. I'm grateful to Dave for offering a target for these stories, which might have remained latent in collective memory otherwise. Some of these columns were later reprinted in the *Kyoto Journal* with the friendly editorship of Ken Rodgers and John Einarsen.

Douglas Newton and Dana Standridge Roberts were part of my "Taiwan mafia," long-time expat friends in Taiwan and America. In the early days of these then-lyric-gonzo stories, Doug and Dana always appreciated the best of what they were, while never hesitating to point out ways they could be improved.

Thank you to James C. Scott for recommending this book to Yale University Press, and for his typically encouraging advice to "keep punching."

Thanks to Wendy Call for early editorial advice through the Victor Hugo House in Seattle.

Parisian ethnologist and experimental fisheries researcher Paul Sorrentino provided important feedback on the text and helpful reflection on questions of identity, culture, and ritual— merci monsieur, "as usual."

In 2007 I traveled to New Caledonia to join Yiming for an artist residency at the Tjibaou Culture Center in Nouméa, to explore connections between aboriginal Taiwanese and Kanack Melanesian cultures. Thanks to Lena Berg and Jeff Soens, residents of the Seattle condo building where I worked as a doorman, for donating frequent flyer miles that covered my travel to Nouméa; and to Joe Roberts and Randall Lane, who bought paintings that helped fund this trip.

My "lived-in" experience in Dulan and Taiwan has been augmented by the rigorous methodology of historians and anthropologists. I would especially like to thank John Thorne, who shared his invaluable dissertation on aboriginal Taiwan with me, and later read the manuscript for anthropological and historical accuracy, helping me avoid generalizations and inaccuracies. Thanks also to Darryl Sterk, Philip P. Arnold, and DJ Hatfield for correspondence about their work. If there are errors in the text despite their good efforts, they are mine alone.

A Far Corner was written and revised over many years and broad geographies. Many people generously supported this process by offering me rooms to stay and work in. Thank you to Henriette Buist, Martin Goericke, Afsheen and Tara Mostofi, Red Pine, Kate and Te-toh Titus, Karen Swenson, Justin and Lauren Ezell, Monty Kim and Clare Perry.

I'm grateful to Rita Kao and Brian Curran for helping verify factual information and names during my absence from Dulan, and for Dulan camaraderie, which included refusing to let me to pay my tab at their restaurant when I left Taiwan in 2004.

I became friends with Taiwanese poet and scholar Shuenshing Lee during my brief grad school career at the University of Washington in Seattle. When I decided to go to Taiwan to study Chinese, Lee arranged a room in Taipei for me, and also sent me an envelope containing two crisp 1,000-NT bills—to make sure I did not starve to death before I made it to a bank to cash my traveler's checks, I guess. This was a precursor to the generosity and goodwill I invariably received from Taiwanese during the many years I spent in their country. Thanks, Lee, for half a lifetime of friendship (so far), and for translating *Ocean Hieroglyphics* and many other poems and songs into Chinese.

None of this would have happened if I hadn't accidentally

taken Dr. Michelle Yeh's class "The Influence of Zen on Chinese and Japanese Literature" at UC Davis in 1990, my first exposure to the Chinese poetry I fell in love with. Thank you, Professor Yeh, for a class that changed and enriched my life.

At the University of Nebraska Press, Matthew Bokovoy handled the beginning of the acquisition process with great amiability and arranged peer reviews that helped the manuscript fulfill its potential. Derek Krissoff was extremely supportive in navigating the editorial process and in arranging the production and positioning of the book. Much gratitude to Derek and Matt, and to Courtney Ochsner, Sara Springsteen, copyeditor Jane Curran, and the rest of the UNP staff.

Many thanks also to the no-longer-anonymous peer reviewers, Mark Spitzer and Kurt Caswell, who pointed the way for the book to go a step beyond what I had conceived it to be.

Additional thanks to Ming-sho, Mike O'Connor, Mike Morical, Da Mooze, Diva, Jeff Hengst, Kelly O'Keefe, Janet Brown, Lan Anh Ha Thi, Dani, and Umi.

. . .

Finally, thanks to my mother and father, for everything else and much more.

Romanization, Names, Transcription, and Currency

Non-English words and phrases indicated by *italics* are Mandarin Chinese unless otherwise indicated. I have used the *pinyin* romanization system for Chinese. Pinyin sounds that may not be at least approximately self-evident are:

> q is a ch sound pronounced at the front of the mouth, *ch* in cheese
> ch is pronounced at the back of the mouth, *chr*
> x is a sh sound pronounced at the front of the mouth, *sh* in she
> shi is pronounced at the back of the mouth, *shr*
> zhi is pronounced at the back of the mouth, *zhr*
> c is *ts*
> z is *tz*
> r is a cross between *r* and *j*

. . .

I have retained some place-names that have standard-usage non-pinyin transcriptions, such as "Taipei," which in pinyin would be Taibei.

Place-names in pinyin and local spelling:

Hualian—Hualien
Gaoxiong—Kaohsiung
Xinzhu—Hsinchu

Taibei—Taipei
Taidong—Taitung
Jilong—Keelung

. . .

Many Taiwanese are called by diminutives that consist of *Xiao* 小 ("small") plus a character of their given name (e.g., Xiao Lu, Xiao Hua). *A* 阿 serves the same function (A-sun, A-cai) but is a Taiwanese language construction, even when used in Mandarin names.

I have written Chinese personal names in pinyin except cases where an individual has personally chosen another spelling. I have transcribed non-Chinese names by ear except where another spelling is established. *P. Chin* is a pseudonym.

The village where I lived is called *Dulan* in Chinese, and this is the name I heard used in (Mandarin) conversation. I have transcribed the Amis language place-name by ear as *Etolan*, but I have seen ethnologists write it *Atolan* and *'Tolan*. Likewise, Amis is written *'Amis* by some academics.

. . .

The currency of Taiwan, or the Republic of China, is the New Taiwan dollar. It is officially abbreviated as NTD, but in common parlance this is often shortened to NT, which is what I have used here. In Chinese a unit of currency is formally *yuan*, but in speaking *kuai* (literally "piece") is more often used. The exchange rate between New Taiwan dollars and U.S. dollars is about 30:1.

A Note on Ethnic Classifications

Nearly all the characters in this book are legally "Taiwanese"—that is, they are citizens of the Republic of China, which practically and geographically consists of the island of Taiwan and a few small outlying islands. However, ethnically and culturally, some finer distinctions can be made. The following designations are approximate, partly because in Taiwan two people of the same background may define themselves differently, according to their political or cultural orientation.

• • •

Taiwanese refers to Minnan/Hoklo people of southern Fujian Province who immigrated to Taiwan starting in the seventeenth century. Taiwanese language, Taiyu, is a slight local variant of Minnanyu, the dialect of Chinese spoken in southern Fujian.

Han is the designation of ethnic majority Chinese and encompasses Mainland Chinese, ethnic Taiwanese, and Hakka—they are ethnic "Chinese," distinct from any of the ethnic minority or aboriginal peoples of China or Taiwan. Han ethnicity is an amalgamation of many peoples through a process of assimilation over millennia. Aboriginals in Taiwan often refer to the Han as Hanzu, "Han tribe."

Chinese or **Mainlander** here indicates residents of Taiwan who migrated from mainland China in 1945 or after, when Taiwan was occupied by the Republic of China. Roughly two million people, mostly soldiers, migrated to Taiwan in 1949 with Chiang Kai-shek and his Nationalist government, in retreat from the Chinese Communist army. Seven million Taiwanese lived in Taiwan at that time.

Hakka are a minority Han Chinese people who speak their own Chinese dialect and remain culturally and linguistically distinct from ethnic majority Han. Hakka are called Kejiaren, in Mandarin, "guest people." Their origins remain unclear, but they have always constituted a minority Han ethnicity.

Aboriginal here refers to any of the indigenous tribal peoples of Taiwan. The number of tribes in Taiwan is a subject for debate as "new" tribes have recently been granted recognition—in 2002 it was ten, and the current official number is fourteen. In some situations aboriginals identify with a pan-aboriginal culture or identity—that is, "aboriginal" as distinct from Taiwanese or Chinese. In other contexts individuals define themselves according to their specific tribes. All indigenous peoples of Taiwan belong to the Austronesian language family.

Aboriginal people in this book come from the following tribes:

Amis
Puyuma
Bunun
Paiwan
Tao
Rukai

Amis (A-mei in Chinese) is recognized by scholars as an exonym, applied by the Puyuma, in whose language it means "north"—Amis territory lies to the north of the Puyuma. I have used "Amis" throughout this text because it is how I heard this group refer to themselves during my residence in Taiwan. An endonym for Amis, Pangcah, is commonly used in the northern half of their range.

SELECTED BIBLIOGRAPHY

Andrade, Tonio. *How Taiwan Became Chinese: Dutch, Spanish, and Han Colonization in the Seventeenth Century.* New York: Columbia University Press, 2008.

Arnold, Philip P. "Indigenous Religion." In manuscript.

Bellwood, Peter, James J. Fox, and Darrell Tryon, eds. *The Austronesians, Historical and Comparative Perspectives.* Canberra: Australian National University Press, 2006.

Brown, Melissa J. *Is Taiwan Chinese? The Impact of Culture, Power, and Migration on Changing Identities.* Berkeley: University of California Press, 2004.

Chiu, Scarlett. "Meanings of a Lapita Face: Materialized Social Memory in Ancient House Societies." *Taiwan Journal of Anthropology* 3, no. 1 (2005): 1–47.

Clastres, Pierre. *Chronicle of the Guayaki Indians.* New York: Zone Books, 1998.

De Busser, Rik. "The Influence of Christianity on the Bunun Language: A Preliminary Overview." In *Proceedings of the International Workshop on "Special Genres" in and around Indonesia,* 59–76. Tokyo: Research Institute for Languages and Cultures of Asia and Africa, Tokyo University of Foreign Studies, 2013.

Diamond, Jared M. "Taiwan's Gift to the World." *Nature* 403 (17 February 2000): 709–10.

Grimble, Arthur. *A Pattern of Islands.* London: Reprint Society, 1954.

Ku, Kun-Hai. "'Who Is Your Name?' Naming Paiwan Identities in Contemporary Taiwan." In *Personal Names in Asia: History, Culture, and Identity,* edited by Zheng Yangwen and Charles J. H. Macdonald. Singapore: Singapore University Press, 2010.

Mauss, Marcel. *The Gift: Forms and Functions of Exchange in Archaic Societies.* New York: Norton, 1967.

Mintz, Sidney W. *Sweetness and Power: The Place of Sugar in Modern History*. New York: Penguin, 1985.

Rudolph, Michael. "The Emergence of the Concept of 'Ethnic Group' in Taiwan and the Role of Taiwan's Austronesians in the Construction of Taiwanese Identity." *Historiography East & West* 2, no. 1 (2004): 86–115.

Scott, James C. *The Art of Not Being Governed*. New Haven: Yale University Press, 2009.

Shepherd, John. *Statecraft and Political Economy on the Taiwan Frontier, 1600–1800*. Stanford: Stanford University Press, 1993.

Sterk, Darryl Cameron. "The Return of the Vanishing Formosan: Disturbing the Discourse of National Domestication as the Literary Fate of the Aboriginal Maiden in Postwar Taiwanese Film and Fiction." PhD thesis, Department of East Asian Studies, University of Toronto, 2009.

Thorne, John F. "The Evolution of Ethnic Identity among Urbanizing Pangcah Aborigines in Taiwan." PhD thesis, University of Hong Kong, 1997.

Weatherdon, Meaghan Sarah. "The Tao People's Anti-Nuclear Movement: Indigenous Religion, Presbyterian Christianity, and Environmental Protest on Orchid Island, Taiwan." Master's thesis, Department of Religious Studies, Queens University, Kingston, Ontario, 2012.

Williams, Tennessee. "On a Streetcar Named Success." *New York Times*, November 30, 1947.